20.20
2/5/09

Tattoos, Desire and Violence

Marks of Resistance in Literature, Film and Television

Karin Beeler

McFarland & Company, Inc., Publishers
Jefferson, North Carolina, and London

LIBRARY OF CONGRESS CATALOGUING-IN-PUBLICATION DATA

Beeler, Karin E. (Karin Elizabeth), 1963–
    Tattoos, desire and violence : marks of resistance in
literature, film and television / Karin Beeler.
        p.   cm.
    Includes bibliographical references and index.

    ISBN 0-7864-2389-7 (softcover : 50# alkaline paper)

    1. Tattooing in literature.   2. Tattooing in motion
pictures.   3. Tattooing on television.   4. Tattooing —
Social aspects.   I. Title.
    PN56.T27B44   2006
    809'.93559 — dc22   2005031062

British Library cataloguing data are available

On the cover: photograph ©2005 Fotosearch.com; artwork by
Annushka Sonek

Manufactured in the United States of America

*McFarland & Company, Inc., Publishers
Box 611, Jefferson, North Carolina 28640
www.mcfarlandpub.com*

To Stan and Amelia, with love

Acknowledgments

This book is the culmination of many years of researching, reading, viewing and listening to tattoo narratives.

I would like to thank the following organizations for their financial support, which was particularly important in the early part of my research program. I am grateful to the Centre for Research in Women's Studies and Gender Relations at the University of British Columbia and to the DAAD (German Academic Exchange Service) for awarding research fellowships during my sabbatical year. Thank you, Dr. Klaus Martens and colleagues in the English department at Universität des Saarlandes, for your kind assistance during my research visit and for inviting me to return to give a paper on my work. Thanks also go to my home institution, the University of Northern British Columbia, for travel funding that allowed me to present papers on my tattoo research at several conferences.

I would like to extend special thanks to Henk Schiffmacher (Hanky Panky) for a wonderful conversation in Amsterdam and for his contributions to the field of tattoo research; he offered a number of interesting ideas on the direction this book could take when it was still in its infancy. I want to thank tattoo artist and writer "Madame Chinchilla" for her correspondence (sorry I didn't make it to that California tattoo convention!); thanks also to other tattoo artists and their assistants for their observations.

Acknowledgments

I also benefited from conversations with tattooed and non-tattooed students, staff and faculty at the University of Northern British Columbia who were interviewed and surveyed on the subject of tattoos. I appreciate Kelly Wintemute's assistance in conducting this survey and in analyzing the data for our joint report *Tattoo Study: The Cultural, Symbolic and Social Significance of Tattoos in a University Community*.

Thanks to Königshausen and Neumann for permission to reprint portions of my article that appeared in the book *The Canadian Alternative* (ed. Klaus Martens).

I would like to extend my appreciation to colleagues Aritha van Herk, Jo-Anne Fiske, Rochelle Simmons and others who were excited about the uniqueness of my tattoo project. I'm especially grateful to my colleague and friend Dee Horne for her ongoing support, for countless discussions over coffee, and for reading versions of the manuscript.

Finally, I need to recognize the many hours of child care that my mother and my husband Stan provided, especially during the latter stages of the writing and editing process. I couldn't have managed without you. Thank you, Stan (as always), for your emotional support as well as for your technical expertise with computers, DVDs and videos! I particularly cherish the hours I spent with my daughter, who learned to say "tattoo" almost as soon as she learned the word "bottle." She reminds me every day, along with my dogs and cat, that there is life beyond the computer!

Karin Beeler

Contents

Introduction:
Tattoos as Narrative

The tattoo is a form of body art that can be traced back to the fourth millennium B.C. in Europe and to about 2000 B.C. in Egypt (Caplan xi). The word "tattoo" stems from the Polynesian word *tatau* which means "knocking" or "striking" (Rowe 18). The term may actually imitate the sound of the tapping that was used to generate tattoos in Polynesian cultures. The Japanese use the term *irezumi* to describe the process of inserting ink into the skin, a concept often linked to the notion of punishment, and in the Maori language, tattoos are known as *moko*, which traditionally involved carving designs into the skin along with the insertion of ink.

Yet tattoos are so much more than a desirable or decorative art form or the end result of an often painful process. They tell the stories of individuals; they express the beliefs of a community, whether these groups consist of aboriginal people, prisoners or circus "freaks." In many cultures, the tattoo symbolizes a rite of passage, a way of marking a particular event in the narrative of life, an expression of defiance or resistance to authority. These reasons for acquiring a tattoo are still part of tattoo cultures today.

Tattoos continue to be a reality in contemporary culture across the globe; some would even argue that the world has experienced a new

1

tattoo renaissance. The current interest in tattoos is evident in count-less ways: advertisements that use tattooed individuals to sell a prod-uct (e.g., records or clothing), images of stereotypical tattooed biker figures in television and film, the availability of temporary tattoos for children (including Hanukkah tattoos!), even the production of a tat-tooed Barbie doll. Not surprisingly, the term tattoo has expanded to include a range of meanings that suggest various kinds of markings or experiences of pain. Temporary tattoos are one example of how the context for what was once thought permanent has been modified. Per-haps this is the result of the development of laser surgery, which has, in postmodern fashion, subverted the once commonly held notion that the tattoo could never be removed. Yet since "real" tattoos are a kind of scar, their affiliation to the scarred body and psyche is often explored by creators of tattoo narratives (e.g. literature, television and film). These artists also draw parallels between the scarred body and the aes-thetic elements of the tattoo.

Tattoos in Narrative and as Narrative

As a clasp around all contradictions and as a subtext beneath every motive, the story remains above anything else: The tattoo is a narra-tive. It is as close to the image as it is to the writing (Mäder 15 in von Glinski, *Masters of Tattoo*).

Tattoos are an art form with a strong visual presence. When one views a tattoo, one is ordinarily struck by the design, the color or the aesthetic aspects of this visual image and how this work of art inter-faces with the contours of the body. While tattoos have been studied in a number of different ways that usually focus on their visual, anthro-pological or historical dimension, tattoos are also present in narrative forms such as fiction, memoir, film and television. Moreover, they function as a narrative or tell stories of their genesis; alternatively, the tattoo can in turn generate a story. (People are fascinated with tattoos and often want to know the story behind their existence.) Yet because the tattoo is a form of body art, the tattoo's narrative is a story of blood and ink. Tattoo narratives may be stories of desire, of trauma and violence, and of cultural preservation — stories that are intimately connected to the symbolic and physical or bodily aspects of the tattoo.

Instead of reading or viewing the image of the tattoo as a symbol that requires historical interpretation or an anthropological context, I propose to read the tattoos in texts, television, and film in relation to the narratives of desire and violence in which they are embedded. In addition, I will examine how the tattoo often tells its own story which runs counter to the master-narrative presented within a text, thus allowing the bearer to perform an act of resistance or subversion.

Tattoos and Ekphrasis

While many people may be familiar with the depiction of visual art forms in print media, they may not be aware that *ekphrasis* is the term used to describe such depiction. For centuries, writers have been fascinated by the power of the visual arts, including painting, sculpture and photography, and have attempted to incorporate images from these art forms into their texts. Poetry which depicts either actual or imaginary works of art such as paintings is not uncommon. W. H. Auden's "Musée des beaux arts" and Earle Birney's "El Greco" are just a few examples of texts that depict visual art.

Why would a writer be interested in describing a different medium? Perhaps because it allows the writer to offer an interpretation of the work of art that is not possible through a graphic image alone, or because the description adds a different dimension to the work. In presenting the visual through the textual medium, writers often capture the paradox of desire and resistance in their works. Their works embed a desire for the visual, yet because these writers represent the visual through the textual medium, the image is often linked to a concept of resistance since there is often a tension created when the textual meets the visual.

Text based art forms and visual based art forms often convey their subjects differently. While not as numerous as images of paintings in literature, tattoos are also represented in texts.

Because it too is a form of visual art, the tattoo must also be considered as an ekphrastic device when depicted in a text. Many critics of ekphrasis have focussed on ekphrasis in lyric poetry, but narratives have become more common as the subject of ekphrastic studies. One of the striking features of the textual tattoo is its ability to generate narratives of desire and violence because of the relationship between tattoos and the body. Such narratives often embed the concept of resistance that is associated not only with tattoos but also with the concept of ekphrasis.

Tattoos, Resistance and Marginality

While many will argue that tattoos are becoming increasingly mainstream, John Gray contends that the tattoo continues to be associated with difference. I too believe that even though they have entered popular culture, there is still a good deal of resistance culture associated with tattoos. In a survey that I conducted at the University of Northern British Columbia (Beeler and Wintemute, *Tattoo Study: The Cultural, Symbolic and Social Significance of Tattoos in a University Community*, 2001), 68 percent of the respondents chose to hide their tattoos on certain occasions:

> ... most of those surveyed chose a spot on the body that could be hidden. Since respondents like the option of revealing their tattoo in certain situations and not in others, they clearly feel that there is still some stigma associated with being tattooed, despite their perception that there is increasing social acceptance of tattoos. Perhaps their tattoos are more potent signs of resistance than they wish to admit [Beeler and Wintemute 8].

Many of the participants in my university tattoo study still believed in the importance of concealing their tattoos; similarly, tattoo narratives continue to depict the tattoo in relation to various kinds of resistance and marginality. More specifically, tattoos are images and narratives of resistance and marginality in a variety of cultural contexts, whether we consider New Zealand Maori narratives or Jewish American texts. (The majority of the texts and films analyzed in this book fall within the post–1970s category because of the extensive use of postmodern, post-colonial, feminist or inter-media techniques in these works which highlight the theme of resistance.) Thus, despite the perception that tattoos are becoming increasingly mainstream, tattoos, tattoo artists and tattoo culture remain on the periphery. The narratives that I have selected depict the tattooed individual or the tattoo artist as an outlaw figure and highlight the subversive potential of the tattoo.

Resistance is a complex concept to define. For me, resistance is associated with a certain amount of instability, with a shift in a paradigm in the relations between text and image. Resistance to hegemony is presented in a number of texts, and usually those who resist occupy the margins of society. However, in the context of tattoo culture (and in many other cultures or communities for that matter), one must also realize that resistance can result in the formation of a community with its own hegemonic or dominant values. Therefore, identifying resistance in these texts will be highly dependent on individual contexts. Yet because this book highlights the relationship between tattoos, gender and desire, I particularly like Shirley Geok-Lin Lim's explanation of resistance in "Asians in Anglo-American Feminism: Reciprocity and Resistance," because it identifies the complexity of sites of resistance depending on the network of cultural and gender related factors. She argues that, in a sense, Catholic doctrine offered a means of resistance to a different mode of patriarchal thought, Confucianism, that dominated her childhood. Thus, oddly enough, Catholicism via the image of Catholic nuns offered the author some form of liberation from the philosophy of Confucianism. In a similar way, tattooed prisoners may be collectively discussed in the context of resistance to various kinds of authority — the legal system or mainstream social values. However, while a neo–Nazi such as the character of Schillinger in *Oz* may resist the authority of the prison system, his resistance to racial diversity may be considered more problematic than the resistance of a tattooed concentration camp survivor defying fascism. Thus the term resistance is used throughout the book to depict a variety of social situations and not simply acts of left-wing resistance.

Clearly, tattoos are linked to various forms of resistance. Historically, and even mythically, the tattoo has been associated with subversion, and it continues to serve this function in contemporary culture. For example, one of the greatest fears of many individuals is getting an incorrect tattoo, because it is a permanent mark. The image of the tattoo as a mistake occurs in a number of narratives and may take the form of a completed tattoo not corresponding to, or falling short of, an individual's intended or desired image. Despite its permanence, the tattoo may also resist images of stability and suggest the possibility of re-invention and re-interpretation. Tattoos are images and narratives of human desire.

Tattoos and Desire

Because tattoos are so intimately linked with the body, it requires very little effort to see the connection between tattoos and the concept of desire. Alfred Gell points out the impact of the tattoo on the one who gazes upon the body of a tattooed "other":

> Marked, patterned, or scarred skin draws in the gaze of the onlooker, exercises the power of fascination, and lowers certain defences. The eye isolates and follows the mazy pathways of the design and eventually, so to speak, enters the body of the other, because the peculiarity of tattooing is that it is inside the skin rather than on its surface [Gell 36].

The correlation between the tattoo, the body and the sexual act — this last being the culmination of human desire — is suggested in Gell's quotation. Even tattoo parlor humor introduces this connection, when tattoo artists refer to "twenty-minute specials" or "quickies" for tattoos that do not take much time to complete.

The images of tattoos, even if these "images" consist of text or numbers (as in the case of prison tattoos), may be a reflection of the tattooed individual's desire. Alternatively, tattoos are an expression of the tattoo artist's desire, particularly if the recipient of the tattoo did not willingly choose to be tattooed. While tattoos have been linked to the sexual domain, the term desire is not restricted to the realm of sexual or romantic possibilities. One of the most common definitions of desire is presented by the psycholinguistic critic Jacques Lacan. His sense of desire is captured succinctly by Vincent Crapanzano, who claims that in contrast to "need," which "is directed toward a specific object, is unmediated by language, and, unlike desire, can be satisfied directly," desire "must always be satisfied, inso far as it can be satisfied by symbolic substitutes for that which it can never possess" (Crapanzano 89). While some may argue that the tattoo itself is an object of desire and that it is an end in itself, others would agree that the tattoo functions more appropriately as a symbolic representation of that which can never be attained, and as such it is a reminder of the elusive character of desire, which sometimes takes the form of a taboo or transgression. As such, the tattoo is inevitably linked to the concept of resistance, since even as it reminds the bearer of the tattoo or those who gaze upon it of some object of desire, it also subverts one's ability to truly possess that object. Thus tattoos often suggest a multitude of narrative possibilities, and those who sport tattoos will often resist telling the whole truth behind their provocative images, which are, after all, the product of ink and blood.

Tattoos and Violence

Most permanent tattoos cannot be created without the tattooed individual's enduring some form of pain. While the tattooing process itself may be painful, the images of the tattoos and the cultural and gendered contexts which produce these tattoos may also be linked to violence. For example, this book examines the relationship between desire, tattoos and violence, prison cultures and violence, tattoos and gangs, tattoos and stories of murder, as well as tattoos and the violence of colonization. Violence is often associated with both desire and resistance culture. The violent aspects of desire can be expressed through sadomasochistic acts, and the tattoo has been represented in narratives that foreground those acts. Other violent sub-cultures such as gangs and prisoners use tattoos to reveal their separation from mainstream society; sometimes violence, gender and tattoos are linked to highlight narratives of transgression and subversion which foreground freak culture or alternative sexualities. As signs, tattoos are rather unstable since they can transcend a single gender, cultural meaning or boundary.

Tattoos, Desire and Violence: Marks of Resistance in Literature, Film and Television will appeal not only to scholars of gender or women's studies, visual culture, and literature, but also to general readers interested in body art and popular culture as well as films that have received international recognition (e.g., *Once Were Warriors, The Pillow Book*). Many readers will be familiar with a number of the works discussed in this book and may enjoy rereading the texts or viewing the films again after reading this study.

This book offers a cross-cultural examination of numerous tattoo narratives, many of which belong to the domain of contemporary popular culture. Highlights of *Tattoos, Desire and Violence* include analysis of the following works or areas: numerous tattoo narratives (fiction and film) about and by women, tattoo memoirs, yakuza gang films, the television prison drama *Oz*, Holocaust fiction, and the long running television series *The X-Files*. (While the majority of tattoos discussed in this book belong to the blood and ink variety, occasionally the term "tattoo" is also used to apply to other kinds of mutilated bodies, e.g., as depicted in Toni Morrison's novel *Beloved* or Peter Greenaway's film and film script *The Pillow Book*.)

Chapter Divisions

All of the book's chapters reveal how the tattoo functions as more than an aesthetic device or visual image in these texts, films or television episodes. While some of the works include drawings or photographs which complement the descriptions of the tattoos in the narratives, I believe that the stories themselves are integral to highlighting the complexity of the tattoos. Although tattoos are represented in literature other than contemporary texts, I have chosen to restrict my analysis of the principal texts to twentieth-century and contemporary works, with the majority of the works falling in the post–1970s category, because of the increasing use of feminist, postmodern or intermedial techniques in these works which highlight the themes of resistance.

Each chapter highlights the tattoo in a different context of resistance and marginality and draws attention to the important interrelationship between the visual and the narrative components of tattoo culture. The different chapters draw on a variety of disciplines or areas such as gender studies, anthropology, history, post-colonial studies, and aesthetics in order to enhance the close literary readings of the narratives.

Chapter one examines the important function of the tattoo in autobiographical writing or memoir. The tattoo serves as a site of memory and resistance for heterosexual or homosexual desires and cultural identities. This chapter also describes the tattoo and its link to resistance in the context of ekphrasis: the textual description of the visual (e.g., a story about a visual art form such as a painting). The phenomenon of ekphrasis can be applied to narratives about tattoos, since these visual marks frequently generate multiple and often subversive narratives which may include images of frustration, suffering and pain as well as pleasure.

In chapter two, I analyze the topic of women and tattoos in the context of an alternative, feminist aesthetic of resistance to masculinist desire. Examples of masculinist bias in tattoo culture and narrative are discussed and followed by a more extensive presentation of tattoo narratives which emphasize the agency of women tattoo artists or tattooed women. These women create an aesthetic or story of desire that is an alternative to an exclusively patriarchal narrative, and the tattoo can offer some form of liberation from an otherwise limited existence. However, the stories of most of these women are not without pain or violence, since their desire to define themselves is also tied to either self-mutilation or some form of psychological suffering.

Chapter three examines "crimes of passion" and further analyzes the relationship between desire and violence that is often embedded in the image of the tattoo and its accompanying narrative. The desire to possess the beauty of the tattoo is linked to the violation of the human body. The tattoo is also viewed as a scar and often reinforces the scarred psychology and bodies of individuals in their respective narratives. Violence in the form of murder is presented in some of these stories, particularly in conjunction with uncontrollable desire. Peter Greenaway's visually arresting film script and movie, *The Pillow Book,* presents the relationship between calligraphy, body painting and the body as a tattooed and mutilated text. Many of the characters in these narratives live on the margins of society, as tattoo artists, as prostitutes, or as killers.

In the fourth chapter, I discuss the relationship between tattoos, love, gang violence and prison violence and group affiliation. I examine the experience of the group mentality as well as that of the alienated or rebellious individual within a gang or group of inmates. The co-mingling of the beautiful and the deadly is expressed through the yakuza (Japanese gang) tattoo; these yakuza narratives also highlight a code of loyalty among men and include homoerotic moments. The female gang experience, lesbian desire and resistance to patriarchal violence are discussed in relation to the film and book versions of *Foxfire.* The text and film present an alternative to the male dominated gang culture. The chapter ends with an analysis of the television series *Oz* as an example of how prison tattoos highlight the identity or affiliation of specific prison gangs or groups. The tattoos in this series also serve as an aesthetic of violence that signifies a prisoner's criminal past or uncontrollable desires through acts such as cannibalism or rape. Chapter five addresses the link between the tattoo and suffering in narratives that focus on the scars on the victims of cultural oppression who have a desire to reproduce or perpetuate pain. In this chapter, I discuss the desire of characters to reproduce the marked and violated body of a Jewish concentration camp survivor, and the desire of characters to imitate or honor the scarred body of a slave in Toni Morrison's *Beloved.* The chapter also examines the traditional New Zealand Maori tattoo in the film *Utu* and the novel and film versions of *Once*

Were Warriors. The transformation of the tattoo into images of desire for a pre-colonial past, as well as other images of the marked or bruised body, are discussed in the context of the perpetuation of violence brought about by colonization.

The final chapter draws on the association of tattoos with freak culture. The tattoo has a long association with circus culture. Sideshow or circus narratives that highlight the freakish aspect of the tattoo constitute the first part of this chapter, and these individuals are examined in the context of unusual appetites or desires. In the second part of the chapter, I extend the concept of the freak by applying the term to a variety of marginalized groups. I develop the link between the "tattooed freak" and other kinds of "freaks" (including transgendered individuals and the marginalization of ethnic minorities) who in turn challenge a uniform, disempowering definition of the term.

The book concludes with some final reflections on the importance of tattoo narratives in telling diverse stories that convey desire, violence and resistance. I stress the relevance of tattoos in examining gender identities and gender relations, and I also reflect on the importance of tattoos as paradoxical forces of mediation and subversion. Finally, I comment on how our tattooed or scarred bodies can be used to tell the stories of our lives.

A Personal Note

The art of storytelling and symbolism is intimately linked to tattoos, whether these images appear on real bodies or on the bodies of fictional characters. While much of this book is devoted to the literary analysis of how tattoos are represented within a narrative, it is important to note that the topic still elicits many personal, rather than academic, responses. During the years that I have presented material on the topic, people have felt compelled to ask me whether I actually have a tattoo: when I have answered in the affirmative, they have also urged me to share my own tattoo's story or narrative (in addition to expressing a voyeuristic interest in the image itself!). Here then is my tattoo narrative which incorporates the images of desire and violence that can be part of a tattoo experience.

I acquired my tattoo during a research visit to Amsterdam, where I visited Henk Schiffmacher's Tattoo Museum. My trip to Amsterdam also included a visit to Hanky Panky's Tattoo Studio, which is in Amsterdam's Red Light district. Even though the area is fairly quiet during daylight hours, one can't help thinking of the area as a haven of desire.

The tattoo I chose is a relatively simple design; yet, like many tattoos, my tattoo of two dolphins intersecting tells many stories. To begin with, there is the story of the design itself. It is a Melanesian design, and — according to the artist (The Caveman, one of the tattooists) — it is often worn by pearl divers in this area of the world, because when there are dolphins in the water there is usually no sign of sharks. Thus it offers protection from danger or violence. At the same time, it is a sign that symbolizes a recognition of the dichotomy of suffering and celebration that occur in various stages of one's career and personal life. My tattoo also symbolizes a kind of resistance to the orthodoxy of a particular social environment.

People are often surprised by the different stories that a single tattoo like this can generate and want to find out the definitive truth[1] behind the image. However, these people will be sorely disappointed because I believe that the power of the tattoo lies in its ability to generate countless stories and multiple truths. Therefore, like many of the people I surveyed for my tattoo study at the University of Northern British Columbia[2] (and like some of the characters in the fiction, television series and films I discuss), I will play coy and keep part of the narrative hidden, thus reaffirming the image of the tattoo as a sign of resistance.

CHAPTER ONE

Narratives of the Self: Tattoos, Desire, Memory and the Flesh

Why do people get tattooed? The act of being tattooed as well as the tattoos themselves often mark a particular event or person in their lives. Such events are often reminiscent of the contradictory images of violence and desire. Tattoos, memories, love and pain are frequently intertwined. Tattoos tell the stories of a past, whether these are stories of violence or stories of desire; they are the site of memory and visual narrative. It is therefore not surprising that an individual describing his or her tattoo will not only comment on the visual features of the image but will often tell a story leading up to the tattoo's creation, thereby creating a personal memoir of the event. These narratives may well include elements of truth as well as some fictional embellishment.

Some tattoo experiences are recorded in the more formalized art of literary memoir or autobiographical writing. These kinds of life writing may be perceived as pictorial narratives that present images of a period or periods in the writer's life. Memoir and autobiography are often used interchangeably; however, C. Hugh Holman and William Harmon indicate that "memoirs differ from autobiography proper in that they are usually concerned with personalities and actions other than those of the writer, whereas autobiography stresses the inner and private life of its subject" (Holman and Harmon 285). Nevertheless, both forms of life writing often resist the idea that the writer can present the past without some degree of adaptation and that memory is unreliable. The truth as others know it may remain elusive since many writers engage in a playful writing style that introduces fictional elements. Autobiographical writing that includes tattoo experiences is even more subversive in its use of narrative techniques because of the history of subversion attached to the tattoo, especially when combined with an image of desire. One only has to think of the tattooed names of loved ones, which may have been removed, covered up or revised after a breakup.[1] Other examples in real life and in fiction may include the concept of the misspelled tattoo. For example, a misspelled name is a common "fear" or almost a cliché for people who acquire tattoos. A recent credit card company commercial capitalizes on this fear by presenting a man who intends to acquire the tattoo of his girlfriend Donna on his arm, but runs out of cash and can only afford to pay for "Don." This example shows the ambiguous qualities of the tattoo. It seems to function as a preserver of a memory, yet the individual's desire to preserve his loved one's memory is also subverted by the incomplete tattoo; thus the tattoo is presented as an element of resistance. Autobiographical tattoo narratives also show the elusive and subversive qualities of tattoos as they are used by individuals to mark their desires and their memories.

An autobiographical essay by the Prague-born, German-speaking writer Egon Erwin Kisch illustrates the paradoxical role of the tattoo as a preserver of past desires and as a means of resisting representation. Kisch's personal essay "My Tattoos" ("Meine Tätowierungen" 1925), translated by Harold B. Segel, is a piece in his book *The Raging Reporter*, (*Der Rasende Reporter*), which presents his journalistic experiences around the world. Even though Segel classifies Kisch's work as reportage or the "literature of fact" (Segel 3), the tattoo essay certainly suggests some fictional or creative embellishment. While this piece was published in the early part of the twentieth century, it heralds the subversive strategies adopted by Stan Persky and Peter Trachtenberg, who are more recent writers of autobiographical tattoo experiences. Segel's translation of Kisch's essay includes a painting of the European journalist's numerous tattoos as a way of complementing the content of the writer's tattoo narrative. Kisch relates the stories behind some of these tattoos in an essay that reflects the ambivalent role of the tattoo as a preserver of cultural memory and desire as well as its function as a rather violent image of resistance.

The discrepancy between the tattoo as a symbol of preservation and its subversive aspect is highlighted in Kisch's autobiographical essay "My Tattoos," especially through the use of the cultural Other. Two key examples illustrate this tension. One narrative involves his 1906 tattoo experience. One of the reasons Kisch gives for wanting to acquire the tattoo on his right arm involved a way of demonstrating his resistance to the establishment — one of Kisch's trademarks in his illustrious career, which included activities such as his leadership of a left-wing faction in Vienna in 1918 and illegal travel through China in 1932 (Segel xi). Kisch had apparently just left military service and appeared to want to mark the end of this chapter in his life by letting himself "be tattooed, where and how [he] wanted, without any officers reading [him] the riot act" (207). He also becomes intrigued by the tattoo advertisement or poster which highlights the romance of the sea and the American identity of Fred A. Lionsfield,[2] the tattooist. The poster indicates that the customer may choose any design according to his own taste. However, the tattoo he receives is not the tattoo of his choosing, thus illustrating how the tattoo acts as a subversive device that may resist the bearer's desire to "capture" or fashion the past. Kisch relates how the American tattooist Alfred Lionsfield (a former chief petty officer of the flagship *Columbus*) has only a single image left, the clownish image of the "famous Negro performer" Bimbo. Kisch describes this variety-theater artist as a "revolting figure" with "a mouth like a chimpanzee's butt" (207); his descriptions obviously reflect racist attitudes,[3] but what is interesting in his description of the tattoo and the tattooing process is how the image of this cultural Other is imposed onto the writer's body despite his protest. The tattoo represents the author's inability to mark his past according to his taste or true desire; the tattoo is a different kind of image which refuses to be managed. For example, the tattoo causes him great pain. And even when the swelling goes down, the poisonous green eyes of the figure "flare up every year" (209). Thus Kisch's initial desire to preserve a piece of Americana (the idea of an American seafarer of the ship *Columbus*) is subverted by an alternative image of the "foreign."

Another one of Kisch's tattoos illustrates the subversive aspect of this visual art form and the inability of the tattooed individual to over-write a hidden kind of cultural memory with his own interpretation. Kisch describes a tattoo on his left forearm which "portrays the head of a Chinese Mandarin with an elaborately tooled scimitar stuck in his temple" (209). The story behind this image involves his decision to select a picture from a book of patterns presented to him by a tattooer of the Adriatic. When asked by the Asian master what he thought the tattoo represented, Kisch answers, "'That's the picture of a murdered Chinaman'" (209). The writer also considers the possibility that the image could represent some secret Chinese order, a Boxer Rebellion society, or some terrorist organization. However, nothing prepares him for the revelation which he receives several years later, when a Chinese criminal tells him that tattoo symbolizes the punishment eunuchs faced if they violated their duties as servants to imperial Chinese women! Thus, Kisch's autobiographical narrative combines the elements of desire, violence and resistance which are such an integral component of so many tattoo stories. Kisch's story illustrates how he is once again duped or tricked by a tattoo, or by a cultural memory which resists European "translation."

Ekphrasis and Tattoo Narratives

Autobiographical writing shows how desire, violence, resistance and marginality define the tattoo and how the tattooed object is pre-sented in the context of ekphrasis as well as memoir or autobiograph-ical writing. The concept, ekphrasis, may be defined as the textual representation of the graphic or visual. It is a concept that has generally been applied to the representation of paintings, sculpture or photographs in literature. These images of art may be fictional constructions which have no reference to actual works of art outside the text ("notional ekphrasis"), or they may refer to actual examples of visual culture (e.g., a poem about an El Greco painting). However, ekphrasis may also be applied to the textual representation or description of tattoos in Kisch's text and in more contemporary texts which are the focus of this book.

While theories of ekphrasis have generally highlighted the intertwining of the visual and the poetic, they have not fully explored the narrative possibilities of this technique, perhaps because of the emphasis on the descriptive component of the ekphrastic image.[4] Descriptions of the tattoo are clearly the most obvious aspect of the ekphrastic dimension of the tattoo in texts, yet the stories or narratives which surround the tattoo — in other words, the reasons behind the acquisition of a tattoo and the cultural story or tradition associated with this body art are equally potent — the textual description of the tattoo not only creates a visual image of the tattoo for the reader, but also serves as the locus for the narrator's development of a story that on the surface intends to supply an explanation of the tattoo's representation. Tattoos usually generate more than a detached aesthetic appreciation. Kisch's reference to his tattoo of Bimbo as "revolting" is a case in point — the viewers of tattoos often experience a desire to discover the tattoo's symbolic value. One could argue that the expectation that a revelation of the tattoo's "true meaning" will accompany the ekphrastic description is more intense in autobiographical writing because this is a form that — rightly or wrongly — has been perceived as closer to "reality" than other prose forms such as the novel or short story. Of course, countless studies of autobiographical writing have demonstrated that there is always an element of creative construction or reconstruction in the telling of a story, even an autobiographical account. It is this possibility of invention that also marks Kisch's ekphrastic account of his tattoos. To begin with, the painting of Kisch that accompanies Segel's translation of Kisch's essay offers only a frontal view of the author's upper body, so the description of a tattoo on his back has no corresponding picture of this image which might suggest that an actual tattoo exists. However, a painting of an author may still be perceived as less reliable than a photograph in terms of its truth-telling ability, so unless there are photographs of Kisch that reveal these tattoos, a visual portrait is not a definitive sign of reality. What is more interesting than the search for correspondences between the textual descriptions of the tattoo and their visual representation in the painting (some might argue that it is important to show that Kisch's tattoos are examples of actual, rather than notional ekphrasis, is Kisch's presentation of the tattoos in a context of narrative play and irony. While Kisch was writing during the post–World War I period and seemed to share an enthusiasm for non-fictional writing or the "literature of fact" (Segel 3), the stories surrounding his tattoos may very well include fictional elements. For example, can we believe Kisch's reluctance to have the image of Bimbo tattooed on his arm, or that the green eyes continued to flare up every year in an almost supernatural fashion, or that he was unaware of the tattoo of the bloodied Chinese man as a symbol of castration? Yet even if these stories are distortions of the original experience of acquiring the tattoos, from a literary perspective they illustrate how the writer uses irony to present the seductive, subversive and mystical power of the tattoo as a sign of desire, violence, resistance and cultural otherness. Although the autobiographical essay proposes to contain or manage memory in some way, in the case of Kisch's tattoos this containment is unreliable, even with the assistance of the painting, thus reinforcing the tattoo's powers of resistance.

The use of the tattoo as an ekphrastic sign of resistance or as a subversive device and as a means of constructing narratives of desire is equally apparent in more recent autobiographical works by Stan Persky and Peter Trachtenberg. Unlike Kisch, who wrote during the post–World War I period, these North American writers published in the 1990s. However, like Kisch, Persky and Trachtenberg illustrate the tension between image and narrative that the tattoo creates as an ekphrastic device, and they also do so in the context of autobiographical writing. As Irene Gammel has pointed out in her collection *Confessional Politics: Women's Sexual Self-Representations in Life Writing and*

Popular Media, there has been a huge wave of interest in "confessional" style writing: "telling all is in." Autobiographical writing is one important expression of this interest. Persky's *Autobiography of a Tattoo* and Trachtenberg's *7 Tattoos: A Memoir in the Flesh* are contemporary book length works that reveal a preoccupation with telling, yet the act of telling is by no means a strictly linear or unified process. These postmodern narratives focus on frustrated desires and the fragmented self. The tattoo serves as an ekphrastic device for initiating this kind of narrative and narcissistic exploration, especially in the context of desire.

AUTOBIOGRAPHY OF A TATTOO

Stan Persky is a Canadian writer and critic who was born and raised in the United States. He has written poetry, essays, and a rather unconventional work called *Autobiography of a Tattoo* (1997), which describes his time in the U.S. Navy and his experience of acquiring a tattoo in San Francisco. This city is not only identified with tattoo and marine cultures, but it also evokes associations with homosexual desire because of its large gay community. Persky, who writes openly about his homosexual orientation, is keenly aware of the interrelationship between tattoos, desire and the navy. The title of his book also establishes a link between the ekphrastic device of the tattoo and the story of the self which is presented in a fragmented narrative form. Persky chooses not to accompany his rather brief ekphrastic description of the tattoo with any photos of the actual tattoos, perhaps because of the floating, nebulous quality of the tattoo in his narrative: "I bear a blue tattoo of a ship's anchor on my left forearm, acquired shortly after the completion of my 'tour of duty' in the U.S. Navy (1961). This is its story" (Persky 2).

The title of the author's book might lead a reader to expect a greater focus on a particular tattoo than Persky actually delivers. Instead, the autobiography turns out to be more about the narrator's exploration of his own desire (homosexual desire), as well as the tattoos of others (not just "a tattoo" but more than one tattoo), thus resisting or subverting a more traditional ekphrastic technique of presenting a

19

detailed description of a visual image such as Kisch provides in his modernist autobiography "My Tattoos." The narrative engages in a deconstructionist play with a reader's expectation that there will be lengthy ekphrastic descriptions of Persky's tattoo, or logical, linear connections between various episodes. And despite the narrator's contention that "[t]he tattoo's autobiography is not all hesitations, false starts, *coitus interruptus*" (183), most of the narrative reads this way because this is a way of communicating the narrator's desire for men and for the tattoos of other men. Persky's own tattoo — which is given a rather brief ekphrastic description, "a blue tattoo of a ship's anchor" — is largely developed through his descriptions of the tattoos of a boy in the navy and his father's tattoo. Thus the reader is encouraged "by indirection [to] find directions out" (*Hamlet* 2.1).

The textual interweaving of Persky's tattoo, a Navy boy's tattoo, and his father's body art is presented in section 6 "The Tattoo," of *Autobiography of a Tattoo*. The father's tattoo is described as a "three-dimensional five-pointed blue star on the outside of his right bicep" and serves as an "object of endless fascination" for the young Persky because his father can make the tattoo move with the use of his arm muscles. It represents an initiation into the world of desire: "Again and again I would ask this *vigorous* [emphasis mine], bald-headed man in a white T-shirt" (201) to make the star move. The blue star tattoo is blue like Persky's anchor, but more importantly, it evokes a kind of desire for the movement of the body.

Yet even though Persky's father believes that Stan has followed in his footsteps by joining the navy, Persky's homosexual orientation indicates that he has resisted his father's heterosexual life. This lifestyle of resistance is reflected in his "admiration" of a fellow Navy boy and his tattoo. The latter sported a tattoo of a blue ship's anchor, which is the kind of tattoo Persky says he wanted to get if he were ever to get one. It is through this piece of information that we, as readers, assume that Persky's anchor tattoo matches this one. What is even more intriguing is the suggestion of body imagery through the different terms used to describe portions of the anchor: "[t]he anchor was an 'unfouled' one, which meant that it didn't have a rope (or 'line') tangled (or 'fouled') in around its eye, arms, torso, or pronged feet" (202). But since Persky never describes his own tattoo in detail, the narrative evades full disclosure and the ekphrastic presence of his own tattoo resists complete identification with the Navy fellow's tattoo, the object of his desire.

The narrator's decision to acquire his own tattoo takes place while he is involved in a homosexual romance in San Francisco. This city is well known not only as a site for sexual otherness and for the prominence of the homosexual community, but also for its tattoo community. The artist who tattoos him is none other than the famous Lyle Tuttle, whose entire body except for his hands, neck, and face "was completely covered by a tapestry of tattoos" (204). Tuttle, a white tattoo artist, becomes part of Persky's own narrative and ekphrastic tattoo tapestry of desire. Although he does not relate the two episodes, after Tuttle shows his tattoos, including the tattoo on his sexual organ, the narrator has a curious fantasy of wishing that he was "a black man so that [he] could get the tattoo of the anchor in white ink" (204). This use of a cultural Other in a tattoo narrative is reminiscent of Kisch's descriptions of the tattoo of a Chinese man and his tattoo of Bimbo, the Black entertainer. However, the subversion that Persky creates in his narrative is not related to the cultural Other's undoing the narrator (the Chinese eunuch symbol and the green eyes of Bimbo which infect every year). Instead, the cultural otherness of Black skin is presented as a bodily state that Persky cannot possibly emulate and remains a desire in the Lacanian sense of a yearning that cannot be satisfied.[5]

While Persky's *Autobiography of a Tattoo* may frustrate a reader interested in more explicit descriptions of tattoos, what Persky does leave us with is a sense of the tattoo's symbolic value: it represents an "initiatory education in desire, art, the world — as a document, testimony, as a vow of *memory*" (205). In this sense, the tattoo does fulfill its role as a symbol which, like desire, cannot be fully grasped; even though it exists as a literal inscription on his left forearm (183), it serves as a device for presenting the fragments of memory and the body that are part of writing the partial autobiographical self.

7 TATTOOS: A MEMOIR IN THE FLESH

Peter Trachtenberg's *7 Tattoos: A Memoir in the Flesh* is another contemporary example of autobiographical writing that uses the tattoo to narrate and visualize the self in the context of various kinds of resistance. As a text, it presents written descriptions of the seven tattoos he has acquired in the course of his life. Even though the tattoos are presented in chronological order, the narratives resist a purely linear movement and include reflections on different periods in his life, offering images of his different selves over some forty odd years, including drug addict, alcoholic, student protestor, womanizer, Jew, child of Holocaust survivors, wannabee Catholic, and writer. Like Persky's, Trachtenberg's tattoo narrative depicts the narrator's desires and the image of the tattoo as a sign of resistance; however, Trachtenberg's tattoos also convey more painful and at times more violent images than Persky's narrative.

Unlike Persky's *Autobiography of a Tattoo,* Trachtenberg's memoir also happens to include drawings of his tattoos (which emphasize the intermediality of the book), but what remains fascinating about his text is the assortment of stories generated by the images that reflect the narrator's desires at various times in his life. The author's tattoos function in a visual and narrative capacity. Each chapter is oriented around the symbolic significance of the visual form; his tattoos are aesthetic images of cultural exploration and appropriation as well as sites of desire, memory and resistance. They reinforce the ambivalent role of the tattoo memoir (or autobiographical writing) as a faithful preserver of the past and its counter-tendency to create narratives of resistance which emphasize the unfulfilled desires of the narrator.

As in Kisch's and Persky's texts, the tattoo in Trachtenberg's text serves as a way of linking both the concept of ekphrasis and memoir. The author's tattoos function as a visible illustration of "something that is absent or invisible" (Trachtenberg 16). In this sense, they are similar to the concept of ekphrasis, which is a verbal or textual description of an absent image. An ekphrastic image is usually accessible only through the textual representation or through our knowledge of an "original" work of art that exists outside the confines of the text. Even though Trachtenberg includes drawings or artistic representations of the tattoos in his memoir, we can still argue that his tattoos remain examples of notional ekphrasis since the descriptions correspond to images embedded within the "text" or book rather than photographs of the "actual" image on the author's body. The "original" tattoos still remain elusive and resist any kind of unified symbolism. (The same point was made in relation to the painting of Kisch's tattoos.) W. J. T. Mitchell has claimed that all ekphrasis is notional,[6] since even in the case of a reference to an actual painting the ekphrastic representation is a re-construction of this "real" work of art.

Like ekphrasis, memoir is a form which represents that which is absent in order to portray past events or individuals. In this sense, ekphrasis and memoir are closely linked to the concept of desire, since all three seek to "capture" that which is absent. The writer of a memoir or autobiography may construct fictions as part of this process of remembering: "We all make up stories about our parents, the way tribal people make up stories about the origin of the world" (238). This fictionalization in turn contributes to the multiple symbolic meanings of Trachtenberg's ekphrastic tattoos and even the pictures of his tattoos which resist any single truth.

Trachtenberg presents his seven tattoos as a way of accessing other cultural, artistic, or religious experiences and as a means of representing the intricate visual narrative of his life, including his own cultural Jewish-American affiliation. The tattoos may be divided into several different categories, each of which allows Trachtenberg to construct the tattoo as a sign of some kind of resistance, sometimes in relation to Jewish culture. Tattoos 1 and 3 include a tribal design derived from the Dayak people of Borneo; tattoos 2, 5, and 7 have religious symbolism; tattoo 4 is a symbol of the worker's/communist resistance; and tattoo 6 illustrates how a tattoo acquired as a copy of a lover's tattoo comes to symbolize a failed love relationship: tattoo 6 thus focuses on desire in the form of romantic and sexual desire. Even though his other tattoo narratives do not focus on desire in the erotic sense, they address how he uses tattoos to capture and narrate various forms of desire and pain in his life.

Tribal Tattoos and Resistance

Peter Trachtenberg's first example of how tattoos reflect a desire to mark oneself with the image of another culture involves his trip to Amsterdam. Here he acquired a tribal tattoo from one of the world's great tattoo artists, Henk Schiffmacher, otherwise known as Hanky Panky. It is not unusual for people to travel to other places to acquire a tattoo, since this often facilitates an individual's desire to inscribe another identity onto the body. Peter describes the design he had adapted from a photo in a book of Dayak art from Borneo. The tattoo is "a set of antlers ... actually adapted from an Iban Dayak pattern from Sarawak" (4). He says that it transforms him into "a jungle thing, into a head-hunting Dayak motherfucker" (7). The image is clearly associated with violence and perhaps suggests the narrator's desire to absorb the power of a cultural Other. A year or so later Peter embarks on a journey to Borneo in order to find this tattoo's "original" (4). However, his search for an authentic tattoo proves elusive since the Ngaju people respond that "no one's been tattooed like that for a hundred years" (15); he is thus presented as an anomaly or site of resistance in this particular cultural context. Eventually he meets a group of natives who react to the visual image of his tattoo; they remember relatives who also had one before the arrival of the missionaries who had claimed that tattoos were wicked. Ironically, Trachtenberg's own body functions as the conduit for their collective cultural memory despite the fact that his "tattoo wasn't exactly authentic" (21). He says that he was "just some Dayak wannabe, a cross-cultural poseur, and here I had traveled twelve thousand miles bearing the key to their past on my skin, without even knowing that was what I was carrying" (21). As a "wannabe" he conveys how his desires to become a cultural Other[7] are often frustrated when he merely focuses on his tattoo in a narcissistic fashion. Yet, interestingly enough, his body still acts as a means of communicating something about the Dayak culture to a group of natives, albeit in a mediated form. While recognizing the problematic aspect of his tattoo as a sign of cultural appropriation, Trachtenberg reveals the powerful dimension of the tattoo as an inscriber of memory (even

***The Bounty* (1984). Orion Pictures. Mel Gibson stars as Fletcher Christian,** **formerly the friend and later the enemy of Captain Bligh. This scene depicts** **the tattoo and the tattooing process as a reflection of the desire for the cul-** **tural Other. This kind of desire is experienced by Peter Trachtenberg in his** **memoir, *7 Tattoos: A Memoir in the Flesh* when he searches for an original** **Dayak tattoo that resembles the tribal tattoo he acquired in Amsterdam. In** **this film still, Fletcher Christian is receiving a tattoo in the Tahitian tradi-** **tion of tapping; the placement of Fletcher Christian's head in the lap of a** **beautiful native woman emphasizes his desire to embrace cultural otherness.**

if the memory must be re-contextualized) and a site of cross-cultural communication.

In *7 Tattoos* the tattoo is an ambivalent image or ekphrastic device which suggests entry into a foreign culture while enforcing the author's own cultural identity. This statement also applies to how Kisch's "white-ness" becomes all the more apparent as his tattoos of Bimbo, "the negro entertainer," and of the Chinese man symbolic of eunuchs indicate that he cannot "manage" or contain a cultural Other. The form of the mem-oir imitates the complex symbolism at work in the tattoos. A tattoo may have initially one kind of symbolic value or cultural association; however, its signification proliferates over time as the bearer constructs new narratives. Similarly, a memoir may consist of key episodes which contribute to the main linear movement of the retelling. However, often the sections of narrative which resist the purely linear progression of the "main storyline" are just as important, if not more so, to the entire construction of events or characters.

The use of the memoir as a narrative form often includes visual images that facilitate this exploration of the self.[8] Memoirs or autobiographies sometimes include either actual photographs (e.g., Denise Chong's *The Concubine's Children*) which are also described by the writer (an example of ekphrasis), or the ekphrastic device of describing photographs (in Maxine Hong Kingston's *Woman Warrior*), or even pictures that draw attention to the discrepancy between the photograph and the ekphrastic description (e.g., Carol Shields' *The Stone Diaries*). Instead of photographs, tattoos serve as the key visual device in Trachtenberg's memoir. They act as a point of departure for his memories of family as well as his discussion of other cultures, aesthetic experiences or desires. The tattoo functions in an interesting way because, like most of the other sections of the story, it allows the author to interweave different desires, memories and cultural experiences. For example, chapter one (which includes the author's discussion of his first tattoo and his trip to Borneo) cannot be entirely disengaged from his memory of his father and parallels between Jewish culture and other cultures: "Now, before we get to Borneo, I need to mention that the other reason I'd been so late in getting tattooed was my father. First off, my father was Jewish, and Leviticus 19 says everything there is to say about Jews and tattoos: 'Ye shall not make any cuttings in your flesh for the dead, nor print any marks upon you'" (7). The author thus postpones his narrative of his travels to Borneo (and the reader's desire to hear more about this trip), as a way of explaining the symbolic value of the tattoo, by offering a discussion of Jewish tradition.[9]

The image of the marked body as a taboo is embedded in his Jewish heritage and causes him some anxiety; the tattoo as a site of cultural memory is further reinforced through the tattooing of the Jews in Nazi death camps and creates a graphic image of the relationship between tattoos and violence: "Tattooing had been the Germans' way of keeping track of the Jews they were killing in such huge numbers" (7). Ultimately Trachtenberg resists these negative associations with tattoos that were forced upon people and chooses instead to become someone who is marked willingly; he views his act as a betrayal of his cultural heritage, believing that he has somehow betrayed his father (and the tattooed people he grew up around) and the memory of the Holocaust. Yet, despite the fear that he has defiled a cultural memory, Trachtenberg's tattoos paradoxically allow him to enter into the past to discuss his family and cultural relations. For example, during his trip to Borneo, one Ngaju native by the name of Clarence asks Peter about his tattoo and his father's reaction to it. This question causes the author to remember his father's death. The section then ends with the unusual juxtaposition of an Orthodox Jewish burial and the death song of the Ngaju. This kind of cross-cultural representation is quite different from the less complex/creative depictions of the cultural Other in Kisch's and Persky's autobiographical works (the negro performer and Persky's desire to be a Black man so that he can have a white tattoo).

The interaction between different cultures is repeated in chapter three when Trachtenberg discusses his third tattoo, also a design from Borneo. It is called the Dragon Dog and resembles a wheel and a swastika. According to Trachtenberg, the Iban and Punan Dayaks of northern Borneo view it as a symbol of protection and cosmic unity of male and female elements. He acquires this tattoo before his second trip to Borneo, during which he hopes to find tattooed native inhabitants. He mentions his own tattoo during an interview with a tattooed Kayan woman from the region of Long Bagun in Borneo. However, instead of articulating the cosmic unity of male and female elements as symbolized by his design, he offends the woman when he tells her that his tattoo is based on those of her people. She responds, "'They're not from here.... My people are Kayan'" (103). His encounter with a cultural Other is thus a disappointing one since her tattoos were shameful to her. They reminded her of a past that had not only vanished but been disavowed. The only tattooed people she saw on the TV in the village meetinghouse would be the gangsters in Indonesian crime shows. She had heard her shopkeeper call her an *orang hutan*. In her own lifetime she had become primitive. It is a term that may be nostalgic to us but can only be humiliating to the people we use it to describe [104].[10]

Instead of symbolizing "cosmic unity" and reinforcing the narrator's desire to communicate this kind of unity in his interaction with a native inhabitant, the narrator's tattoo evokes the violence often associated with gangsters in Indonesian crime shows or the lack of respect for a "primitive" past. Trachtenberg's cross-cultural encounter thus reinforces the image of the tattoo as a sign of resistance. The Kayan woman is constructed as a social outcast; similarly Trachtenberg's tattoo resists any identification with unity and contributes to the cultural tension in his encounter with a native inhabitant.

This cultural rift and lack of male/female unity is re-presented in his memory of his relationship with Dinah, one of his many former lovers. Here, Trachtenberg emphasizes desire in an erotic context but still relates this form of desire to the narrator's desire to communicate with other cultures. Dinah's partial American Indian heritage compounds the guilt he already feels for maintaining a relationship with her while betraying another lover: "Am I making Dinah my white man's burden?" (98). His guilt (whatever the source) results in their cultural tension; she thinks he does not wish to continue the relationship because she is not white, and he is unable to see beyond the mask that he has constructed for her, a mask of physical attributes he thinks of as "Indian" (99). Like his encounter with the Borneo woman, he has superimposed his notion of the primitive onto Dinah. However, despite his breakup with her, he still perceives some kind of enduring connection. The chapter ends with an episode that occurs after his return from Borneo. He sees Dinah again as she is sitting on a bus; he wants to talk to her, but unable to communicate verbally, he pulls off his shirt and shows Dinah his tattoos, especially the Dragon Dog on his left biceps (109). Somehow, the visual image expresses this message more succinctly and dramatically than any verbal utterance.[11] It functions as a kind of mediator much like the concept of desire, which often finds no direct object but moves along through an endless chain of signifiers. The tattoo is a record of their past life together, including the ironic resistance of their relationship to the concept of the union of male and female elements embedded in the image of the Dragon Dog tattoo. The narrative draws attention to the author's desire for unity, a desire that is best articulated through the tattoo, which becomes a device of mediation, since words prove inadequate.[12]

Left Wing Resistance

Trachtenberg's fourth tattoo permits the author to shift his discussion of tribal or "primitive" cultures to the field of American politics and the issue of leftist resistance. The layered effect of this memoir chapter, "I Keep the Red Flag Flying," intertwines his memory of different political eras in American history with his father's socialism and Peter's involvement in the New York tattoo scene. The tattoo which represents this form of resistance is created by Peter's female tattoo artist for a competition:

> The tattoo Slam had given me was a drawing of a wrench placed diagonally between two gears. She'd rendered the spanner with punctilious thoroughness, down to the highlights on its chrome-plated shaft, while leaving the gears black silhouettes, and she'd unified the composition by framing wrench and gears with a red triangle that sat athwart my deltoid [119].

As an ekphrastic and aesthetic device, the tattoo contains a foreign cultural element; it draws on Russian Constructivism, a short-lived artistic movement that highlighted the aesthetic of the machine. From 1917 to the late 1920s, Constructivist artists sought to "express the aspirations of the revolutionary proletariat and enhance the physical and intellectual conditions of society as a whole" (Honour and Fleming 687–688). The movement is described by Trachtenberg as "the last unfettered breath drawn by revolutionary art before Stalin strangled it with the noose of Socialist Realism" (Trachtenberg 119). Trachtenberg views his machine tattoo, which he acquired in 1992, as an "emblem of sabotage" used to wipe out the representatives of conservatism and corporate greed that dominated America: "the bankers and the arms dealers and the lumber barons, the fag-bashing preachers, the judges and the lobbyists, and the lawyers...." (120). However, it is also a fitting visual symbol for his anti–Vietnam war activities (in the 1960s) and his earlier brick-throwing acts of resistance to Nixon in 1972, when he joined a group of student protestors to show "solidarity with all oppressed peoples" (113). The author thus imbues the tattoo with an aesthetic of violence and resistance that are presented as alternative weapons to combat the forces of right wing tendencies.[13]

The tattoo also serves as an image that leads into Trachtenberg's narrative about his father's socialism. He had been a "Socialist in Austria in the 1930s" (121) and had marched for the workers against the Nazis (121). When thinking of some of his father's remarks over the years that suggest a *lack* of sympathy with leftist struggle, Trachtenberg concludes that these statements were part of his father's "cover." In the memoir he desperately wishes to sustain an image of his father as a leftist, despite all of the evidence to the contrary. However, he eventually realizes that, like his father — who claimed that "sometimes you got to vote for your bankbook" (134) — he has also compromised his socialist values: "I fret about property values. I grouse over my taxes. I stomp past the dread-locked white kids who panhandle on Avenue A, my spine thrumming with indignation" (142). This shift in political and cultural values crosses cultures (from Austria to the United States) and generations.

This questioning of resistance culture is reinforced in Trachtenberg's discussion of the tattoo milieu or scene, which is usually associated with marginalized groups of people who resist mainstream aesthetics and values. From 1976 to 1981, the author spent four nights a week at the club CBCG where the New York Tattoo Society held its meetings. He saw "unrepentant lawbreakers" including the tattooist Tommy DaVita, who had opened a shop in 1961 after the city made tattooing illegal[14] due to a hepatitis outbreak. However, the image of the tattoo community as a force of resistance is questioned by the author when he returns for a tattoo competition in 1992. During this time he perceives that the radical tendencies have transmuted into concerns about business[15]:

> The truth is tattooists are craftspeople and small-business owners, and they tend to be conservative. Even Slam bitches about the junkies who panhandle on her front stoop ... the most painful truth of all, is that in the 1990s deviance is a marketing strategy ... [144].

This view of resistance groups being coopted by mainstream power sources is not new. It is a reality that is evident in many different groups associated with alternative practices (e.g., the popularity of gay characters in the television sit-com *Will and Grace*) and thus demonstrates how the tattoo and tattoo artists may occupy an ambivalent position: affirming connections to a particular form of marginality while also suggesting connections to established institutions.

Religion and Images of Resistance

Trachtenberg's second tattoo is an example of how this visual art form may be associated with an established religious institution while also suggesting a subversion of religion. The tattoo depicts dripping blood imitative of Christ's wound; it is even placed along his rib cage and ends just above his waist (67). His fifth and seventh tattoos are angels. All three tattoos permit the author to examine religion and the question of resistance or ways of challenging orthodox practices, whether Jewish or Christian.

The second tattoo, copied from an Albrecht Dürer woodcut, is described as a "document of a particular kind of suffering" (37), which is not surprising given the fact that it is a stigma, ["one of Christ's wounds" (39). Trachtenberg recognizes that it is "an outré thing for a Jew to want" (39) or desire; however, its trangressive quality does not end there. He mentions how difficult it was to find a tattooist who was willing to execute this design. Even within the alternative world of tattooing it is considered taboo. He also comments on how the tattoo would be perceived differently by Christians and Jews. According to Trachtenberg, "if you're a Christian, getting one of Jesus's wounds might be considered a laudable thing to do. You know the *Imitatio Christi? The Imitation of Christ?*" (42). However, according to the author, if one is a Jew, such an image is a sacrilege. Not only is he marking his flesh, but he is defaming Jesus and "violating the tacit rule that Jews do nothing — *nothing* to chafe the sensibilities of the people whose tolerance [they] depend on for [their] lives" (42).

As for his reasons for choosing this tattoo, the author does mention that at one time he had become fascinated with Catholicism. He was particularly struck by the images of wounds on the heart of Saint Teresa of Avila that had supposedly been made by God (55). He also found moving the gospel story of Thomas, who touches Jesus' wound, because in some Gnostic versions of the story Thomas is Jesus' twin, and, since twins "are the sundered halves of a single egg," when Thomas placed his hand in the rift in Jesus's side he was "touching his other self" (63). His fascination with wounds (not to mention his heroin addiction[16]) may explain his interest in tattooing, which also involves blood and pain. This relationship between tattooing, wounds and religious fervour is presented in the film *Stigmata*, which offers visual parallels between tattooing and the mysterious phenomenon of stigmata.

Trachtenberg takes his obsession with wounds even further when he convinces himself that he is Jesus' secret twin. This conviction or "madness" stems in part from his feeling that what he had suffered from all his life "was the loss of a twin ... who had died before I was born, maybe in another lifetime" (64). He explains this belief that there were "other selves who were now gone" (63) as a feeling that may be common to all children of Holocaust survivors: "maybe we have the equivalent of an amputee's phantom limb syndrome: a pain that emanates from absence" (63). This focus on absence can in turn be linked to the concept of desire, since desire can never be satisfied. Furthermore, the explanation of phantom selves through the image of Jesus' twin illustrates how Trachtenberg's exploration of Christian religious imagery is presented in a way that only serves to illuminate his Jewish heritage. The tattoo, which appears to resist Jewish culture, is actually transformed into an inscription of the suffering and loss that mark this culture. The image of the tattoo as a sign of "something that is absent or invisible" (16), a desire that can never be truly fulfilled, and as a symbol that resists an easy explanation, is articulated in Trachtenberg's account just as it was in the earlier works by Kisch and Persky through the authors' use of ekphrastic and narrative techniques. Ekphrasis is by definition a textual representation of a visual image; however, the tattoo may well resist representation either because there are no drawings or photographs of the tattoo or because the bearer of the tattoo symbolizes loss or the unattainability of a particular state. In Kisch's case, the tattoo of the Chinese man represented not only the suffering of the eunuch, who is an image of mutilation and frustrated desire, but Kisch's inability to transform the cultural Other into a "he-man" (Segel 210). Persky's constant resistance to providing detailed descriptions of his tattoo indicate the attraction of the tattoo as a sign of loss or a symbol of the inexplicable, which for Persky is closely allied not only to sexual desire but also to the way memory operates. For Trachtenberg, the tattoo serves as a sign of memory as well, but the desire to access this collective memory of suffering and loss may be accomplished only in an indirect or mediated way — through an alternate religious image.

Trachtenberg builds on the image of absence through his ekphrastic presentation of tattoos that depict a particular kind of angel. These tattoos are also captured in the titles of the respective chapters. Chapter five, "I Do the Right Thing," presents a scowling archangel holding a sword and the scales of Justice, while chapter seven, (the final chapter, "I Fall Down") depicts a similar kind of angel falling down. In chapter five, the angel is described as the Archangel Michael, and the tattoo is conceived by the author as a mark of penance. He wishes to atone for wronging his father and his mother over the years by wearing the tattoo as a kind of sentence on his body (Trachtenberg 150) like the penitents in Kafka's *Penal Colony*. Interestingly enough, he chooses a design that also has potent Christian symbolism:

> But the design, after all, was from the early Middle Ages. Some say that crusaders used to get the tattoo of the Archangel Michael to commemorate a journey to the Holy Land. Another story has it that the device was worn by Egyptian Copts, as a sign to their Moslem rulers that they, too, were people of the Book: The Tattoo was a kind of pass that spared them the treatment that was generally meted out to other infidels [179–180].

Yet what is important for Trachtenberg is not the Christian association but the concept of "wrongdoing," which he emphasizes in his discussion of criminals in different cultures, including the figure of Cain, who bore the first tattoo. Trachtenberg subverts the story of the disempowered tattooed criminal who is marked by God, the divine father, without his consent. Unlike Cain, Peter actively chooses his own tattoo. The narrator engages in the ritualistic act of being tattooed as a way of apologizing to his dead father. His act is accompanied by an interesting ekphrastic device, the textual description of his father's photographs (180). Thus the photograph, which Roland Barthes has characterized as "absence"[17] or as a way of remembering the dead, reinforces Trachtenberg's earlier characterization of the tattoo as a sign of something absent. Both the photograph and the tattoo serve as mediators for a desire that cannot be expressed directly.

The seventh and final chapter of *7 Tattoos* focuses on images of falling, resistance and the narrator's struggle with the concept of death in different religious or cultural contexts. The seventh tattoo is a fallen angel, the mirror image of his other angel tattoo: "...he would be falling, falling as though struck by lightning. His sword would be broken. His olive branch would have dropped from his hand. And there would be a look of terror on his face" (232).

For Trachtenberg, the angel also serves as a symbol of resistance in an ironic sort of way. He acquires this tattoo after a physical fall, and acknowledges that he has "never heard of anyone being tattooed after the fact, as a measure against injuries that have already been incurred" (227). His decision to do so subverts the notion of a tattoo as protection against future disease or danger (227), which is the belief of various cultures.[18]

Even though the tattoo appears to be a way of marking the author's physical fall, it is also associated with his identity as a "lapsed Jew" who resists some of the articles of his faith and turns to Buddhist teachings, including the Tibetan Book of the Dead, for solace. His resistance to the notion of a single truth or way of seeing is reinforced through the fictions he constructs throughout his memoir. In this final chapter, he admits that he has lied about the fallen angel tattoo. He told people that the angel was acquired as a memorial to his mother, even though it was "done nine months before she died" (262).

He concludes that even though the angel could represent his mother, perhaps the angel really is Lucifer, and he constructs a new narrative of Lucifer's Fall from heaven, thus ensuring a strong identification between his angel tattoo and this legendary fallen angel.[19] Yet ultimately the object of the narrator's desire cannot be contained neatly in either the image of his mother or that of Lucifer; he resists a simply binary opposition between mother and Lucifer just as he resists the simple binary thinking of a God who would "carve his creatures up into the preterite" (or the non-elect) and "the saved" (262).

Desire and Writing as Resistance

Trachtenberg's narrative of his sixth tattoo offers his reader stories on the topic of romantic desire rather than filial love. In this chapter, "I Kiss Her Good-Bye," the narrator discusses his failed love relationship with a woman by the name of Tara. The chapter highlights the relationship between the tattoo and desire, which is also evident in both Kisch's and Persky's tattoo narratives, and it also presents desire in the context of some kind of resistance. Like Persky, Peter acquires a copy of another individual's tattoo; however, like Kisch, Trachtenberg is aware of the tattoo's capacity to reflect the ironies of eros and life. For example, Peter acquires a copy of his girlfriend's tattoo of dancing stick people, not because he thought that they would stay together, but because he knew they wouldn't (187), thus reinforcing the concept of desire as a state that cannot be fulfilled. Tattoos are often acquired as a way of indicating the permanence and success of a relationship, but for the narrator, his copy of his girlfriend's tattoo suggests the opposite. His pessimistic "reading" of their relationship is also evident in his ekphrastic description of Tara's tattoo, which differs from her own "reading." Tara describes the tattoo as "'dancing people! See their arms?'" (204). Peter, however, elaborates on the description by describing them as the kinds of dancers you see "at Grateful Dead concerts, swaying with the boneless languor of sea anemones. But they might also be people who've been reunited with their loved ones after a long parting, flinging up their arms in the prelude to an embrace so fierce, so greedy, that it could be an act of violence" (204). Here the narrator links desire and violence and develops the reference to violence even more fully in the narrative as he describes the pain involved in acquiring a copy of Tara's tattoo. This experience seems to be an omen of a relationship that will go awry. The tattooist appears to harbor the sadistic tendency of making Peter bleed more during the process, leaving him with "a thick black biscuit of scab that peeled painfully and unevenly, taking off a good deal of the pigment underneath. Many of the figures came out blotched and prematurely faded. It was a bad tattoo" (189). This sadism is an echo of what may be viewed as Peter's own sadistic approach to love relationships — the tendency to leave the women he loves: "S&M is not so much about pain as it is about power, and in sexual relationships power resides with the one who is willing to leave" (198). The masochistic aspect of Peter's desire is evident in his decision to acquire a tattoo that will remind him of the loss of the relationship and in his ability to endure the pain of the tattooing process.

The ekphrastic description of Peter's tattoo also reveals how this tattoo functions as a sign of resistance to the spirit of Tara's original tattoo (dancing people). It embodies the fierceness and violence that Peter ascribes to Tara's stick people, thus suggesting their relationship will not endure. Such a description illustrates that it really does not matter whether a visual image in a text corresponds to some kind of actual image, since the reproduction often resists complete identification with the original.

Trachtenberg not only uses his own tattoo — a failed copy of his lover's tattoo — to convey his inability to sustain his relationship with Tara, but he also introduces stories in order to embed his tattoos in narrative forms such as fiction and film: "Stories are the way we tell the truth and the way we change it into something bearable, encasing the original irritant in the pearly layers of narrative. I've given my irritant another name and another past. I've put words in her mouth. I've done everything I can to hide her" (215). Like tattoos, stories act as a vehicle of mediation for the expression of desire. While this tattoo narrative does not include a cultural Other like some of his other chapters, it does emphasize how individuals construct themselves as Other in stories, because they have difficulty communicating directly. *7 Tattoos* reflects the fiction-making qualities of autobiographical writing, which Trachtenberg highlights through two key techniques. One device is his presentation of stories that Tara sends to Peter to read. The stories include accounts of physical abuse and a self-reflexive story about a woman who sends stories to a male writer. The stories are Tara's way of asking Peter to love her ["'Do I have to spell everything out? I want you to love me!'" (213)]. However, Peter has difficulty removing himself from the world of her "story" and talking about himself in the first person, since he continues to talk about Tara's male character as "he" rather than "I." ["Stop talking about 'he.' This isn't a story anymore" (213)]. This embedding of a story within a story is similar to Peter's tattoo which is a copy of Tara's tattoo, a layering effect that highlights the process of resisting identification with "an original." Like desire, which cannot completely capture a loved one, the reproduction of Tara's tattoo conveys difference or absence rather than sameness.

The use of another technique of embedding a narrative within a narrative is evident in Trachtenberg's inclusion of a film dialogue to indirectly tell the story about the narrator's life with Tara. This narrative takes the form of a film plot. It has elements of a 1940s film noir thriller, which is a genre that often includes some romantic tension between a leading male character and a mysterious woman who may be dangerous (a *femme fatale*). Films based on the crime fiction of Raymond Chandler are good illustrations of the kinds of male/female relationships portrayed in these films. However, as the narrator points out, the film is still his creation despite the stylistic resemblance to a well known genre: "Back to my movie. Let's call it *Riptide* or *The Undertow* or, my personal favorite, *The Mark*, which has the further advantage of being a double entendre" (199). The movie is about a man who leaves his lover to go to war, but before doing so, he acquires a tattoo of "an anchor with a chain wrapped round it and the name 'MONA' written underneath in a finicky Palmer script" (189). The movie's parallels to Peter's own tattoo are evident in the sense that his movie also becomes a story of a failed love. While Peter never acquired a tattoo of his lover's name, his copy of her tattoo is a visual (rather than a textual) recreation of the same, since when he looks at it he remembers her. The movie ends with the male character, Nick, acquiring a different physical identity and postponing a reunion with his lover because she has since married another. At the end of this film, the male character is shot by Mona. Here, Peter uses the film script to invest the woman with a kind of sadistic power that he has in his relationship with Tara. Trachtenberg's technique of including this kind of script has the effect of disrupting the continuity of his "real" autobiography, but it serves the important purpose of illustrating how access to a "real" self is an illusion even in a genre such as autobiographical writing: "...just by using that 'I,' that black hole of English grammar, you are automatically re-creating all the stories you ever told about yourself: You are telling them all over again" (205). This image of narrating the self and reinventing the self is also present in how Trachtenberg uses his copy of Tara's tattoo, and the anchor tattoo in his film script, to capture in an indirect or mediated way some truths about his life. The ekphrastic description of the tattoo that the character Nick bears on his arm describes the sadomasochistic tendencies of lovers: "How could I forget her, when her name was right there on my skin? I couldn't look at my arm without seeing it. I was wrapped around her the way that chain was wrapped around that anchor. And even then I knew I couldn't get loose. I didn't want to get loose. Not even if she took me straight to the bottom" (200). The tattoo, like the process of being tattooed (especially if the tattoo is a poorly done tattoo like Peter's stick people), is a reminder of some of the sadomasochistic aspects of love, as well as the impossibility of fulfilling some romantic desire — hence the use of film noir. This blackness associated with the more pessimistic aspects of film noir is made visually concrete through the narrator's reference to the "black hole" of the autobiographical "I" which includes a layering and seemingly endless reinvention of the self. Furthermore, the image of the horrible black scab, a reminder of Peter's "bad tattoo," is eventually redone, thus demonstrating how tattoos can reinvent the self, just as the endless narrative layers of autobiography can reconstruct the self and resist any simple identification with one original self.

Even though tattoos are visible scars on the body, they may represent that which cannot be grasped or achieved. In this sense they are fitting representations of desire which embeds elements of resistance, since that which is desired is by definition unattainable. Both Stan Persky's and Peter Trachtenberg's narratives show further signs of mediation because their stories are ekphrastic narratives; they offer verbal representations of visual images: tattoos. These autobiographical accounts emphasize that even though a tattoo has the appearance of a concrete image, the memories that it generates may be fragmented. The symbolic fictions that Persky and Trachtenberg construct for different tattoos reinforce the art of autobiographical writing as a way of remembering desires of the self through the reconstruction of other people. In telling stories about others, these writers often arrive at some awareness of their narrative selves. The tattoo thus serves as an ekphrastic metaphor which facilitates this process of creating narratives of mediated identities. Like any other autobiographical art form, tattoos convey a kind of creative narcissism: the bearers of these images are often watching or creating other people in order to watch and create themselves.[20]

CHAPTER TWO

Illustrating the Feminine: Women, Desire, and Resistance in Tattoo Narratives and Culture

The construction of the tattoo as a work of art has been intimately linked with the erotic possibilities of this visual form and with the gender of the viewer and of the bearer of the tattoo. Traditionally, women have been the object of the male gaze, whether in the context of visual art such as painting or in the context of tattoo culture. Even though the tattoo is largely a marginalized form of artistic expression, it has still been dominated by a masculinist[1] aesthetic, resulting in the representation of women as objects of male desire. The popular song "Lydia the Tattooed Lad" illustrates woman as the object of male pleasure and as a book or encyclopedia for the male reader. The fact that Groucho Marx, who played characters known for their lustful interest in the female sex, sang this song is an extra-textual (if not extra-sexual!) reinforcer for the dominance of a masculinist aesthetic.

Other representations of tattooed women as the object of the male gaze include the images of women as stereotypical pinup girls that have been tattooed on men's arms. These images, along with nude tattooed women in magazines, have served the same function as the female nude in Western painting and in certain Eastern depictions of the ideal female form; all of these were created for the male heterosexual gaze or aesthetic. However, there are also signs of a feminist aesthetic developing within tattoo culture as more women shift from their role as *objets d'art* or master-pieces to artists or creators. For example, women tattoo artists, who were once a small minority among tattooists, are increasing in numbers.[2] This shift from object to agent, which is facilitating the development of a feminist aesthetic, is also evident in the context of literature or visual media such as film and television. The representation of tattoos in twentieth-century literature, film and other forms of cultural production often establishes a connection between the concept of a masculinist aesthetic experience and women who resist a masculinist aesthetic, narrative or world view. Tattooed women or female tattoo artists in both literary and non-literary contexts function as examples of feminine empowerment. They create new narratives and possibilities for women as they resist pre-existing masculinist narratives.

The Masculine Aesthetic in Tattoo Culture and Narrative

Tattoo culture has traditionally been a very male-centered culture, since the majority of the tattoo artists across cultures tend to be male and more men than women tend to acquire tattoos. When women are tattooed they are often restricted to objects of male, heterosexual desire. This is predominantly the case in Western tattoo culture but is also evident in Japanese culture, where the majority of tattoo artists have been male and tattooed women served as a canvas much like the idealized women in the art of Japanese printmaking. While the tattoo is still a transgressive kind of art form, women often appear to have more limitations imposed upon them by the patriarchal structure of tattoo communities. The 1983 Japanese film *Irezumi* (discussed further in chapter three) highlights this relationship between the master tattoo artist and the tattooed woman. The woman serves as a source of voyeuristic pleasure for the artist because he observes her sexual relations with another man while he tattoos her.

Like the real world of tattooing, which has been dominated by a masculinist aesthetic, texts and films about tattooing have focused on women in the context of male pleasure. An image of the tattooed woman in the context of sadomasochistic desire is evident in an early-twentieth-century Japanese story about a tattooed woman. The narrative of a male artist's desire and the use of a woman's body for creative, narcissistic and sadomasochistic purposes is expressed in "Shisei" (1910), a short story by Japanese writer Junichiro Tanizaki. The story, which has been translated as "The Tattoo" (1910)[3] or "The Tattooer," is about a tattoo artist, Seikichi, who selects a beautiful geisha as the canvas for his tattoo work. He shows her two paintings, each of which depicts a woman whom this geisha resembles in appearance and (according to the artist) in spirit. The first painting presents an image and a narrative of a Chinese princess with a sadistic character who watches the beheading of a prisoner, and the second picture represents a woman gazing "at a group of men's corpses" with a look of "pride and satisfaction" (Tanizaki 95). Tanizaki's story uses the image of a foreign culture and an evil woman to enhance the sadomasochistic experience for the tattooist. This style of painting was known as *ukiyoye*, a seventeenth- and eighteenth-century genre which often adopted Chinese elements and transformed them into scenes that catered to popular taste: "Pictures of such scenes tend to vulgarity, but so skillful had the painter portrayed the expressions of the princess and of the condemned man that this picture scroll was a work of consummate art" (95). This comment by Tanizaki's narrator could just as easily be applied to the Japanese perception of the art of tattooing in Japan, which has still not been recognized as a legitimate art form outside the tattoo world.

After displaying the paintings, the tattoo artist proceeds to tattoo the image of a spider onto the woman's back as a way of embedding these "femme fatale" qualities into the gcisha. In medieval Japanese legends, the spider is a malign creature, "invulnerable to sword or arrow" (Hall 47), and so it is an "appropriate" image for conveying the tattooist's fear of woman. The tattooing of an isolated image was practiced before the development of the full body tattoo during the first half of the nineteenth century (McCallum 122). In fact, the placement of a single tattoo such as the name of a lover was practiced by seventeenth-century courtesans (Daly 105). In selecting a single object such as a spider for a tattoo, Tanazaki enhances the fetishistic dimension of the tattoo so as to facilitate the artist's fixation on the one, ideal object. Fetishism involves the obsession with a particular object or element which functions as a substitution or replacement for the whole. As Donald McCallum points out in his analysis of the story, the tattoo artist realizes that he has found his "perfect female subject" when he sees Seikichi's "stunningly beautiful foot" (McCallum 125). The foot is the initial fetish object which is eventually replaced by the tattoo of the spider on her body. In his introduction to Fellman's *The Japanese Tattoo* D. M. Thomas argues that *irezumi* (or Japanese tattoo and tattoo communities) and fetishism are "largely the preserve of men" and that viewing the tattoo as fetish reflects the fetishist's need "to interpose a symbol — fur or leather, garter belt or high-heeled shoes — between himself and his naked lover" (Fellman 9). Thomas thus reinforces the image of woman as tattooed canvas for male spectatorship or pleasure.[4]

The translation of the story's title as "The Tattoo" emphasizes the power of the image of this woman as a fetishistic work of art which comes alive and engenders both fear and desire in the spectator. However, in some ways the translation "The Tattooer" better highlights the narcissistic element of the artist's creativity. The text tells us that "it was as if the tattooer's very spirit entered into the design, and each injected drop of vermilion was like a drop of his own blood penetrating the girl's body" (Tanizaki 96). This passage also suggests the correlation between tattooing and sexual intercourse (Gell 36). The translation of "Shisei" (tattoo) as "The Tattooer" obviously highlights the power of the artist, who alone has "the power to make of [her] a beautiful woman" (96). She also exercises a dangerous power over her viewer; he will become the first of many male victims (100). While the geisha may be invested with some degree of power in the sadomasochistic experience of the male artist/victim, the tattooed woman is still demonized and completes the narrative that has been constructed for her.

TATTOO

Tanazaki's story is an early-twentieth-century example of how tattooed women serve as images of male desire in tattoo narratives. However, even a later work such as the novel/film *Tattoo* limits woman in this capacity.[5] *Tattoo* (1981) is an American text/film which offers a rather disturbing portrayal of a man's desire for woman as an aesthetic object. Lee Hays' book *Tattoo* (published in 1981, the same year as the film directed by Bob Brooks) presents the story of an American sol-

Tattoo (1981). 20th Century–Fox. Maddy (Maud Adams) and Karl (Bruce Dern) depict the relationship between desire, tattoos and captivity. Maddy has been tattooed against her will, and her captor, Karl, shows his dominance over her since he is upright and she is in a reclining position. The relationship between the act of tattooing and the sexual act is suggested in this scene; however, near the end of the film, Maddy engages in an act of resistance by grabbing a sharp instrument and killing Karl, thus reinforcing the link between the tattooed body, desire and violence.

dier (played by Bruce Dern in the film) who, having studied the art of tattooing in Japan, returns to the United States and establishes himself as a renowned tattooist. He is employed by a modeling company to paint some of the models with his tattoo designs. This contract leads to his obsession with one of the models, Maddy, whose body initially serves as a canvas for painted or pseudo-tattoos and ultimately as the "tabula rasa" for a permanent full body tattoo, which he tattoos on her body after taking her hostage.[6] Although the film has moments of feminine resistance to a patriarchal code of oppression (Maddy kills her captor at the end), Frances Mascia-Lees and Patricia Sharpe have argued that the film essentially upholds a kind of male fear of women's liberation. One could further argue that this male framing or containment of woman is mimicked by men who sport tattoos of pinup girls or sexually provocative women. A history of American and European tattooing also reveals countless images of women that have served the male heterosexual gaze. Tattoos of pinup girls have been pervasive in the history of Western tattooing, not unlike the dominant aesthetic of the female nude in Western painting.

While there are "class differences" in the case of traditional "lowbrow" tattoo culture and "highbrow" fine art, both cultural phenomena have perpetuated the Pygmalion myth of feminine beauty that is "made flesh by the warming glow of masculine desire" (Nolan 76). According to Margo DeMello, "biker" or "lowbrow" tattoo magazines have tended to emphasize nude female photos, and only fairly recently have decreased the number of these photographs in their magazines (DeMello 114). Pictures of women that fall outside the clichéd image of pinup-girl pose are rare. DeMello also mentions that this kind of tattoo magazine (e.g., *Tattoo* and *Easyriders*) has not exactly welcomed gay and lesbian tattoo culture; they are "marked by fairly regular queer bashing" (123).

Feminist Agency in Tattoo Narratives

The American film/novel *Tattoo*, like many of the so-called "lowbrow" tattoo magazines, clearly offers images of women that serve a masculine aesthetic. However, there are a number of twentieth-and twenty-first-century fictional texts and non-fictional examples which provide evidence of feminine empowerment through women who resist the images of containment that are so rampant in other aspects of tattoo culture. These texts, films and non-literary examples often draw on the male preoccupation with the feminine form, and challenge this way of containing or managing women. Within the last decade or so, a number of magazines (most of these belong to what Margo DeMello considers to be the highbrow variety) have tried to move beyond the exclusivity of the heterosexual, masculinist aesthetic by including a variety of images of tattooed women that challenge the hegemony of the pinup girl pose. These images include pictures of older tattooed women, pregnant women and lesbians — images which do not generally fit the traditional Western aesthetic of the "beautiful" woman.

While Margo DeMello argues that a shift in the construction of feminine images (e.g., fewer nude photos) may be due to a class phenomenon (more members of the middle class acquiring tattoos), another likely reason is the increase in the number of female tattoo artists. As Margot Mifflin indicates in her 1997 book *Bodies of Subversion: A Secret History of Women and Tattoo*, women tattooists used to be rare, but in the 1990s women represented about 15% of American tattooists (Mifflin 9). Many of these contemporary artists actually advertise tattooing by female tattoo artists for their female clientele. For example, a Canadian studio based in Alberta is called Sisters' Inc. Body Art Studio, and it advertises itself as a studio "exclusively for Women by Female Artists." Another example of the rise of woman-centered tattoo culture is evident in "The Tattoo Baby Doll Project," a collaborative project started in 1998 by a female embroiderer and female tattoo artists across the United States. The philosophy behind the "tattooing" of dolls reveals how women are using their agency as artists to empower themselves and to create their own images of themselves.

The development of a feminist aesthetic in the world of the tattooed is also evident in how women have used tattoos in creative ways to challenge narrowly defined or masculinist concepts of the beautiful, feminine body. (Women with full body tattoos are one illustration of this phenomenon, since such tattoos are often deemed "unfeminine" by masculinist culture.) Another group consists of breast cancer survivors who have used art to heal their "broken" bodies. Pam Huntley's tattoo of an eagle's feather and an abalone shell suggests the power to heal oneself and to connect with other women. The eagle feather is a symbol of sacred healing, and the abalone is a symbol of the feminine rite of passage for Native American women (Huntley). Breast cancer survivor Pam Huntley tells the story of the restorative power of tattoos and how cultural symbolism can heal the body and the psyche:

> My girlfriend designed my tattoo, it's a redwood branch with an eagle's feather and a small abalone shell hanging from it. The eagle feather is a sacred healing symbol for Native Americans, and I feel birds are my connection to the natural world. The abalone shell brings the water element and is a symbol of the feminine. North Coast Native American girls had the ceremony for coming of age where their mothers would hold up an abalone shell and the girl was suppose[d] to jump up and see the reflection of the woman no longer a girl.... I use the visualization of myself inside a Redwood Circle and have had many ceremonies inside redwood circles. To me they are Mother Earth and I will always be proud to have her on my heart [Huntley, "In Celebration of a Scar: Women, Breast Cancer and Tattoos"].

For Huntley the Native American cultural elements of her tattoo serve a therapeutic function, contrary to the horror experienced by Maddy in *Tattoo,* who does not choose her own design. The woman-centered aspect of Huntley's tattoo conveys the control women exercise over their own bodies through the selection of feminine imagery and through the subversion of patriarchally defined expectations. As a breast cancer survivor, she resists the aesthetics of normalization surrounding the image of breast implants and creates a feminist "narrative" of healing through her tattoo imagery.

The development of a feminist aesthetic in tattoo culture is also evident in twentieth-century images of the tattoo experience in various tattoo narratives, including fiction, film or television. Not surprisingly, this feminist aesthetic in the fictional context is also linked to women who become artists or agents instead of objects or images of masculine desire.

THE ILLUSTRATED MAN

Ray Bradbury's science fiction collection *The Illustrated Man* (1951), which was also adapted into film (1969), is one of the best known literary works about tattoos. In fact, the very term "illustrated man" has become synonymous with tattooed individuals (e.g., Peter Trachtenberg's reference to the tattooist Lyle Tuttle in his memoir *7 Tattoos*).

However, unlike *Tattoo* and Tanizaki's story "The Tattooer," which focus on the male tattoo artist and his female subject, Bradbury presents a woman as artist and a man as her canvas. The narrator of the prologue encounters someone called "the Illustrated Man," a man who is looking for carnival or sideshow work. He is a walking work of art since he has tattoos all over his body (which is not unusual for someone associated with circus life); however, they produce unusual aesthetic effects, because they move at night and predict the future.

Their unusual aesthetic quality is explained by the man, who says that he was tattooed by a woman: "A little old witch who looked a thousand years old one moment and twenty years old the next, but she said she could travel in time" (Bradbury 3). This female tattoo artist is also depicted as a woman who practiced the art of deception, because her advertisements or signs read "Skin Illustration! Illustration instead of tattoo! Artistic!" (3) Bradbury's focus on a woman as tattooist is highly unusual (yet perhaps entirely appropriate for the genre of science fiction), because during the first half of the twentieth century women with tattoos, let alone female tattoo artists, were relatively uncommon.

As Margot Mifflin states in *Bodies of Subversion: A Secret History of Women and Tattoo* (1997), "[U]nlike women who worked in their husbands' parlors, the rare maverick who set up her own shop was anathema to her male competitors" (Mifflin 35). One could conclude that the female tattooist in *The Illustrated Man* is demonized for her appropriation of what was during Bradbury's time (the 1950s), and certainly during the historical period of the story (the 1900s), a craft primarily associated with male practitioners. However, since Bradbury establishes a link between the moving tattoo images and the art of narrative, this tattoo artist may also represent the displacement of any domain of male creativity, including the act of writing. The Illustrated Man's horror at the magical nature of the moving images symbolizes a resistance to female generated texts or images: "When I find that witch, I'm going to kill her" (Bradbury 3). [7]

This resistance is further highlighted by the interaction between the two male characters, the Illustrated Man, and the narrator or spectator of these images. The images on the back of the Illustrated Man are aesthetically pleasing at first to the narrator, but then become dangerous for the spectator. On the back of the man's body, a special spot or jumble of color fills up with the image of the person who gazes at this tattoo, portraying the death of the individual and filling the viewer with fear. The character who sees his own reflection experiences the death of his desire for image and narrative. He escapes his literal death by fleeing and leaving behind the Illustrated Man and the stories which Bradbury's reading audience has also just finished reading, thus putting an end to their own narrative desire. As Eugene Goodheart argues in *Desire and Its Discontents*, "Knowledge and possession are the death of desire" (Goodheart 4). In this sense, the images reinforce the narcissistic aspect of the tattoo for the viewer. Thus, the narrative attempts to minimize the creative agency of woman, since the male spectator's narcissistic desire to contemplate the self as mediated by the Illustrated Man mirrors the masculine desire expressed by the male artists in *Tattoo* and Tanizaki's story. Despite *The Illustrated Man*'s focus on male anxiety associated with the female tattoo artist's craft, woman is still constructed as the creator of tattoo images instead of merely serving as a tattooed object of masculine desire as is the case in *Tattoo* and in the Japanese story "The Tattooer."

"The Tattooed Woman"

A story that aired on the radio in 1975, some twenty years after Bradbury's text, illustrates another attempt to introduce a feminist aesthetic into a tattoo narrative. However, in Marian Engel's story "The Tattooed Woman," the central female character is both the tattoo artist and the bearer of the "tattoo." Engel's story even re-evaluates the concept of the tattoo in order to highlight this shift from a masculine to a feminist aesthetic. The tattoos in Engel's story are not the ordinary ink variety. They are cuts or scars that her female protagonist carves into her flesh.

Marian Engel's short story uses the concept of the tattoo or marked body as a metaphor for the pain experienced by a forty-two-year-old woman whose husband has left her for a twenty-one-year-old "girl." (The 1975 story has certain autobiographical elements, since Marian Engel separated from her husband in 1975 and divorced two years later.) The narrator constructs an image of the other woman's body as "young and firm and unscarred" (Engel 5) and contrasts this image with her own body, which "was not new or neat or pretty" (4). She therefore resists the aesthetic of feminine beauty represented by her husband's lover (also an extension of his ideal of feminine beauty) and proceeds to "tattoo" herself through acts of self-mutilation. This woman carves a star on her forehead and creates an alternative aesthetic, drawing parallels between the bumps on her aging cheeks and the "beautiful slashes" on the ebony skins of African women in a *National Geographic* magazine (6). She becomes devoted to the ritual of scarring herself, carving images that resemble the letter A. This act is presented in terms of an artistic technique since the narrator is "not interested in hurting herself" (6):

> I am an artist, now, she thought, a true artist. My body is my
> canvas. I am very old, and very beautiful, I am carved like an
> old shaman, I am an artifact of an old culture, my body is a
> pictograph from prehistory, it has been used and bent and
> violated and broken, but I have resisted. I am Somebody (8).

The image of marking the body is a concrete manifestation of the narrator's desire to create an aesthetic of survival which runs counter to the Western masculine ideal of unmarked feminine beauty. Christl Verduyn offers the following reading of Engel's story:

> Making her (own) marks(s), the tattooed woman moves from
> a passive to an active stance. She refuses to be engraved by age
> or by the anonymity Western society would ascribe her as
> "just another old lady." Instead, she inscribes her own marks,
> stepping out of the stereotypical female role of reproducer
> into that of active producer and marker (Verduyn 11)

The narrator is both artist and a work of art and thereby creates an alternative aesthetic to the traditional image of woman whose beauty is defined by a male artist. Yet while the narrator attempts to resist a patriarchal worldview by taking ownership of her own body (albeit in a rather disturbing way), the story still shows the pervasiveness of the masculine aesthetic. Her male doctor offers a prescription for transformation of her carved-up body into the ideal feminine body by urging her to acquire a tan: "You should go somewhere hot. It will make a very striking tan" (Engel 9). Thus, while Engel's character uses her body to disrupt the masculinist defined image of the ideal female form, the danger of subjecting herself to a male-defined ideal of beauty that will cover up her marked body (the beginning of feminist agency) is ever-present.

THE TATTOOED MAP

Another Canadian text which links the tattoo to images of resistance and feminine desire in a highly experimental fashion is Barbara Hodgson's intermedial work *The Tattooed Map* (1995). In this book the tattoo and the map are used as metaphors for the physical and psychological journey of Lydia, the text's leading female character. The alternative form of the book reinforces the dual visual and narrative forces at work in this story, because Hodgson combines narrative sections with a collage of drawings, photographs, and bits of letters. The text is reminiscent of the visual/textual interplay found in Nick Bantock's "novel" *Griffin & Sabine: An Extraordinary Correspondence* (1991), a book consisting of pages of postcards and letters between two people whose desire for one another is expressed through the mediated form of letters, postcards and visual art. Near the end of the correspondence in *Griffin & Sabine*, Griffin says: "Sabine, you don't exist. I invented you. You, the cards, the stamps, the islands, you're a figment of my imagination.... I've started to think I'm in love with you" (n. p.).

Bantock's narrative of desire has some key parallels with Hodgson's text, which is also a true intermingling of the visual and the textual and which, like Bantock's book, also abandons the printed page's convention of page numbers. The narrative is laid out in the form of journal entries (initially Lydia's and then those of her friend Christopher, or C), and acts as a travelogue and a map of their journey through Morocco. However, their travels through this exotic land take a strange turn when Lydia acquires a pattern of red marks that resemble a tattoo. Shortly thereafter, she encounters a café owner by the name of Layesh, who has a map tattooed onto his arm and who declares that he will never stop traveling (n. p.). She identifies with this individual because of her own travels and because of the tattoo which she now bears. Initially one might perceive Lydia's own tattoo as an imitation of a masculine aesthetic for at least two reasons. To begin, with her name evokes associations with the figure of Lydia in the famous song "Lydia, the Tattooed Lady" sung by Groucho Marx, who played the role of the womanizer in film and in his comedy routines. Furthermore, she may also be viewed as a Sabine figure or as an extension of the masculine experience if one compares her to Sabine in *Griffin & Sabine*. However, this is a rather limited way of reading her experience. The focus of the text is clearly on Lydia, and even when she disappears, she remains the focal point of this visual narrative.

Like Maddy, the woman who is taken hostage in the film *Tattoo*, Lydia is initially the unwilling recipient of a tattoo, and "reel[s] with nausea" at the thought that it is a part of her. This feeling of horror is symbolic of the psychological fear individuals may experience at the notion of being permanently altered. The superimposition of a tattoo on an unwilling recipient also suggests a form of violation similar to sexual violation. However, after the initial shock experienced by Lydia, the physical manifestation initiated by the tattoo also reflects an inner transformation in Lydia's life, a transformation from passivity to activity. As Lydia's later journal entries indicate, the pattern on her own body grows in size and begins to resemble a map.

The metaphor of the map or mapping is a powerful one that enhances the link between the tattoo as a visual form and its narrative qualities. While cartography has its foundation in a masculine worldview of exploration, the concept of mapping has also been used by feminists to comment on women's experiences as a way of resisting traditional teleologically oriented narratives. Feminist geographers and scholars in other disciplines have made use of theories of space to discuss feminine ways of seeing. According to Helen Buss, mapping "recognizes that the world changes over time" (Buss 10). "Indeed, mapping itself and its technologies change constantly, shifting and readjusting our concepts of the self and the world" (11). Buss uses the images of maps and mapping in her feminist study of Canadian women's autobiography in English. In a sense, Lydia's tattoo narrative is a woman's autobiography of a tattoo narrative. Like maps, tattoos are signs or signals of change. Therefore it is not surprising that Lydia's cartographical autobiography of her tattoo signals multiple transformations:

> It's beautiful, but it's ugly, too, like the veins and arteries that you can trace on the inside of your wrist. My arm no longer belongs to me. It's become another thing to be admired and studied but not a functional object. It no longer carries my watch; it feels too precious to be made to hold things and I can't bear to touch myself in case it spreads even further. As I become detached [sic] from it, I can admire and appreciate its physical beauty as though it *were* a map drawn out over months of exploration and study... (n. p.).

The aesthetic disinterestedness expressed in the passage allows Lydia to see herself in the context of a larger narrative "drawn out over months." Yet Lydia eventually disappears out of her time after a fantastic metamorphosis that marks a transition to a feminist aesthetic:

As I lay on a rough stone block I can feel myself being pummeled and massaged and a voice, in a foreign language, says over and over, "We'll rub this off, then you won't have to leave again. We'll rub this off." I watch the map peel off in one piece and slither to the floor. The women emerge from the dark corners and slowly walk, bent over double and with arms outstretched, towards my map lying on the damp tiles. I sit up and watch them coming closer and closer, and then, suddenly afraid and cold, I grab the map, step into it one foot after the other. I draw it on like the skin of a cheetah, pull it up over my shoulders, stick my arms into it, until I am once again totally enveloped. The women begin to wail, and I understand, I finally understand. I have something they want. I had been someone chosen, but now I am someone who has made a choice. Secure in my map I leave, as rapidly as I can, and my last sight of the room is the image of the women returning to their darknesses and silences, confined by the steam left by my tears.

The map does indeed cover my whole body now. (n. p.).

The rubbing or peeling of this tattooed map challenges the image of a tattoo as a stable or permanent form by emphasizing the erasable art form of Middle Eastern henna patterns. This passage suggests Lydia's identification with the practice of women from other cultures and establishes a kind of feminist aesthetic that may facilitate a kind of cross-cultural communication. The fantastic scene of Lydia's physical transformation involves her change from a woman who is the unwilling bearer of a tattoo, to a woman who puts on her own tattooed skin as an agent of change. She therefore becomes a kind of mythic icon to other women who have not made active choices in their lives and who return to "their darknesses and silences." Like Engel's "tattooed woman," she too becomes an artist figure or an agent: "I am someone who has made a choice." In keeping with her interest in documenting her life (e.g., journal entries), she photographs her arm as the tattoo covers more and more of her body.

Through Lydia, Hodgson creates a feminist aesthetic, another way of seeing, which is defined by the character's own ability to see a tattoo that is not initially perceived by her male companion. Like the male character Griffin in *Griffin & Sabine,* who wonders whether Sabine even exists, Christopher, Lydia's traveling partner, doubts the existence of her tattoo. However, paradoxically, her physical disappearance and Christopher's reading of Lydia's journals eventually permit him to see the tattooed map on the photographs of her arm, which he was previously unable to perceive. He is only able to "see" Lydia in a mediated fashion, through photographs of her tattoo and through the medium of narrative. In other words, Lydia has created a feminist way of reading or viewing for her male companion which is dependent on her words and images. When his own arm develops the tattooed pattern of "red and blue lines of rivers and roads," he realizes that they will be his "passport back to Lydia." In this narrative of desire, individuals do not make contact with one another directly, but via the tattoo, whether it appears in a mediated visual form (through photographs) or in a narrative form (through Lydia's journal entries). Thus the tattoo serves as an alternative, feminine way of reading and viewing desire.

"Never Again" (The X-Files)

The link between feminine empowerment and tattoos is also apparent in television series such as *The X-Files* which present women in the context of fantasy or science fiction genres.[8] While it is important to note that some of the women in these works are not entirely free of patriarchal restrictions, they are still presented as women who attempt to resist a masculinist worldview. Thus, they become agents in a counter-narrative to male authority. For example, in "The Curse," episode 19 of *The Hitchhiker Series* (1986), a male landlord promises a tenant that he will make repairs to her building. He then becomes involved with another woman and shortly thereafter discovers a snake tattoo on his body. Both women try to tell him how to get rid of the snake, thus suggesting the magical powers of women. Their powers echo those of Bradbury's female witch-like tattoo artist, who also regulates the male body. While these women appear to be demonized as seductive women, they are also agents who do not merely serve as objects of masculine desire.

Another woman who is associated with a counter-narrative is the character of Donna in the sitcom *That '70s Show*. While most of the episodes follow the ground rules of a "real" world, one of the episodes in season 4, "It's a Wonderful Life," places Donna in a fantastic storyline and links her with tattoos. In this episode the character of Eric wonders what his life would be like if he had never met Donna. In the same spirit as the original film *It's a Wonderful Life*, an angel shows Eric what his life and the lives of others would have been like if things had been different. The angel reveals to Eric how Donna ends up kissing his friend Hyde (a rebel figure) instead and acquiring a tattoo on her stomach with the words "Question Authority." She thus becomes part of a narrative of resistance; in a sense, this fantastic image of Donna in an alternative world is still an extension of her character in Eric's former reality. As the angel points out to Eric, it is Donna who gave Eric the confidence to stand up to people, and the tattoo seems to convey this image, albeit in a more extreme form.

However, the image of the tattooed woman and resistance is a complex one, because, while the alternative story of Donna initially resists Eric's image of the wholesome girl next door, in the course of this new narrative she becomes the object of another master narrative. Donna's second tattoo reveals how resistance operates in this complex fashion. Her second tattoo reads "Property of Hyde," and the angel makes the ironic comment "Classy!" in response to this image. Thus, while Donna is presented as a woman who resists the safe, middle class sensibility of Eric's value system, she leaves one masculine aesthetic behind only to adopt another. She is also contained by the male dominated biker-style tattoo culture which constructs woman as property. (This reflects the image of woman presented in many of the lowbrow tattoo magazines discussed by Margo DeMello.) As the fantastic storyline continues, a heavily tattooed and pregnant Donna is seen marrying the rebel figure Hyde. Thus, while her tattoos continue to convey the image of a counter-culture, the storyline reveals how she is confined within this culture with a husband who ends up in prison or away from home most of the time. The conflicting image of the tattoo as a symbol of resistance and containment may be due to the hybrid nature of the series, which parodies the values of the 1970s from a 1990s and twenty-first-century perspective. What may have been considered an image of resistance at one time is often viewed as an image of assimilation from a contemporary perspective. Thus resistance is a relative concept which shifts according to different factors such as class, gender relations and historical context. In "It's a Wonderful Life" the tattoo functions as a subversive element, but not necessarily in a way that allows women to remain images of feminist resistance.

An example of a 1990s television series which places women and tattoos in a more empowered context is the fantastic storyline of an episode of the popular *X-Files* series which explores extraterrestrial and fantastic phenomena. "Never Again" (1997), a tattoo episode about "illustrated women" and feminine empowerment, introduces a tattoo design of a Betty Page-style pinup girl along with FBI agent Dana Scully and her decision to acquire a tattoo. Both may be viewed as rather complicated images of feminist resistance in the context of a masculinist culture. The storyline of "Never Again" (written by Glen Morgan and James Wong) involves a recently divorced man by the name of Ed Jerse, who enters a tattoo parlor and, ironically, selects a Betty Page-like design which also bears the accompanying words "Never Again." Here the visual image of the desirable Betty Page tattoo interacts with the written script "Never Again" to suggest that this divorced individual will never again experience desire or pain through a woman. Betty Page is a fitting aesthetic for these conflicting images of desire and suffering. She was a 1950s pinup girl, often represented as the girl next door, but also depicted in sadomasochistic rituals. (The brilliant red dye used by the Russian tattoo artist to create Ed's tattoo furthers the aesthetic of beauty and violence in this story.) In the course of the narrative, Ed hears the mocking voice of a woman emanating from the Betty Page tattoo; he attempts to silence it with a burning cigarette, thus causing the tattoo to bleed. This female voice claims to be his protection against other women and slowly drives him insane whenever he thinks of the opposite sex, until he is driven to kill a woman. His desperation and the impact of the tattoo on his life echo the plight of the Illustrated Man, who also blames a woman for his condition and whose tattoos predict the death of others. Ultimately, the story suggests that the source of Ed's undoing has not been the feminine principle, but Ed's own actions. Ed ends up doing to himself what his tattoo, a disguised image of his hatred for women, had planned for other women, including Scully. Like Bradbury's Illustrated Man, and Karl Kinsky in *Tattoo*, he is defeated by the forces of femininity and by his own enduring, albeit repressed, desire for the feminine.

The Betty Page tattoo functions in a curious way. On the one hand, it may simply be seen as an extension of Ed's desire to contain women as he has done by acquiring the Betty Page tattoo. (This containment is an imitation of the tattoos of nude women on men's arms, or the proliferation of nude tattooed women in magazines geared to a male readership). However, the tattoo may also serve as a kind of postmodern feminist aesthetic or commentary; it resists or subverts the aesthetic that has historically been created for tattoos that depict women as objects of male desire; the Betty Page tattoo is transformed from an object of desire to an "agent."

This creator/created dynamic and the tension between a masculinist and a feminist aesthetic are also played out in agent Dana Scully's case, since she meets Ed in the tattoo parlor. Scully tells him about her desire to rebel after spending her life following around "father figures." Her feminist resistance translates into a classic image of rebellion: the decision to acquire a tattoo. Scully chooses an oroboros, the image of a snake eating its own tail (from the Greek, "tail devouring"). In ancient myth, this image symbolizes the forces of destruction and renewal and thus serves as a fitting parallel to the Betty Page tattoo with its sadomasochistic tendencies. During the Renaissance it was revived "as a symbol of time, eternity and the universe" (Hall 44). Dana's own desire for creative agency and renewal is hinted at in this episode as she takes charge of her life by acquiring a tattoo, then by dating Ed, and finally by saving her own life when Ed's tattoo tells him to push her into an incinerator. The final words of the episode reveal Scully's desire to escape a life dominated by a masculine aesthetic or world view as symbolized by her partner Fox Mulder: "Not everything is about you, Mulder. This is my life."

The X-Files 4.13: "Never Again" (1997). Gillian Anderson as agent Dana Scully acquires her tattoo of an oroboros, a snake eating its own tail. The scene depicts Scully in a moment of pain and ecstasy as she glances up at her new love interest during the tattooing process.

COVER ME

Most of the tattoo narratives with examples of female empowerment have foregrounded women who appear to be over 30 or who are
trying to break away from a pattern that was established in their earlier life. However, there are also tattoo narratives which highlight the
experiences of teenaged women or "girl culture." In the 1990s, the term
"girl culture" became pervasive as the all-female rock band the Spice
Girls tried to promote songs centered around women's experiences.
Their songs appealed to very young girls as well as teenagers, and while
their popularity soon made them part of a mainstream phenomenon,
there were still elements of "resistance" in their image that contributed
to their message of feminine empowerment. One of the members of
the group, known as "Sporty Spice" or Melanie C., sported several tattoos. As a fan site for Spice Girls wannabes pointed out, two of her
tattoos with Chinese characters on her right shoulder apparently "stand
for 'woman' and 'strength' or, in Spicetalk, 'girl power'" ("Spice Girls").

While the Spice Girls phenomenon has been criticized for its rather
saccharine promotion of the concept of "girl power," there are tattoo
narratives which offer a more radical image of this concept. A Canadian text which offers a twenty-first-century articulation of a younger
woman as a figure of resistance is Mariko Tamaki's novel *Cover Me*
(2000). Tamaki is a young writer of Japanese heritage who is also a
musical performer. She has made a point of challenging limited per-
ceptions of women's experiences through various art forms. She has
performed in a short film on lesbian relations called *Shelf Life* (Cole)
and formed a performance troupe called *Pretty, Porky and Pissed Off*
in order to challenge women's obsession with the thin female body. As
a big girl herself, she offers a feminist critique of limited fashions for
heavy women: "They don't make black unitards for big girls. They're
all a size too small... "(Cole). Tamaki's resistance to the "proper" feminine form was also evident in her private high school experience, when
she wore "a low-cut vintage dress so everyone could see [her] tattoos"
(Cole). Tamaki's novel *Cover Me* extends this fascination with alternatives for women by presenting a character who uses her body for cre-

ative expression. Her work thus makes an interesting counter-narrative to the image of the tattooed woman depicted in Tanazaki's "The Tattooer," who essentially serves as the extension of the male artist's creative spirit.

The character Traci in *Cover Me* has some parallels with Engel's "Tattooed Woman," because Tamaki's character also carves her body as a way of expressing agency. While both women resist a dominant aesthetic, they are from two completely different time periods. Tamaki's character Traci is a teenager of the '90s instead of a woman who is probably informed by the attitudes of the '60s and the '70s (Engel's story first aired in 1975). The book jacket describes the central character as a figure of resistance in the context of 1990s North American youth culture: "With purple hair and sequined boots Traci Yamoto stars in a wicked riot-girrl[9] rumble against family expectations and private school poseurs. Craving the protection of a thick skin, she picks up a razor and begins to carve. A slip of the hand lands Traci in psych ward 7, but a tattoo gun, a Goth, and a microphone offer her a way out of the 'burbs and into her own skin."

This teenager's decision to become a singer in a rock band allows her to put an end to her self-mutilation. The act of carving her own skin appears to be a more disturbing way of articulating autonomy, even though it is presented in the context of some kind of individual, creative expression. A healthier alternative for using the skin as a site of creative expression is Traci's decision to acquire tattoos. They too become associated with a kind of feminist ability to control her own life: "Unlike feeling my scars, feeling my tattoos gives me a sense of power. I am the *mistress* [emphasis mine] of my domain" (Tamaki 107). Traci's image as a force of resistance is also evident in how her tattoos challenge institutions of authority such as school and parents. For example, she is the first person in her school to get a tattoo (58), and she has arguments with her parents, who disapprove of her tattoos:

> "For years I cut my body in pieces and no one in this house notices until I land myself in the hospital. Now, I get a tattoo and suddenly everyone's all in my face. Everyone's pissed off.

Why? Because I've finally taken control of my body? Decided that my body is mine?" [114].

Her six tattoos are a means of establishing an identity for herself outside the context of her family environment, including her money-conscious father and her mother (who spent time in a psychiatric hospital).[10] Yet because tattoos and tattoo narratives are subversive, the tattoo that Traci thinks about getting first is not actually her first tattoo. She would like to acquire a tattoo depicting wings to symbolize how she feels when she is singing "Like I'm an angel" (195). At the end of this chapter in the novel, however, she indicates that this initial desire is delayed or postponed: "I had a revelation that would delay my acquisition of wings" (105). Just as the reader is prepared to read about the all-important experience of the wings tattoo, the narrator subverts her narrative by writing about her acquisition of her beetle tattoo. This becomes her first tattoo. It is a giant black beetle in the center of her chest. Interestingly enough, the tattoo has some connection to her father despite her desire to use tattoos to distinguish herself from her family. He is fond of rewriting the Beatles' song "She Loves You," and ten of the twenty songs are about his daughter (16). In choosing the beetle tattoo, Traci may be embedding a memory of her father into her skin. However, because desire is a mediated concept, it is even more likely that she is embedding herself into her skin via her father's image of her in his rewritten versions of "She Loves You." This mediated representation in the form of the beetle tattoo would still seem to indicate a link to a masculinist perspective. It is, nevertheless, possible to see the tattoo as an image of resistance. Even if Traci had tried to echo her father's fascination with the Beatles through her tattoo, this "echo" is not recognized by her father. Thus the duplication or reproduction of the beetle/Beatles idea is more of a transformation, and may very well be viewed as a young woman's desire to transform the images that have been handed down to her by her parent. Traci's father merely sees the tattoo as an expression of the ridiculous (115), while Traci insists that the tattoo is her way of finding out who she is.

While the beetle on Traci's body functions as a pun that alludes to the Beatles, a group linked to her father's musical taste, her body art offers the possibility of resisting parental authority. Traci's father seems to be obsessed with financial matters and can only communicate with her about her tattoo in economic terms: "Who paid for that?" (113). The tattoo which she acquires three months after the beetle tattoo has healed provokes a similar response. It consists of the word MINE, and Traci's father can only "read" it as an economic statement: "'It means you paid for it?'" (117). However, for Traci, this particular tattoo is intended to express her ability to control her own body image and her inner self. The blue and purple colors are reminiscent of the psychological and physical pain which she endured while cutting herself. The tattoo also marks her body as her own in her dual attempt to resist complete identification with either her father, who has "thick skin" like Traci, or with her mother, described as Traci's "own phantom twin" (20). Thus the presence of this particular tattoo in *Cover Me* reaffirms the power of the tattoo as a sign of resistance to prescribed identities as well as the tattoo's potential as a sign of self-creation.

According to Hilde Hein, "With the help of feminist aesthetics we are able to appreciate old things in new ways and to assimilate new things that would be excluded by traditional aesthetic theory" (Hein 455). Hein's comment about the benefits of analyzing "new things that would be excluded by traditional aesthetic theory" applies nicely to the discussion of tattoos as a visual art form. A discussion of tattoos as Art (with a capital A) is certainly not the kind of topic that falls within the realm of traditional aesthetics, which has highlighted Western painting or sculpture by male artists. Feminist aesthetics should definitely engage in a critical examination of "new things," such as women as producers of texts and images (e.g., Engel's "The Tattooed Woman"), in order to examine how earlier models have been challenged. However, while some of Hein's statements are valid, it is unlikely that feminist aesthetics will always enable readers or spectators to "appreciate" old things in new ways; surely one of the purposes of a feminist critical practice is to expose and challenge a masculinist aesthetic that simply reinforces an image of woman as victim or *femme fatale* in narratives or artistic situations determined by men (e.g., *Tattoo* and Tanizaki's

"The Tattoo"). Furthermore, in order to be most effective, feminist aesthetics should not limit itself to texts or images authored or generated by women; while these texts (e.g., *The Tattooed Map,* the personal narratives of breast cancer survivors) may well convey some more liberating narratives, it is still important to offer critical analysis of other forms of cultural production (e.g., television series) which depict women as aesthetic objects of masculine desire in order to identify even an attempt to resist such an aesthetic (e.g., "Never Again"). Tattoos still have a marginalized status within the visual arts and literary studies, but despite this marginalized status, a patriarchal perspective still dominates much of the imagery. A feminist analysis of the tattoo experience in personal narratives of the body, in film, in television, and in literature can show how even alternative forms of art may be appropriated by a masculinist aesthetic that controls the representation and participation of women.

CHAPTER THREE

Crimes of Passion: Tattooed Bodies as a Site of Struggle

Tattoo narratives often highlight the interrelationship between desire and violence. The tattoo artist has frequently been presented as a male and as the dominant power over the woman who is his captive. However, this male artist is often a marginalized individual in his own right with a history of violence in his life (he may even have been held captive), and this perspective plays a role in his view of women as objects of desire. Narratives such as *Tattoo* (film and novel) and *Skin Art* depict this kind of captor/captive relationship. The idea of containing the object of desire is also presented in Takagi's *The Tattoo Murder Case* and *The Pillow Book*. Takagi's work of fiction presents images of tattoo and marginalization as well, but in this case the role of the tattooed female body operates in a greater capacity as a site of resistance and creativity. In *The Pillow Book*, both male and female bodies are the subjects of body art and desire and become tattoo texts. All four of these narratives incorporate images of marginalized bodies, desire, and resistance. In these tattoo fictions, which also happen to mention Asian cultures, the tattooed body is perceived in an aesthetic capacity but is closely linked to desire and violence, thus undercutting a purely dispassionate or disinterested view of the tattoo. Thus, tattoos are viewed as an extreme form of art, perhaps because they are imprinted on the body, and because of this, some narratives of desire and violence culminate in the consummate, violent act of murder.

Tattoo Tales of Captivity and Desire

TATTOO AND SKIN ART

Tattoo captivity tales foreground the themes of violence and violation and link these themes to an aesthetic or artistic sensibility. The novel and film *Tattoo* (1981) and the film *Skin Art* (1993) present tattooed bodies and tattoo artists in the context of imprisonment or captivity.[1] In these narratives, the male character is the tattoo artist and the woman is tattooed by the artist. What *Tattoo* and *Skin Art* have in common is how the tattooed female figures are presented as the artistic canvas and mirrors of the male tattoo artist's feelings of marginalization or own sense of captivity.

TATTOO

The similarities between the two films are outlined in the *Video Movie Guide 2000* in the description of *Skin Art*: "His [the artist's] obsession to turn her into a living canvas reeks of *Tattoo*, starring Bruce Dern" (Guide 1025). Both narratives are stories of desire, and both tattoo narratives are also stories of violence. Karl (*Tattoo*) and Will (*Skin Art*) turn to tattooing after their experiences as soldiers overseas and are influenced by Asian cultures. In both Lee Hays' novel *Tattoo* and its film version no information is offered on Karl's activities as a soldier, except that he went to Japan for some "R & R, to drink, find women perhaps, to look at the shrines and the monuments, but not really to absorb the culture" (Hays viii). Given the release date of the film *Tattoo* (1981), it is probable that he was an American soldier in Vietnam. Although the violence of the war experience is not described, one cannot help but wonder whether his decision to abduct a woman to turn her into his captive was perhaps influenced by what he experienced as a soldier. Frances Mascia-Lees and Patricia Sharpe have argued that Karl's actions may be seen as a backlash to the freedoms promoted by the feminist movement in the 1960s and early '70s. However, it is also possible that Karl's desire to control the body of another could be a response to the chaos and upheaval of a war which marginalized the American soldier, who was not widely supported in his own country.

While nothing is said about Karl's experiences as a soldier, the film and novel versions of *Tattoo* begin with a focus on the mind-and body-altering power of Japanese culture, specifically in the form of tattooing. During his visit to Japan, he witnesses the presentation of tattoos as a new aesthetic and an expression of desire. After observing a group of tattooed men perform in a celebration, he becomes obsessed with the aesthetic and spiritual ideal of tattoos, especially full body tattoos. Yet he is also aware of the "sensual" nature of the images on the bodies of these men. He experiences this sensuality first hand when he is tattooed by a great Japanese tattoo master: "The soldier had a look of ecstasy on his face" (vii) and decides that he will learn the art of tattooing from a Japanese master and practice the art.

Karl's retreat into the realm of the private, or into the realm of the artistic imagination, may be viewed as a resistance to the demands of public service or duty as represented by his former life as a soldier. His unwillingness to engage in direct interaction with individuals is expressed through voyeuristic behavior such as his contemplation of the fashion model, Maddy, through the mediation of video or photographs. When he finally does imprison Maddy in his home, he treats her as an aesthetic object and does not engage in sexual intercourse with her until his artwork is complete. Even then, she functions primarily as a substitute for some elusive object of desire that is associated with the aesthetic of bondage; perhaps she signifies the creation of a scarred body under his control, unlike the scarred and mutilated bodies of soldiers and civilians during a war.[2]

Karl Kinsky's interest in the Japanese tattoo and his connection with this exotic cultural practice places him in the marginal world of the 1970s tattoo artist. A man who lacks the social skills necessary to integrate into mainstream society, Karl has difficulty expressing himself directly and uses the mediated form of the tattoo for creative expression. This is also indicative of how he receives or processes the images of others in a mediated form, perhaps as a way of managing or containing the image. For example, the desire he develops for Maddy, the fashion model he later takes hostage, is established through the "screen" or filter of art. He is actually introduced to Maddy through television. He sees an image of her modelling on the screen, which in turn mediates his desire and reinforces the voyeuristic tendency of Karl's character: "...a beautiful blonde girl in what was obviously a commercial for a product called Aphrodite. When the girl came on the screen, there was something about her that captured Karl's interest..."(11–12). The fact that Maddy is selling a product called Aphrodite after the Greek goddess of love emphasizes the link between Maddy and desire in this tattoo narrative.

When Karl is on the verge of leaving the office, he sees a photograph of the girl in the television commercial, another indication of how other media, in this case photography, reinforce the visual image of tattoo art in the novel/film. The videotape of Maddy's modeling serves as yet another mediated image of woman, which Karl can "process" and contemplate in private. Interestingly enough, this reference to photography echoes the image of the camera that is introduced at the very beginning of the novel *Tattoo*. For example, Karl had been viewing a Japanese man carrying a Buddhist shrine through his camera; however, he does put the camera away and stares at the bearers of this shrine directly when he realizes that they were tattooed. When viewing Maddy, Karl's initial experience of her is in a mediated form, via photographs or other media or even other bodies, and his subsequent perception of her continues to maintain this mediated form of contact, unlike his more direct gaze at the Japanese men.

The mediated nature of Karl's desire for Maddy is perpetuated through another female body via a sex shop. After seeing Maddy at a modeling office, he goes to a sex shop where he imagines Maddy while contemplating the body of one of the erotic performers. Once again the context for his spectatorship is presented in a contained framework where the female body has been presented for male consumption. He is able to "capture" Maddy, albeit in an altered form. While this act would suggest the satisfaction of his desire for Maddy, the mediated quality of this viewing of the female body only serves to emphasize that desire is twinned with the concept of resistance, since he unconsciously resists direct contact with Maddy.

Karl's obsession as a tattoo artist with the mediated presentation of the female body echoes that of Pygmalion, the sculptor from Greek mythology. Pygmalion is described as a woman-hater (Ovid) who finds fault with members of the opposite sex. As a result he decides to shape an image of a perfect woman (when Venus transforms her into a real woman, she is known as Galatea) by creating a statue. Karl is a contemporary Pygmalion figure because he searches for some ideal object for his desire. Like Pygmalion, whose desire for his statue intensifies, Karl is determined to transform this very public fashion model into his own private object of aesthetic and religious adoration.

For Karl, Maddy's image as an ideal is not only a reflection of his desire to find an ideal woman, but also a logical extension of his memorable aesthetic and religious experience in Japan and his ongoing interest in Japanese art. Maddy mentions that Karl's tattoo designs look like the Japanese prints of Utamoro. Interestingly enough, this Japanese artist was known for his prints of idealized women, some of which served as designs for tattoos. Like other artists who have "captured" women as art, Karl captures his ideal woman. He expresses the need to regulate, to control every move in his interaction with Maddy including the regulation of her language. Thus his desire becomes intertwined with violence. His extreme act of anti-social behavior involves the abduction of this woman so that he can control her without the influence of others. He holds her hostage and commits an act of violation which is justified in the name of art: his desire to turn her into a "master"-piece, that bears his mark (much like Pygmalion's shaping of his ideal woman).[3] Furthermore, by tattooing her entire body in stages, he attempts to tame or manage this woman in a ritualistic fashion. As Jay Clayton and Jessica Benjamin have argued, "Confining violence to a protected aesthetic realm resembles the ritual process in which violence is limited to a sacred victim who has been set apart from the rest of the community" (Clayton 44; Benjamin, "The Bonds of Love," in Clayton 45). Maddy becomes the unfortunate victim of these acts of violence and violation. Karl sees her as his "sacred victim," but, in marginalizing her through the art of tattooing, he also seems to reaffirm his own marginalized status as an individual alienated from the rest of society, including his own family. [His Aunt Teresa implies that he could have made something out of himself if he had helped his father with his business instead of becoming a tattoo artist (25).]

Karl's difficulty communicating with his own family is repeated in the difficulty he has communicating with Maddy directly. His desire for Maddy is characterized by his need to control or dictate the terms of his aesthetic and erotic experiences, and so he initially uses various media to access her image indirectly. For example, the use of the television set and the photographs of Maddy mediate Karl's introduction to the actual woman. However, mirrors also serve as a way of accessing the image of Maddy in an indirect manner. For example, they facilitate a voyeuristic experience: "Neither she nor the young man were aware of his presence. He watched their reversed reflections in one of the mirrors" (58). The mirror not only serves as a medium for desire but is also linked to violence when Maddy smashes Karl's full length mirror after seeing the beginnings of the tattoo on her body. The smashing of the mirror is symbolic of her wish to destroy not only the image that Karl has imposed upon her, but Karl himself. Since she cannot destroy the tattoo without injuring herself and is unable to harm her captor directly, she takes a mirror and destroys this object of mediation. In *Tattoo*, the novel, there is greater emphasis placed on how the tattoo on Maddy's body is a mirror image of Karl's tattoo: "They were mirror images of one another. He had said they would be one" (180).[4]

Karl articulates his love for Maddy in terms of a mark or shield that he must apply to her in the concrete form of a tattoo; this mark will apparently allow her to become one with him. Until the tattoo is completed, until her body becomes a mirror image of his own tattooed self, he cannot have direct contact with her (167, 180). This state of deferral aptly fits Lacan's definition of desire as displacement and deferral since desire "can never be satisfied by an object" (Clayton 40).

Tattoo **(1981). 20th Century–Fox. Bruce Dern as Karl, the tattoo artist, embraces Maddy (played by Maud Adams) in an expression of masculine desire. He reveals a Pygmalion-like desire for Maddy, who becomes his image of the ideal work of art. In this scene they are positioned as a mirror image of one another.**

Unlike many creative acts which can be interpreted as "a healthy manifestation of narcissism" that create concrete works of art as "a kind of reconstruction of the ideal self or self-object" (Layton and Schapiro 23), Karl's creative act is a pathological narcissism that violates and imprisons a woman's body in the name of aesthetics (a concept that feminists have criticized in their analysis of the Western aesthetic and the visual arts). While Karl is himself a marginalized artist, a "freak" who resists society's expectation of more mainstream occupations, he still expresses patriarchal dominance in his treatment of a woman. The totalizing impact of the narrative which serves the leading male character's desire makes it difficult to locate instances of feminine resistance; however, we can identify a few. Even though Maddy is a fashion model whose very profession suggests that she is not entirely in control of her image, the novel includes an explicit reference to her ability to question the controlling aspect of art. For example, when she is posing for the camera, she is able to throw back her head and laugh "at her own parody of a sexpot" (41), thereby exposing the artifice of the art of fashion photography. This ability to manipulate art actually makes it possible for her to escape her captivity at Karl's house. She draws on Karl's interest in using art as a mediated form of experience to trap him. Maddy shows Karl a color photo of a doll in a book on Japanese tattoos and draws a parallel between the picture of this doll and the Hakata doll in porcelain that sits on Karl's own mantel:

> The doll was of a woman reclining on silk cushions strewn across a mat on the floor. A man bent over the woman. At first Maddy had believed he was about to embrace and enter her, but in the picture she could see that he held a bamboo needle....
> Karl looked at the doll, at her, then his eyes glanced down at the picture in the book on the couch (174).

Maddy persuades Karl that they should imitate the scene in the book during their next tattoo session. He is overjoyed and agrees. Once he finishes the complete tattoo on her body, thus creating a mirror image of himself, they actually have intercourse, and she grabs the tattoo needle and kills him. This scene would appear to serve as the ultimate form of victory for a woman in Maddy's situation, for she has redirected the tool used to subjugate her against her oppressor. However, as Frances Mascia-Lees and Patricia Sharpe argue in their study of the film *Tattoo*, "the female fear which the film arouses about male control is not assuaged either despite Adam's[5] [sic] seeming triumph" (Mascia-Lees and Sharpe 154). She is ultimately unable to escape the master narrative of the text and the hegemony of male desire, since her act of violence is described as an unconscious act[6]; she did not know "what she was doing" (181). Furthermore she is unable to resist experiencing sexual pleasure during intercourse despite her hatred of the man who has taken away her individuality. While it would appear that Karl's desire and violation of Maddy ended when he had sex with her, this is not entirely true. Since Maddy bears the mirror image of Karl's tattoo on her body, she in a sense acts as the site of mediation for his desire. She is marked for life, and has had no choice in determining the new aesthetic on her body.[7]

SKIN ART

Like *Tattoo*, the film *Skin Art* (1993) foregrounds a male tattoo artist whose life is marked by violence and desire. The relationship between the tattooed body, the marginalized tattoo artist, war and captivity is established through the flashback sequences in *Skin Art* (1993). Like Karl Kinsky, the film's main character Will also served as a soldier. He was stationed in Vietnam and was held captive. Like Karl, whose contact with Asian culture inspired him to become a tattoo artist, Will becomes a tattoo artist upon his return to the United States. Will's main occupation consists of tattooing Asian prostitutes for a white pimp who views the tattoos as evidence of his ownership of these women. The pimp's treatment of these women is similar to Karl's view of a tattoo on a woman as a sign of her readiness to be marked or taken by a man.[8] Thus this tattoo narrative incorporates the themes of desire and violence which are so often identified with tattoo culture and establishes a connection between two different kinds of captivity: Will's imprisonment in Vietnam and the restricted lives of the prostitutes that he tattoos in the United States. When Will is asked to tattoo a woman by the name of Lily, who is highly prized by the pimp, he remembers his experiences as a prisoner of war in Vietnam, thus establishing a clear link between tattoos, desire, violence and scars (both physical and psychological).[9]

Most of Will's memories of his Asian experience are of an intensely negative nature, while Karl's memories of Japanese tattoos in *Tattoo* involve moments of ecstasy. Will's captor in Vietnam was a horribly scarred colonel, but his face remains hidden until the end of Will's recollections. Many of Will's memories involve his conversations with Sophia, the Vietnamese-French mistress of this man, who attends to

Will's wounds after his beatings. In some ways, Will experiences the victim role that is assigned to Maddy in *Tattoo*. However, his wounds and scars are the result of beatings while Maddy's scars are tattoos. Nevertheless, like Maddy, the colonel's mistress in *Skin Art* is the bearer of a tattoo (Sophia's is a butterfly). Like Maddy, she was tattooed by a man — in this case, her father. At the end of the film she is killed by the colonel for betraying him by sharing an intimate moment with Will. In an act of retaliation, Will murders the colonel and remembers how Sophia had told Will that a tattoo represents the ultimate commitment between the tattooer and his canvas. He takes these words to heart, by inscribing his memory of her onto the body of Lily, the Asian prostitute.

Will chooses the image of a spider for Lily's tattoo perhaps because he remembers that Sophia kept a tarantula as a pet. Yet the tattoo also conveys a predatory or dangerous quality of spiders and women — the latter are therefore linked to both violence and desire. Even though Will shared an intimate moment with Sophia, it is also clear that she was complicit in the colonel's torture of Will. Thus desire and violence are intertwined in this film. Although the film does not reveal any tattoos on Will's own body, he bears a mark of another sort: the scars of beatings on his back. While his tattooing of women seems less disturbing than Karl's capture of Maddy in *Tattoo*, because he has not kidnapped them, he is still carrying out a patriarchal imperative by marking their bodies to satisfy the desire of another man (their pimp) and his own. Like Karl, Will is a Pygmalion figure who approaches woman as an artistic canvas that represents an extension of either his or another man's masculine desire. He also inscribes a memory of his violent past onto the female body. When he tattoos the image of the spider on the back of Lily the prostitute, her tattooed body serves as an extension of the suffering experienced by the tattoo artist. Will's choice of the spider image may also indicate a desire to use his art to offer himself and Lily some psychological and aesthetic release from imprisonment and violence. The film portrays how he is haunted by his memories of torture and death in Vietnam and locks himself away in his apartment, where he practices his tattooing and views videos of his tattooed subjects (much like Karl's mediated experience of Maddy via photographs or television). Will appears to have a twofold desire: he wants to remember Sophia indirectly through his tattooed subjects, and he wants to be able to purge the memories of his torture. After he completes Lily's tattoo he engages in sexual intercourse with her, perhaps as a way to accomplish both of these desires. Yet it is important to realize that Lily does not represent a direct object of desire; she is simply the vehicle that allows Will to re-experience Sophia and to purge himself of his negative memories of captivity. The film attempts to suggest that the fact that Will was the first man to have sexual relations with Lily may be an act of subversion. He is able to place his mark on this woman before the pimp can (just as his intimacy with Sophia could be seen as an act of defying the colonel). However, feminist viewers are unlikely to be convinced by this apparently subversive act, since the women in the film are largely limited in their role as an extension of masculine desire. Therefore Will's status as a figure of resistance to an oppressor figure such as the pimp must be considered alongside his own use of women as objects that serve his Pygmalion-like tendency to marginalize women by defining them as his *objets d'art*.[10]

Tattoo Art and Stories of Murder

Both *Skin Art* and *Tattoo* show the interrelationship between tattoos, desire, violence, and captivity — a relationship that often presents the tattoo artist and the tattooed body as marginalized or criminal bodies. In both of these works, the male artists' perspectives are highlighted. Furthermore both artists are influenced by Asian culture in one form or another as the narratives depict crimes of passion. The women clearly serve the masculine imperative in these two films. Two other narratives which develop the relationship between the artist's aesthetic sensibility and the tattooed body are *The Tattoo Murder Case* and *The Pillow Book*. These two works include a focus on Japanese culture and thus reinforce the impact of the Asian tattoo experience in narratives of desire and violence. Akimitsu Takagi's *The Tattoo Murder Case* is a Japanese detective novel, and Peter Greenaway's film script/film *The Pillow Book* is the work of a British director who creates a narrative which reinforces the connection between text and image in Japanese culture. The script and film present pseudo-tattoos in the form of body painting (a kind of Japanese calligraphy), as well as the image of the body as tattooed text, in order to show the transgressive and violent relationship between body, image and text or narrative.

One narrative genre which has included representations of tattooed bodies in the context of love and violence is the detective novel, often considered a genre which highlights the theme of concealment as a way of resisting disclosure or the unraveling of a crime. These novels are populated with characters who commit criminal acts or crimes of passion. They thus resist figures of authority or the image of reason often symbolized by the detective in these narratives. Because tattoos serve as an obvious mark of identification, it is not surprising that they should appear in this genre. Texts such as *The Snake Tattoo, The Million Dollar Tattoo, Blood Money, The Concubine's Tattoo*[11] and *The Tattoo Murder Case* present the image of the tattoo as a means of initiating the detective's quest or desire to solve a mystery and as a source of knowledge. Tattoos are therefore linked to the concepts of revelation or recognition.[12] Even classical mystery or murder narratives such as the story of Odysseus and the story of Cain make use of the technique of identification. In the case of the Greek hero Odysseus, his scar functions much like a tattoo in that it is a permanent mark which would lead to his public identification. (His childhood nurse sees the scar and becomes aware of his true identity.) He needs to conceal his identity from the suitors of his wife Penelope in order to surprise them and murder them. Thus, the narrative of Odysseus and Penelope also happens to be an ancient narrative of desire and violence. Another character whose actions are linked to an identifying mark is the Biblical figure Cain, often called the bearer of the first tattoo. Cain slew his brother Abel in an act of resistance to God's preferential treatment of Abel; the permanent mark which God places on Cain not only identifies him as a criminal but also serves as a visual reminder of Cain's secret or act of concealment, the murder of his brother. Both the narratives of Cain and Odysseus involve crimes of passion, an important facet of the tattoo in contemporary detective fiction.

THE TATTOO MURDER CASE

Yet tattoos do not only serve as a simple sign of identification, which is such an important feature of the detective novel, but also function as a sign of resistance to the rational discourse of the detective's world view. This is certainly the case in *The Tattoo Murder Case* (1998), a Japanese murder mystery by writer Akimitsu Takagi. This novel was published in 1948 under the title *Shisei Satsujin Jiken* and received the Mystery Writers Club Award of Japan in 1949. It was translated by Deborah Boliver Boehm into English in 1998, so (despite its original publication date) the 1998 translation transforms the text into a kind of contemporary novel which may appeal to an English-speaking audience interested in tattoo culture. The novel is set in post–World War II Japan and deals with the murder of Kinue, known as the most beautiful tattooed woman in Japan (Takagi 18), whose tattooed body is the object of desire and violence in aesthetic, economic, and sexual contexts. The post–World War II setting is important because it reminds the reader of the atmosphere of death and desolation that permeated Japan during, and after the war. Anti-American statements reinforce this mood, and tattoo culture is used to express a kind of resistance to the American victory. Although tattoos are identified with a marginal culture within Japan, they are used to promote the superiority of a Japanese aesthetic in contrast to the American art of tattooing:

> "Have you seen the ridiculous Americans strutting about, showing off their pathetic 'sushi' tattoos?" He pointed toward a small clump of G.I.s who were chatting with two young Japanese women in identical short red dresses. "Unlike the Japanese tattoo, which flows over the contours of the body like a river over stones, the Americans cover their arms with a hodge podge of unsightly, obvious designs — hearts, anchors, flags, and the like…. There's no excuse for the total lack of artistry" [10].

Further comments are made on the different techniques in tattooing used by American and Japanese tattoo artists, the former using only a single needle while the latter use multiple needles that allow for more subtle shading techniques. Thus technical complexity results in a superior aesthetic appearance of the tattoo design. A rich folkloric tradition in Japanese culture is also cited as a reason for the more aesthetically pleasing designs. This element of superstition and folkloric story will add significantly to the mystery surrounding the alternative world of tattoo culture. It is interesting to note that the discussion concerning the comparison of Japanese and American tattoos seems to be based on a Japanese envy of the American G.I.'s who are talking to two young Japanese women in "short red dresses" (10). These women could be prostitutes, and, like the tattooed prostitutes in the film *Skin Art* whose lives are enmeshed in violence and desire, these women are also connected to tattoos, only in this case the tattoos are on the body of American soldiers.

The analysis of tattoos in two different cultures in the early part of the novel is Takagi's way of emphasizing the tattoo as a beautiful art form that affects and seduces the viewer of body art. Tattoos and desire will be linked even in the context of science as the narrative unfolds. However, initially, this link between tattoos and the erotic dimension is suppressed, as the narrative highlights the science of tattooing. The scientific dimensions of the tattoo are presented in one of the early episodes of the novel involving a leading character, Kenzo Matsushita. This 29-year-old has medical school training and plans to join the police medical staff with the help of his older brother, Detective Chief Inspector Daiyu Matsushita. His early exposure to tattoos involved a brief visit to the famous specimen room at Tokyo University, but beyond this, he had "no particular interest in or affinity for tattoos" (7). The narrative thus continues to focus on the scientific aspects of tattoo culture, with very little focus on tattoos and desire. The specimen room described in Takagi's novel is undoubtedly a reference to the collection of tattooed skins at the Medical Pathology Museum of Tokyo University. According to D. E. Hardy, "the air raids of 1945 destroyed the University Medical buildings, and along with it all photographs and extensive documentation of the tattoo work" (Hardy, *Life and Death Tattoos* 75). The actual tattooed skins were stored in a separate location and were preserved.

The character Kenzo thus initially serves as a means of linking the tattooed body to the world of science or rational thought. Kenzo decides to further his knowledge of tattoos — strictly in the interest of science, of course — by attending a tattoo competition, since "a passing knowledge of the tattoo culture might be useful to a future doctor of forensic medicine, if only because tattooed people (whose ranks included a great many gun-toting gangsters) had a tendency to become involved or implicated in crimes" (Takagi 6). Thus the novel develops the polarization of the world of science and detective work with the chaotic underworld of tattoo culture. The rational discourse of science is initially separated from the crimes of passion executed by tattooed individuals; however, in the course of the narrative, this rational perspective is increasingly challenged by the tattooed body, especially when this body is a woman's. According to one of Kenzo's old school friends, many of the fully tattooed women consort with members of the underworld: "By getting tattooed all over and cutting themselves off from normal society, the women show their commitment to a particular man and to the renegade-outlaw life in general" (17). This statement reinforces the outlaw quality of the speaker, Hisashi Mogami; according to some rumors, he was an experimental chemist, "living an unconventional, rootless life" (16). More importantly, it foreshadows an outlaw quality or an alternative aesthetic that will be associated with the woman Kenzo knows as Kinue. In the course of the narrative, he develops an appreciation for tattoos as an art form after watching Kinue's exhibition during the tattoo contest. However, his aesthetic appreciation, which is equated with a kind of Zen enlightenment (31) similar to the state experienced by Karl in the American novel/film *Tattoo*, is intertwined with erotic pleasure. Kenzo eventually has a sexual encounter with Kinue, which in turn reinforces his aesthetic pleasure and interest in the artistry of tattoos on the human body.

Another member of the scientific community who expresses a fascination with tattoo art is professor Hayakawa (known as Dr. Tattoo).

He covets Kinue's skin, since he would like to add it to his collection of tattooed skins after she is dead. His obsession with tattoos suggests that they are dangerous because they destabilize even the rational mind of a scientist. The professor functions as a site of intersection between the rational and the irrational in this murder mystery, because when Kinue is murdered her tattooed torso is stolen, and he becomes one of the prime suspects. His character is most likely based on Dr. Masaichi Fukushi, a doctor of medicine specializing in pathology who began a collection of tattooed skins at the Medical Pathology Museum of Tokyo University: "he began to study and catalog motifs and designs of more than two thousand people, and collected over three thousand photographs of the work" (Hardy, *Life and Death Tattoos* 75). However, unlike Kenzo, whose aesthetic experience of tattoos is closely tied to the erotic, Dr. Tattoo's obsession is linked to the concept of aesthetic and perhaps even economic value or desire. He calls Kinue's tattoo "a national treasure" (Takagi 5) and expresses his desire to preserve her tattoo for posterity. She indicates that she plans to be cremated, thereby frustrating this desire. Unfortunately her resistance is futile; when her tattooed torso is recovered at the end of the murder mystery, it is contained and hung from the ceiling of the specimen room. Clearly her vocal resistance to this kind of scientific containment is unable to prevent the will of science from prevailing.

Even though readers expect corpses in detective fiction as well as the connection between desire and violence, the concept of dismembering a body to obtain a tattoo is a truly gruesome detail. However, Takagi does not include this action merely to titillate the reader. Clearly there are also parallels with the time period of the novel. Since it is set in post-war Japan, the brutality and suffering of those involved in the war serves as an important undercurrent in the novel. The mutilated tattooed body, and even the art of tattooing in general, function as metaphors for those who died at Hiroshima as well as for the scarred psyche and bodies of those Japanese men and women who survived the bombing. The murder and mutilation of Kinue may also serve as an extreme illustration of the pain and scarring that are a part of the Japanese tattooing process, especially in the case of full body tattoos. Thus the end product, the beautiful tattoo designs, are actually the result of suffering.

The aesthetic of death is further embedded in the ekphrastic imagery of the tattoo designs on Kinue's body and on those of her dead siblings. The novel suggests that the images themselves are somehow responsible for the death of tattooed individuals. Kinue's tattoos depict the character of Orochimaru, an evil mountain sorcerer from Japanese folklore, and a big snake on her back. Yet like most tattoos, the images also tell a story — a story which Kinue's own life imitates. She tells Kenzo that her father saw an old woodblock-print version of the story of Orochimaru and two other sorcerers, Jiraiya and Tsunedahime, who competed with one another to create the most powerful spells. This story reinforces the link between tattoos and other art forms like woodblock prints, which are part of Japanese art history. At the same time it highlights the narrative of taboo desire as embedded within a visual art form. Kinue tells Kenzo how her father tattooed the different sorcerers on each of his children's bodies, along with each sorcerer's accompanying animal: Jiraiya on her older brother, Tsunedahime on her sister Tamae, and Orochimaru on Kinue. Her two siblings apparently succumbed to the curse of death during World War II, and the woman Kenzo knows as Kinue also fears for her life and is apparently murdered later in the story.

Professor Hayakawa later explains to Kenzo why these images of the sorcerers and their animals contribute to the belief in a curse: "'The sorcerer Jiraiya always appears riding on a giant toad, Orochimaru on a snake, and Tsunedahime on a slug. If anyone ever tattooed a snake, a frog, and a slug on one person's body, the three creatures would fight to death'" (56). When Kenzo asks if these three curses were to appear on three different bodies, the professor indicates that normally the curse would not take effect; however, in the case of three siblings, this would be considered a reckless act indeed. The alternative world of folkloric superstition thus underscores the macabre aspect of the tattoo world depicted in Takagi's text. Even a man of science such as professor Hayakawa believes in the story of the Three Curses (56) or the forbidden tattoo, a fact that Kenzo finds quite unsettling. During another conversation with the professor, Kenzo also tries to understand in rational terms how anyone could acquire a body tattoo, since he views this procedure as an act of self-mutilation. Yet even as Kenzo himself questions this obsession, he too becomes seduced by the image of the tattoo, and at the conclusion of the novel he goes so far as to kiss the disembodied skin of his dead lover as a final farewell.[13] This desire for the tattooed body is a desire that his older brother the detective does not share; he simply finds them grotesque and thus attempts to uphold the master-narrative of rational discourse in this detective novel (105).

While the textual descriptions of tattoos in *The Tattoo Murder Case* constitute one kind of ekphrasis (or textual representation of the graphic) in the novel, they are by no means the only visual art form that contributes to the aesthetics of desire, death and resistance in this text. References to photographs of tattoos complicate the narrative of this murder mystery even further and serve as an important form of mediation just like the photographs and mirrors in *Tattoo*. Despite their identification with revealing the truth, photographs are actually used to disguise or defer meaning rather than to reveal "the truth." The photographs of the three Nomura siblings initially lead the police to believe that the three individuals were actually tattooed with the three curses, each bearing one of the curses. One of the photographs plainly shows the sister Tamae with the Tsunedahime tattoo. However, as Kyosuke, a former medical school student and intellectual who solves the case, points out, the investigators had assumed that a photograph only reflects reality, an assumption that critics of photography have often questioned.[14] The police and Kenzo believed that Tamae Nomura bore the Tsunedahime tattoo, "an assumption that is based on the fundamental notion that a tattoo can never be erased" (300).[15] However, the picture in question depicted a pseudo or drawn-on tattoo, not a permanent tattoo; thus the photograph exercises a mediating influence on the presentation of the tattoo by resisting the truth. This intermingling of tattoo images, photographs and pseudo or temporary tattoos leads the character Kyosuke to a complicated series of conclusions. He reveals how Kinue had actually colluded with her boyfriend, Hisashi Mogami (Kenzo's former school friend), in the murder of her sister

Tamae, and that it was Tamae's body that had been mutilated to give the impression that Kinue had been killed for her tattoo. The "real" tattooed Kinue does not escape death either, however. She is eventually shot through the heart by her lover's stray bullet.

Kinue's association with the renegade Hisashi Mogami and the fact that she is a tattooed woman are signs of her outlaw status within the context of Japanese society. As Willem R. van Gulik points out, despite the fact that the bourgeois aristocracy in Japan did participate in the activities of the "townspeople" (van Gulik, in Hardy, "Japanese Tattooing" 59), tattooing is still often linked to the activities of the lower classes in both moral and economic terms. "Because it takes place on the body, it remains taboo for most of the populace" (Hardy, "Japanese Tattooing" 66). In addition to engaging in this act of tattooing that is often associated with the lower orders of society (including prostitutes), Kinue chooses a lover who is a man on the margins of society.

Yet Kinue's proclivity for deception is not only viewed as a social condition, it is also presented as an inherited condition. According to Kyosuke, the man who solves the case, Kinue's attachment to the man who committed the murders of her brother and sister "was exacerbated by the criminal blood that was flowing in her veins, the outlaw legacy of her adulterous mother" (316). The focus on the outlaw, tattooed body as a site of deception is thus reinforced through Kinue's association with another rebel figure, her mother. The latter had abandoned her husband and children and then became a female burgler (Takagi 198). Desire and violence therefore flow in the blood of these two women, which cement their images as figures of resistance.[16]

The Tattoo Murder Case is a fine example of how tattoos are presented as an aesthetic of resistance to the rational world of science and police work. They generate narratives of desire and death that are false, yet they still maintain their erotic qualities for those who are seduced by their beauty. Like *Tattoo* and some of the content of *Skin Art, The Tattoo Murder Case* foregrounds the female body as the site of desire and violence; yet, on a cultural level, Takagi's text also illustrates how tattoos create an unstable, shifting narrative that reinforces the scarred psyche and bodies of post-war Japanese society.

Tattoos, Desire and Violence

THE PILLOW BOOK

The Pillow Book (1996) is a film by British (Welsh-born) director Peter Greenaway. It presents images of desire and various forms of violence including suicide, murder and the mutilation of a body. Desire and violence are in turn linked to the concept of the body as a tattooed text. Although much of *The Pillow Book* deals with body writing or painting rather than tattooing, the idea of writing on the body with indelible ink and preserving the body as text may be viewed as an act of pseudo-tattooing.[17] Peter Greenaway also highlights the parallel between tattoos, painting and writing in the 1984 outline of what developed into his film *The Pillow Book*. At that time he was considering "a tentative cinema project to be organized according to the 26 letters of the alphabet and to be called *26 Facts about Flesh and Ink*" (Greenaway 5). In this preliminary outline, under the letter "E" heading he indicates that the key character of the film is a contemporary Sei Shonagon who is "an exile from Japan, from a personal background of culture familiar with exquisite scholarship and refined sensuality; familiar with a history of decorating the body with cosmetics and tattoes [sic], and familiar with a literature that, through calligraphy, is half-way to painting" (6). The interrelationship between the visual and the textual[18] as well as the medium of the body therefore allows Greenaway to engage in multi-media play and display that resist the separation of text, image, and body into mutually exclusive categories.[19]

The Pillow Book focuses on the activities of Nagiko, who is a contemporary Sei Shonagon figure living in the 1990s in Hong Kong. Sei Shonagon was an eleventh-century Japanese woman who wrote *The Pillow Book*, a diary of observations on Japanese court society, including the subject of love or desire, which is a focal point of Greenaway's film. This book was apparently "kept in the drawer of the wooden pillow on which the authoress laid her head at night" (6). Like her predecessor, Sei Shonagon, Nagiko combines the textual with the proximity of the body, her text does not simply include images of desire; instead, the body becomes an art form associated with desire and death much like Kinue's body in Takagi's novel *The Tattoo Murder Case*.

However, unlike Takagi's Kinue — who is generally viewed as the object of desire — Greenaway's character Nagiko is an active subject, a writer who uses male bodies as the medium for her text. Her book or series of books is described as "The Thirteen Books Written on Skin." These books consist of short texts or poems written in Japanese on the bodies of men who are sent to a publisher for "consideration." Unfortunately, one of these men, Jerome, on whom she has written "The Book of the Lover," commits suicide by swallowing sleeping pills and indelible ink. His body is stolen by the publisher, who has his skin "made up into a book" (87) for his private enjoyment. Nagiko arranges to have the publisher killed, reclaims Jerome's body text, and has the text transcribed onto her own body in the form of a tattoo. Like the tattooed body in Takagi's novel, the medium of the body in *The Pillow Book* is the message of both desire and violence.[20]

Greenaway's film is an astonishing narrative and visual experience, which is not surprising given his own abilities as an artist. He produced and exhibited drawings, paintings and collages which have influenced his film-making (Elliott and Purdy, "Artificial Eye/Artificial You" 200). While it has an original storyline as well as creative visual images, it does offer parallels (intentional or not) with previous Japanese films on Japanese visual art forms from printmaking to bodypainting to tattooing. Films such as *Utamoro and His Five Women* (1946), *Irezumi* (1982) and *Kwaidan* (1964) may well have influenced the director in the making of *The Pillow Book,* with its focus on desire and violence. The first film introduces the link between tattoos and the prints of the famous painter Utamoro; *Irezumi* presents voyeuristic images of tattooing and sexual desire, and *Kwaidan* is a film based on the stories of the English writer Lafcadio Hearn. This last film includes images of painted and mutilated bodies and presents the concept of a marked body as a sign of resistance.

While the film *Kwaidan* probably has the least number of parallels with Greenaway's film, it offers an interesting depiction of the relationship between an artist, ink, the body and mutilation. *Kwaidan* is a series of four short stories based on the work of the writer Lafcadio Hearn.[21] In the story of Hoichi the earless, a musician by the name of

Hoichi is bewitched by spirits to play his music. In order to prevent the ongoing appearance and demands of these spirits, a Buddhist priest writes a holy text on Hoichi's body to protect him, thereby indicating the power of the marked body and its ability to generate some form of resistance to the supernatural. Unfortunately, the priest forgets to write the protective script on Hoichi's ears, and the musician's ears are removed by a visiting spirit. The film points out the danger for an artist whose work is desired by others. The scenes of the painted and mutilated body have interesting parallels with Greenaway's character Nagiko, who paints her own body and the bodies of others in Greenaway's film. Like Hoichi's severed ears in *Kwaidan*, the body of Nagiko's lover Jerome is mutilated after his death; Jerome's body is then transformed into a kind of tattooed text. While Hoichi's body is not tattooed, the theme of desire for a mutilated body is certainly re-presented in *The Pillow Book*.

A film that has more obvious parallels with Greenaway's project is a much earlier work called *Utamoro and his Five Women*. Utamoro was a famous Japanese woodblock-print artist whose designs grace all kinds of Japanese products today from calendars to T-shirts. Greenway as a filmmaker, would quite likely have viewed Kenji Mizoguchi's 1946 black and white film on this artist. Mizoguchi presents Utamoro as an artist challenging the Kano school of painting with his late-eighteenth-century Edo woodblock printing (Dalle Vacche 199). It offers various images of resistance, including those of a tattooed woman (prostitute) whose desire for a man challenges the traditional image of the submissive Japanese woman. The artist is also depicted as a figure who challenges convention. As Angela Dalle Vacche states in her chapter on this film, in "late eighteenth-century Edo, woodblock printing challenged the Kano school of painting" (199).[22]

The film presents Utamoro as an artist willing to experiment with new techniques, including painting images on the back of a woman as the preliminary stage of a tattoo.[23] His artistic rival observes that Utamoro creates flesh and blood paintings; this emphasis on living flesh explains the transition to tattooing in the film, not unlike the parallels Greenaway makes between body writing and the tattooed body in *The Pillow-Book*.

The narrative of "Uta" and his struggles to find new forms of inspiration for his art (including a variety of women) alternates with a narrative of a courtesan's love for a man who already loves another woman. The courtesan, Tagasode, chooses to have herself tattooed as a pledge to her lover. Her status as a marginalized figure is emphasized in the film when she is described by a woman called Okita as a courtesan who talks with an accent, and because her back is tattooed with the image of a legendary woman. Her fate, however, is to die at the hands of Okita, the jealous lover of Shozaburo. The tattooed back of the courtesan is revealed as she dies, as a reminder of tattoos' transgressive power to seduce men. (A character in the film says that the words of this courtesan, along with her tattoo, seduced Shozaburo.) The film ends with a transition from this image of the tattoo to various comments on art and the images of women in the prints of Utamoro, who will "draw the beauty of women one after another." Presumably his art will enshrine their images just as the tattoo of the legendary woman is enshrined on the courtesan's back.

Peter Greenaway's character Nagiko has some affinities with the courtesan figure in *Utamoro and His Five Women* because she also violates the norm of traditional decency by encouraging men to write on her body. Like the tattooed courtesan's, Nagiko's body is marked, although initially only in a temporary fashion with ink or paint that can be removed. Her desire to be marked is considered all the more "forward" (Greenaway 66) when she meets a European by the name of Jerome, because he is a "non-Japanese" man. While Nagiko uses her own body as a "page" to experience pleasure, she develops into a more active figure who paints or writes on the bodies of others. Like the artist Utamoro, she paints the bodies of her human subjects, but while Utamoro used the bodies of women as his canvas, Nagiko uses the bodies of men. This is significant in the context of a culture where women's bodies have traditionally served as the objects of desire. Her European lover Jerome urges her to use his body and to treat him "like the page of a book" (Greenaway 67). This represents a turning point in Nagiko's life, since she is beginning her training as a writer even though she has difficulty with the concept of becoming the agent rather than the canvas or paper.

The image of the tattooed woman is developed even further in the contemporary Japanese film *Irezumi* (1982), which may also be viewed as a forerunner of Greenaway's *The Pillow Book*. As Lucy Fischer indicates in her article "*Irezumi*: Tattoo, Taboo, and the Female Body," many of the issues raised in *The Pillow Book*, including questions of writing, eroticism and the female body, were broached in *Irezumi* (also known as *Spirit of Tattoo*) (Fischer 11). The title of the film that embodies the image of Japanese tattooing involves a former tattoo master, Kyogoro Yamato, whose beautiful tattoos were created through rather unusual means, thus presenting him as a kind of unorthodox figure within the alternative world of tattoo culture. While tattooing his female subjects, he demands that they have sex with a man; in the case of his most recent subject, Akane, he enlists the aid of his young assistant Harutsune to make love to her. The images of desire and violation are presented through the merging of tattooing and sexual intercourse. Yet even though much of the film focuses on the woman as a *tabula rasa* for male artistic expression and masculine desire, the tattooed woman is also transformed as a result of her tattoo. She acquires a new sense of empowerment and complicity with the artist. She had initially been persuaded to acquire the tattoo by her lover, who insisted on making love to a tattooed woman, but after acquiring the tattoo she distances herself from this lover and appears to become a more independent person, thus suggesting the possibility of resisting an image of feminine passivity.

Like Mizoguchi's film *Utamoro and His Five Women* and *Irezumi*, Greenaway's film uses the body as a canvas for artistic expression; however, he reverses the traditional role of man as artist and woman as the object of the creative impulse. Instead, he focuses on a woman as creator and primary producer of meaning. Nagiko uses male models as well as her own body for her artistic expression. Her development into a writer, however, remains firmly entrenched within the world of the visual and the context of voyeuristic desire and violence. The art of photography contributes to Nagiko's development as a writer and her search for a more permanent art form that approximates that of the tattoo. During a sexual encounter with a "client," she makes love in a

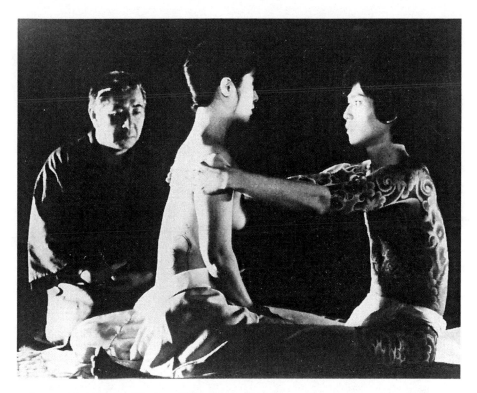

Irezumi (1985). Pacific Arts Video Records. Masayo Utsonomiya plays Akane (center), a woman whose lover encourages her to acquire a tattoo. The tattooing sessions, however, involve sexual relations with the tattooed male assistant (right) as the master tattoo artist Kyogoro Yamato (left) tattoos and watches the interaction between Akane and Harutsune in a voyeuristic fashion. The film literalizes the relationship between tattoos or artistic creation and sexual desire, and acts as an important precursor to Peter Greenaway's film *The Pillow Book.*

"lettered sarcophagus" (Greenaway 69) whose letters leave an imprint on her back. The client in turn takes photographs of Nagiko. The photograph in this and other scenes is a way of offering the illusion of a permanent mark on Nagiko's body, much like the photograph of what appeared to be a real tattoo on the back of a character in Takagi's *The Tattoo Murder Case.* Yet while the photograph is an attempt to convey the appearance of a permanent mark, the mark is not the same as the permanence of a tattoo. The photograph does serve as an interesting

The Pillow Book (1996). CFP Distribution. **Ken Ogata plays the father of Nagiko (played by Vivian Wu), the main character of *The Pillow Book*. He paints her face as part of a birthday ritual. Nagiko will reverse the process by becoming the artist or writer figure later in the film, when she writes her books on the bodies of men. At the end of the film she acquires a tattoo of the text that she wrote on her lover's body.**

mediation device much like the camera or video in *Tattoo* which is used to facilitate a voyeuristic view of a desirable woman. In Nagiko's case, her friend Hoki, the photographer, desires Nagiko's body, and because she will not interact with him directly in the doubly erotic act of sexuality and textuality, he must be content with accessing her indirectly through the mediating power of the photograph. He writes on photographs of Nagiko's body (since he cannot write on her directly): "Nagiko, I love you, I love you" (72). The permanence he seeks with the use of the photograph is akin to the permanence associated with a tattoo, but at this point in the narrative or film, the impermanence of text and skin are still highlighted.

Nagiko continues in her quest for the ultimate act of writing that will acquire a permanent quality. The film script of *The Pillow Book* suggests that one of her clients, the printer, may have offered her some special ink that would be permanent (69). In a subsequent act of writing, she eventually uses a kind of indelible ink which approximates the image of a tattoo since it does not wash off.[24] She writes the first of her thirteen books on Jerome's body, and he visits a publisher, who also happens to be his former lover. The publisher tries to lick off the letters, but they "do not erase" (78). This is Nagiko's first articulation of permanent text, which approximates the concept of a tattoo: a combination of flesh and ink.

Desire and violence are further enmeshed in the image of the textual body, when Jerome becomes jealous of Nagiko's encounters with other men who become the erotic medium for her writing (83). Ingesting pills supplied by Nagiko's photographer friend, Hoki, Jerome commits suicide. Nagiko begins writing her sixth book on Jerome's naked body before she even realizes that he is dead. In the film script of *The Pillow Book*, an English version of the Sixth Book addressing the relationship between the body and ink is included in Appendix 2. Nagiko writes this text on the corpse of her lover. The content of the Sixth Book offers a clear parallel between tattooing and writing on the body:

> Body and book are open.
> Face and page.
> Body and page.
> Blood and ink [107].

The combination of blood and ink is suggestive of a tattoo, which is formed through the injecting of ink into the skin and the scarring process resulting from the bleeding of the skin. In the "book" the speaker (presumably Nagiko) reveals her desire to "keep this book forever" (107) — the permanence evoked in this combined image of body and ink also suggests the permanence of a tattoo.

While tattoos are an art form and function as images of desire, they are created through an often painful physical transformation of the body. This link between violence and the body as art is evident in Jerome's death and in the violation of his body by the publisher; Jerome's skin is transformed into a book or textual tattoo for the pub-

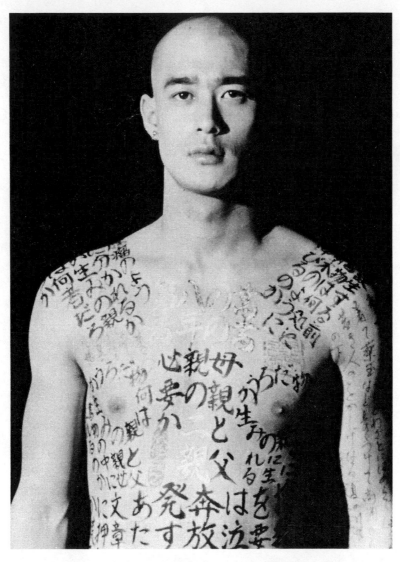

The Pillow Book (1996). CFP Distribution. The young man is an image of
the male body as text; he is one of the human texts sent by the writer Nagiko
(played by Vivian Wu) to her publisher in exchange for her dead lover's body.
The body of Jerome (Ewen MacGregor) had been transformend by this publisher into a textual tattoo through the mutilation and transformation of his
textual body into a book. These masculine bodies or texts stimulate the literary and homosexual desire of the publisher in the film.

lisher's private enjoyment. He actually uses the book as a "pillow book" which he reads in bed. The publisher's desire for Jerome's textual body is similar to Professor Hayakawa's desire to add Kinue's tattooed skin to his collection of tattoos in *The Tattoo Murder Case*; however, the publisher has a more erotic interest in Jerome, while professor Hayakawa's interest appears to be more scientifically motivated. Both Kinue's corpse and Jerome's dead body function in an unusual capacity because they are not simply images, narratives or poems about the violated body — they ARE permanent and mutilated works of art.[25]

In order to highlight both the textual and violent aspects of his narrative even further, Greenaway includes a reference to Kafka's *Penal Colony* as a way of cementing the parallel between tattooing and text. It is highly ironic that, earlier in the narrative, Jerome actually carries Kafka's book. In the film script of *The Pillow-Book,* Greenaway describes Kafka's *Penal Settlement* (Greenaway's translation of the title) as "the story of the possibility of a man's crimes being written on his body by a writing-torture machine" (79). According to Kafka, the link between art, violence and the suffering of the artist was undeniable. Jerome seems to epitomize this intersection, since his death and sub-sequent mutilation causes Nagiko, the artist in the story, much distress. She continues to write her remaining seven books on the bodies of various men and sends them to the publisher, who cannot resist reading them. The thirteenth and final book is called "The Book of the Dead." It is written on the body of a man who poses like a sumo wrestler. After reading the book, the publisher hands "the book of Nagiko's lover" (97) to the man, who will return it to Nagiko. The man then murders the publisher according to the instructions in the "book": *"you have desecrated the body of my lover. You and I know that you have lived long enough"* (97).

Despite some of the horrific elements in *The Pillow Book*, it is important to note that Nagiko's memory of Jerome is not exclusively within the domain of violation. After Jerome's death, Nagiko has the text of this book tattooed onto her breast "In blue-black and orange-red, with a design that incorporates the last calligraphic writing on Jerome's body" (98), thus symbolizing a re-union with Jerome and the restoration of her own text. This tattoo is somewhat reminiscent of the practices of Japanese courtesans who "tattooed *kisho bori* (promise engravings) on hidden parts of their bodies, visible only when naked or in the act of love" (Fellmann 16). The act of tattooing the name[26] of a lover onto one's body was also practiced in Japan (Hardy, "Japanese Tattooing" 59), although, in the case of Nagiko's tattoo, the image is not just a name that represents the lover, but the image of the lover as text, desire and death.

In the final images of *The Pillow Book*, the child that suckles at Nagiko's tattooed breast not only is part of the past narrative of death, blood, and ink but also symbolizes the desire for future creative expression. Thus the female creator of this human book subverts the desire of the male publisher who had desecrated the writer's lover and her original work of art. *The Pillow Book* culminates in an image of the tattoo as a permanent memory of a lover's text; it provides an interesting study of the development of body texts from erasable art forms which resist permanence to the creation of a permanent, yet private, record. In a slight adaptation of Marshall McLuhan's famous statement, "the medium is the message," the film reveals that the body is indeed the final message.

The Pillow Book, *The Tattoo Murder Case*, *Skin Art* and *Tattoo* show how body art or the marked body is associated with desire as well as acts of violence or violation. There is a criminal element in each of these works, whether in the form of kidnapping, prostitution or murder. The concept of desire for a tattooed or marked body is part of the violent context. In *Skin Art* and *Tattoo* the tattoo artist's own obsession with the self affects his relationship with women, who are his tattooed subjects and held captive in one way or another. The alienated or psychologically scarred male artist often expresses his feeling of alienation and his desires in a mediated fashion through the viewing of other media such as photographs or videos. Women may also serve as the vehicle for his original desire, which cannot be satisfied. Even though the tattoo artist may resist other dominant or mainstream forces, his image as a figure of resistance is problematic, since he still fosters the containment of women through his perception of them as canvases for his artistic expression. *The Tattoo Murder Case* presents a more varied role for one tattooed woman as the perpetrator rather than the victim of a crime; the tattooed female body functions as a means of resisting the discourse of science and the rational world of police work that dominates the genre of the detective novel. However, tattoos are clearly presented as dangerous rather than liberating. In this novel, other art forms such as photographs function in a mediating capacity in order to conceal or defer the truth about a mutilated tattoo. In *The Pillow Book*, Greenaway addresses the danger associated with the marked body. The painted body can be a site of desire, but the body marked with permanent ink is even more desirable; the female creator of this human tattoo discovers how one reader's or publisher's desire to read the text results in an obsession to contain and possess the text. The publisher violates the textual body and transforms and mutilates the human body into a different kind of tattooed book consisting of individual pages of skin. However, one crime of passion — the theft and mutilation of this human text — is countered by another crime of passion: the eventual murder of the publisher. Thus, *The Pillow Book* articulates the message present in many other tattoo narratives — art is desirable but dangerous.

CHAPTER FOUR

Members Only: Tattoo Stories of Gangs and Inmates

In the minds of the general public, tattoos are often linked to violence in the context of gangs and prison culture. The stereotypical image of the biker sporting a demonic tattoo comes to mind in relation to gangs, and the prisoner with a crudely fashioned prison tattoo is another. However, beyond the initial shock factor of such tattoos, the tattoos of gang members and prison inmates reflect some interesting connections to the concepts of desire and violence. Both groups may use tattoos to signify a sense of belonging to a particular group as well as their resistance to the mainstream or to non-gang communities.[1] Within gang culture, there is a desire to follow the code of the gang and to identify with a group mentality by using clothing or the tattooed body to signify a spirit of resistance. Gang or gangster culture can include many different groups, including biker gangs. The latter have been studied in many contexts other than tattoo culture, so they will not form a major part of this tattoo study. However, one group that may offer an intriguing way of relating the tattoo to narratives of desire, violence and resistance is the Japanese gang known as the yakuza. This group is an organized crime presence that has parallels with the Mafia. Another kind of gang experience can be examined through the depiction of a female gang in literature and film. Female gang literature or films are far less common than works about the male gang experience. However, Joyce Carol Oates' *Foxfire* offers a creative examination of female gang culture, desire, violence and the importance of the tattoo for group members.

One could say that the inevitable outcome of some gangs is the prison experience.

Prisoners have also incorporated tattoos along with the images and realities of violence into their worlds of experience. In tattoo narratives about prisoners, the tattoo operates in a capacity similar to the gang tattoo because it appeals to an exclusive community of individuals who resist authority. The tattoos of prisoners may reflect the image of these prisoners as one large group or community that resists the Law — however these inmates define it. Tattoos can also symbolize their individual desires or mark their affiliation with a group within the prison.

A Gang of Men: The Yakuza

A number of the tattoo narratives in this book (including *Skin Art* and *The Tattoo Murder Case*) have mentioned various outcast figures such as prostitutes or gang members (e.g., yakuza) who are linked to the underbelly of their respective societies. Not surprisingly, when outcast figures or criminal elements appear within these narratives, there is a strong possibility of violence and passion. Desire is expressed in yakuza narratives through male/female relations, homoeroticism and even death.

As in other gang contexts, the connection between tattoos and resistance to authority or the establishment is quite apparent in the world of the yakuza (pronounced ya'kuza). The yakuza are a Japanese brotherhood or gang culture, often seen as the Japanese equivalent of the Mafia in American society. The name stems from a Japanese card game in which the combination of numbers 8–9–3 (ya-ku-za) is worthless or useless (Fellman 15). As Fellman points out, they "take pride in being worthless or useless members of an outcast social group" (15). The yakuza trace their origin to a seventeenth-century hero bandit,

Banzuin Chobei, who was depicted in Kabuki plays and in tattoo images. Gang members are adorned with tattoos "starting at the collar in an all-over pattern which sometimes covers their bodies clear down to the ankles" (Rome 54). These striking tattoos simultaneously suggest beauty and invite the viewer to admire these tattoos, while also reminding the spectator of the violent and dangerous life led by members of the yakuza. Clearly, the yakuza, like the Mafia or other international gangs, see themselves as practicing outside the boundaries of the law. Yet, ironically, they create their own code of ethics and allegiances within their respective organizations.[2] Depictions of the yakuza in film often highlight their tattooed bodies in order to present the conflicting images of beauty and violence which appeal to the voyeurism of the audience. These films affirm the role of the yakuza as criminals as well as their code of allegiance to the group. In *The Tattooed Men* (1975), Florence Rome, an American reporter, offers some comments on the representation of yakuza gang culture in Japanese film. Rome notes that Japanese writer Yukio Mishima (213) wrote long essays in praise of the *yakuza-eiga,* the yakuza films, for their artistic merit; however, Rome suggests that the genre is quite formulaic: "the style is broad" (213) and, as in old-time Westerns, "there are certain obligatory characters and obligatory scenes" (213). Yakuza films tend to involves scenes in which tattoos are revealed after kimonos are shed (to the delight of the voyeuristic, cheering movie going audience). This revelation of the tattoo can take various forms in contemporary yakuza movies, but the scenes are usually linked to the interrelationship between desire and violence.

BROTHER

While Rome refers to an earlier era of yakuza films produced during the 1960s, a more contemporary yakuza film such as Takeshi Kitano's *Brother* (2000) also includes some tattoo content.[3] Although tattoos appear only twice in *Brother,* they are still highly suggestive of outlaw status combined with desire. In this film, Yamamoto, a yakuza member in exile, travels to Los Angeles where his younger brother is organizing a drug ring. He eventually becomes the leader of this organization until he is killed by the Mafia at the end of the film. The first tattoo scene includes a view of Yamamoto's own back, which consists of a full-back tattoo of a beautiful Japanese woman. The tattoo initially functions as a visual announcement of his alien presence in the United States, because full-body tattoos in the Japanese style are not the norm, especially within American tattoo culture. His outsider status[4] is also reinforced through his poor knowledge of English and by the way Americans treat him as an unusual foreigner. Yet the image of the beautiful Japanese woman on the back of this man may also suggest his ability to use his Otherness (whether this Otherness is equated with Japanese culture or with femininity) to his advantage. In true gangster style, he capitalizes on what may be perceived as an initial image of marginalization and carves out his own territory in a foreign land.

The second tattoo scene develops the concept of desire for the feminine even further in relation to the violent world of the yakuza. This scene involves the figure of Yamamoto's former "lieutenant" or "right hand" man in Japan. He is a rather feminine looking character who also has a back tattoo, thus linking him to Yamamoto in a visual capacity. However, the tattoo also offers a curious comment on gender relations between members of the yakuza. Prior to this scene the lieutenant expressed surprise at the fact that Yamamoto appeared to like women now. This comment draws attention to the possibility of some secret homoerotic past between the two men or between Yamamoto and other men. The tattoo scene is followed by another curious scene in which Yamamoto practices English by alternating the words man and woman while looking out the window to observe people. The tattoo thus signals a level of sexual transgression or gender relations that fall outside the mainstream code of heterosexual relationships.[5] At the same time it emphasizes the "brotherly" bond between members of the yakuza. After Aniki Yamamoto's death, the African-American character Denny, who had become his new right hand man, utters the words, "I love you man."

THE YAKUZA

In addition to the presence of the yakuza in Japanese made films, this culture has also been represented in American films and literature. *The Yakuza* (1974) stars Robert Mitchum as American private eye Harry Kilmer, who travels to Japan to seek out Eiko Ken, a former love interest (who happens to be Japanese), while also becoming involved in the Japanese underworld.[6] The co-star of *The Yakuza* is Japanese actor Takakura Ken (who plays Tanaka Ken, Eiko's brother), a major star in Japanese yakuza films. The film shows a heavy Western influence, largely because of the Hollywood influence on this genre (*Tokyo Wars*, DVD reference material). At the same time, it shows how Eastern and Western cultures interact through images of desire and violence.

While the use of the tattoo in this film is not extensive, there are some scenes which reinforce the link between desire, sexuality, violence executed by members of the yakuza, and Japanese tattoos. The opening scenes showcase the heavily tattooed backs of Japanese men (who are presumably members of the yakuza). A key section in the middle of the film involves a swimming pool or bathhouse setting, which is an ideal scene to depict the kind of voyeurism that was typical of Japanese yakuza films. The scene opens with a view of a towel sliding away from the back of a Japanese man swimming, thus allowing the viewer to participate in a kind of voyeuristic experience of the tattoo. The tattoo on this man's back depicts an angry man with a snake across his mouth. The snake seems to signify danger. Nearby, the American detective Harry Kilmer, played by Robert Mitchum, is relaxing in the water and talking to his younger friend, Dusty, who is admiring the naked bodies of Japanese women showering behind a barrier of frosted glass. Dusty tells Harry how he had just been remembering his Japanese girlfriend making dinner. The dangerous image of the Japanese man's tattoo, combined with the interest or desire expressed by Dusty in women, establish the relationship between violence and desire in the film. Dusty also observes some of the differences in Japanese and American society and uses weapons or images of violence to establish these distinctions. For example, he explains that the

Japanese sword, the katana, slashes inward while Americans slash out. A Japanese saw is pulled towards the person whereas an American saw works with an outward motion. Finally, he says; "when an American cracks up, he opens up a window and shoots up a bunch of strangers. When a Japanese cracks up, he closes a window and kills himself. Everything's in reverse, isn't it?"

Shortly after talking about the two apparently unrelated topics of women and violence, Harry's friend and Harry are approached by a tattooed swimmer with a striking image of a demon-like animal on his back. The demon has fish-like scales and tentacle-like red patterns suggestive of blood. The swimmer stabs Harry with a knife; however, Mitchum's character grabs the knife and successfully kills his assailant. Sexuality and violence are linked in this scene, since the death struggle in the water alternates with images of desire. Before and throughout this attack, the film alternates between reflections of violence and desire, and the tattoo images only intensify these connections. For example, in the swimming area there is a large glass cylinder that houses bright orange fish. The fish swimming around in the bowl are similar to the people in the swimming pool, especially the colorful tattooed swimmers. The nude Japanese women showering behind the frosted glass barrier resemble the fish in that they may also be perceived as trapped or contained.

Like the fish in the fish container and the women showering, the two Americans, Harry and Dusty, are trapped within the pool, a site of danger. The fish container and the swimming pool therefore serve as sites of mediation where Japanese and Americans meet in the context of death and desire. During the Japanese swimmer's attempted stabbing of Harry in the pool, the camera cuts quickly from one image to another. The viewer sees the scales of the fish on the swimmer's back, then Harry Kilmer wrestling with the assailant, then the nude women behind the frosted screen, back to the man with the knife. The attack is violent yet intimate at the same time, so that it suggests both a sexual and an aggressive interaction. The Japanese man was sent by Harry's former friend George Tanner to attack Harry, so the image of the snake in this individual's tattoo and in the tattoo of the earlier

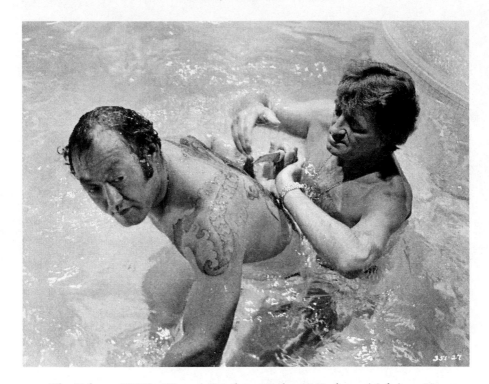

The Yakuza (1970). Warner Brothers. Robert Mitchum (right) as Harry Kilmer defends himself and stabs the tattooed member of the yakuza or Japanese gang who planned to kill him. The man's tattoo is a colorful image of a serpent or fish-like creature with red tentacles and highlights the image of deadly beauty associated with the gang member's tattoo.

swimmer may suggest betrayal as well as danger. The entire scene in the bathhouse or swimming pool may indicate that the American male who contemplates Japanese beauty in the form of women will be punished for this cross-cultural transgression or will run the risk of death. It is therefore fitting that a Japanese man sporting the terrifying beauty of a tattoo is a bearer of this message. Beauty (in the form of a tattoo, and in the shape of a woman) can be dangerous. In the case of a tattoo, beauty may be on the back of a member of the yakuza, and in the case of Harry's Japanese girlfriend, beauty is partly responsible for luring Harry to Japan.

A later segment of *The Yakuza* develops the link between sexuality and violence even further as it focuses on the killing spree initiated by Tanaka Ken, a former yakuza and the brother of Harry's girlfriend Eiko. Ken dislikes Kilmer but feels that he owes him a debt of gratitude for saving Eiko's life in the past. He and Harry enter a dwelling where a group of tattooed and semi-clad Japanese men sit playing a game with clothed men and women. The mixture of semi clad and clothed individuals in this opening scene foreshadows the tearing of Tanaka Ken's clothes in the following scenes and the revelation of his tattoo. Harry wields a rifle or shotgun (perhaps as a sign of an American weapon), while Harry's friend uses a Japanese sword. As Harry's "partner" engages in battle with members of the yakuza, searching for a man by the name of Tono, his shirt is ripped apart by an opponent. The gradual opening of the ripped shirt to reveal more and more of the tattoo is somewhat like a strip tease, and so sexuality and desire are never far removed from the violence of this segment of the film. The revelation of the tattooed body simulates the revelation of the yakuza tattoos that are commonplace in Japanese yakuza films. When Tanaka Ken's shirt has been ripped open sufficiently, the viewer is eventually able to see a tattoo consisting of orange flames and a blue demonic face. Tanaka Ken's skin is also covered with blood, blending with the colors of the tattoo so that it is difficult for the viewer to determine if the red color is blood or part of the tattoo. He uses a Japanese sword during his fight sequences; the camera focuses on the intimacy of the killing since he is right up against his victim when he stabs him with the sword. The phallic associations with swords are so apparent that it does not require much imagination to see the sexual overtones of this scene. Clearly the act of violence and the sadistic pleasure associated with the murder of the victim have sexual ramifications. The connection to the realm of desire is all the more apparent when Tanaka Ken finally finds Tono. By this point in the film, Tanaka Ken's shirt is no longer on his body. Moreover, the man that he plans to fight also engages in an act of revelation: he takes off his hat and reveals a tattoo of a spider on his head, perhaps signifying danger or evil. As the discussion of Tanazaki's spider tattoo in his story "The Tattooer" revealed, in medieval Japanese legends the spider is a malign creature, "invulnerable to sword or

The Yakuza (1970). Warner Brothers. Takakura Ken (left) plays Tanaka Ken, who battles a member of the yakuza (right) in a scene that depicts the gang member's tattooed back. Tanaka Ken's own back is also tattooed since he was a member of the yakuza. The men's semi-clad bodies and phallic-like swords suggest machismo and homoeroticism.

arrow" (Hall). Ironically, this man will not be invulnerable to the sword despite the image of the spider as a powerful creature. As Tanaka fights this man, he experiences brief flashbacks of Harry's Japanese girlfriend as well as a memory of Dusty's girlfriend, who had been killed by other yakuza. Here the film reaffirms the relationship between desire and violence and once again suggests that desire leads to violence as an inevitable outcome.

After Tanaka's killing spree comes to an end in this segment of *The Yakuza*, the camera includes a closeup of his tattoo. It reveals the face of a demon with one eye open and the other eye covered in blood. The demon's red lips are also prominent. They could suggest love, an important theme in the film, or bloody violence. The fact that one of the eyes is stained in blood or visibly absent foreshadows the mutilation of a finger (an important yakuza ritual) which occurs later in the film.

It becomes obvious that the tattoo in *The Yakuza* represents gang membership (both present and former), loyalty, and desire as well as violence. As a sign of the bloodied body, the tattoo is easily tied to the scenes of dismemberment which take place near the end of the film. Harry's friend Tanaka Ken severs his own little finger and gives it to a person whom he has betrayed. Harry imitates this Japanese gesture by doing the same and giving his finger to Tanaka Ken as a way of repaying his debt. The finger functions not only as a site of exchange, but as a phallic symbol of power and homoeroticism. The exchange of fingers suggests not only a cross-cultural exchange,[7] but a sexually suggestive interaction.

THE MAN WITH THE RED TATTOO

The Man with the Red Tattoo (2002) continues the American fascination with the machismo of yakuza culture and also includes some comments on the culture included in critical commentary on the yakuza. "According to Koji Kata, the ex-*yakuza* turned writer, the *yakuza* have a male-chauvinist attitude toward women, and they express it in their slogan, 'Be a man, live like a man,' which stems from the feudal attitudes of old Japan" (Rome 214). In some respects the male dominated world of the yakuza serves as appropriate subject matter for a James Bond novel, since the famous British spy operates within a world of adventure and technology that privileges the male sphere of endeavor as well. *The Man with the Red Tattoo* is a novel by an American who has written continuations of Ian Fleming's original James Bond series. In this novel Bond travels to Japan and learns about the yakuza, who are also involved in taking over pharmaceutical companies and controlling the production of a biological weapon or virus. One member of the yakuza is Goro Yoshida, the man with the red tattoo. His tattoo is quite appropriate in the criminal world of the yakuza, whose own tattooed bodies may be beautiful but also serve as constant reminders of the blood and violence they create in other contexts.[8] The color red is particularly evocative of both beauty and death. In her description of the color red, a real Japanese tattoo artist, Mitsuaki Ohwada, describes it as a beautiful color. However, there is also danger inherent in the color red within the context of tattooing, because this tattoo ink contains cadmium, a metallic element that can poison the body (Fellman 12).

In Benson's novel, Yoshida's tattoo is primarily red: "its red color dominated the design." The red contributes to the dual effect of the beautiful and the deadly. Death is present in the tattoo's depiction of a site of struggle: "an ancient battle between samurai and dragons ... it was at once marvelous, beautiful and terrifying" (Benson 37). The dragon image hearkens back to the popularity of this design in the prints of Japan's Edo-period artists; it is an image that was often depicted in conjunction with a hero or warrior figure. For example, the artist Utagawa Kuniyoshi (1797–1861) created a series of prints called "108 Heroes of *Suikoden*," including "The dragon-tattooed Shishin engaged in a fight" (McCallum 122). This character was one of the many heroic outlaws from the *Suikoden*, Bakin's Japanese translation of the fourteenth-century picaresque Chinese novel *Shui-hu Chuan* (known in English as *The Water Margin*). Many of the full-body tattoos on the backs of contemporary Japanese men, including the yakuza, depict images of legendary heroes such as the tattooed hero

Heikuro engaged in a death struggle with a serpent (Fellman 40). While many might question whether the yakuza should be viewed as heroic figures, the dragon tattoo on Yoshida's back still serves an important purpose since it includes a visual and an inter-textual reference to an earlier story or narrative of death and beauty.

The image of Yoshida's tattoo offers some interesting insight into his sense of self as a member of the yakuza, but even more revealing is the amount of pain he endured in order to acquire the tattoo. When Yoshida had the tattoo work done, he experienced many hours of pain, "one hundred for the back alone" (Benson 37). Since the traditional art of *irezumi* involves manual tattooing as opposed to the use of electric devices, Yoshida's ability to endure this kind of pain does paint him as a rather brave man even though he is clearly a villain in the context of the James Bond narrative.

Yoshida's tattoo also links him to another artistic yet violent heritage: the ritual art of *seppuku,* or Japanese suicide, and the masochistic connection between desire and death. Chapter 15 of the novel reveals this uneasy relationship in the title "The Desire for Death." In this chapter, Benson creates a fictional narrative outlining Yoshida's connection to the famous Japanese writer Yukio Mishima. Yoshida's identity as a member of the yakuza involved in the practice of violence seems to complement his idolization of the famous right wing writer Yukio Mishima. As Florence Rome indicates in *The Tattooed Men,* Mishima commented on the merits of yakuza films, perhaps because he valued the importance of courage and ritual including the willingness to commit *seppuku,* a form of suicide. However, author Benson presents Mishima as an individual who apparently disapproved of Yoshida's involvement in organized crime despite his own belief in many of the yakuza principles (147). In the fictional context of Benson's novel, Mishima apparently dismissed Yoshida from his private army, the Shield society, which was dedicated to the traditional values of Japan.

The rift between Yoshida and Mishima in *The Man with the Red Tattoo* reinforces Yoshida's status as a tattooed outcast; yet after Mishima commits *seppuku* in 1970, Yoshida has the desire to reenact the bloody

narrative of Mishima's death through his own. In a preliminary enact-
ment of this ritual, Yoshida presses the blade against his skin, "feeling
the sharp tip's desire to penetrate his body" (149). The imagery is not
only evocative of potential violence, but also has a clear sexual sugges-
tiveness, implying Yoshida's homoerotic attachment to Mishima. When
Yoshida finally ends his life, he does so by cutting his stomach. The
crimson color of his tattoo reflects his bloody death at the end of the
novel. Yet, strangely enough, he would still have considered his death
"beautiful" because he died "the way he wanted, as Mishima did" (291).
In an earlier section of the novel Yoshida remembered Mishima's words:
"'A man's determination to become a beautiful person is very different
from the same desire in a woman; in a man it is always the desire for
death'"(149). The novel not only cements the image of a tattoo as a
sign of resistance to British (perhaps even American) attitudes, but it
reveals how the tattoo functions as a continuation of an earlier cultural
narrative and aesthetic: the "beautiful" suicide of Mishima.

The red tattoo also reinforces the bond of brotherhood that exists
for members of the yakuza. In yakuza films and literature, the tattoo
may also be used as a device to highlight the strict codes or rules within
the "gang" as well as the image of an individual as a social outcast. In
The Man with the Red Tattoo it suggests the kind of homoerotic element that is also present in yakuza films such as *Brother* and *The Yakuza*.
In *The Yakuza*, the element of finger mutilation or removal is used to
highlight the sense of loyalty or debt one individual owes to another;
the mutilated finger is another image of the altered or bloody body and
is thus linked to the tattooed body, which represents the intersection
of pain and loyalty to the yakuza group. This ritual of severing the finger
is described in Benson's novel as *yubitsume*. Apparently, when a member of the yakuza does something wrong, he has to cut off the joint of
a finger and then give the piece of finger to the *kaicho* or leader as an
apology (81). The image of the bloody finger acts as another reminder
that this is a story about blood, but, as mentioned in the analysis of
The Yakuza, it also provides phallic imagery that may suggest either
machismo or a sadomasochistic homoerotic relationship between male
members of the yakuza.

Finally, the redness of Yoshida's tattoo also reinforces the narrative of blood and the body that is part of the yakuza plan to take over companies and use technology and science to engage in biological warfare. Mosquitoes are used as "an ingenious delivery system" (130) for a virus, and like tattoos they become part of the image of blood and death in the novel. Perhaps their predatory nature also becomes a metaphor for the yakuza, who may have a lust for blood. This desire to experience pain may take the form of acquiring painful tattoos, practicing the ritual of finger mutilation, or committing suicide with a sword. The comparison between mosquitoes and the yakuza is not exact, however, since most members of the yakuza are male, and the only harmful mosquitoes are the females. These tend to live longer than the males and are sometimes called "red widows" (132). Nevertheless, even with this modification of the original parallel, it is possible to connect Yoshida, a member of the yakuza, to the mosquito. He can be viewed as a male version of a "red widow" with respect to his homoerotic feelings for Mishima, who died before he did. Thus the image of the man with the red tattoo intersects with many other references to the color red and to the images of blood and desire that are part of the gang culture of the yakuza in *The Man with the Red Tattoo*.

A Gang of Girls

FOXFIRE

The majority of yakuza narratives involve a focus on male culture; a film that focuses on female involvement in gang culture is a rarity.[9] In order to examine the dynamics of female gang members in a fictional context, one must leave the yakuza genre and analyze another kind of work about tattooed gang members. Joyce Carol Oates' novel *Foxfire: Confessions of a Girl Gang* (1993) is a tattoo narrative which offers a view of female gang culture and focuses more on the concept of the tattoo as a rite of passage[10] than the yakuza genre tends to do. The tattoo serves as a way of showing a change in the lives of several young women as they become part of the gang called Foxfire. The tattoo reaffirms the membership of these individuals in a particular group and tells the story of these young women.

The novel *Foxfire* was adapted into a film starring Angelina Jolie as Legs Sadovsky, the rebellious leader of this teenaged gang. Both the novel and film promote a girl-centered gang culture of resistance, albeit in different historical periods. The novel and the film depict tattoos in the context of resistance to institutional and masculine authority. The tattoo ritual and symbol incorporated into the plot of *Foxfire* also establishes relations between teenaged girls as an alternative form of love and loyalty to heterosexual relations dominated by patriarchal attitudes. There are a few differences between Oates' novel and the 1996 film by director Annette Haywood-Carter, even though the scene involving the collective tattooing is quite similar. Oates' book is set in the New York of the 1950s, a time when girl gangs were not as prominent a phenomenon as in the 1990s: "...there were gangs in Hammond in Lowertown in the Fairfax neighborhood but they were all boys or young men in their late teens, early twenties, there were no girl gangs nor were there stories of or memories of 'girl gangs'" (Oates 35).[11] Oates' female gang is comprised of five white girls who, along with other characters, hold some of the racist attitudes typical of the time. The film transforms the setting into a contemporary time, and in keeping with the 1990s emphasis on cultural diversity, one of the girls, Goldie Goldberg (who is a white girl in the novel), appears to be the Asian daughter of a white father.

In the novel version of *Foxfire*, a 50-year-old-woman, Maddy Wirtz, narrates and writes the story of a young rebel by the name of Legs Sadovsky who enters the lives of four other girls, Maddy, Goldie, Lana and Rita. Legs helps these girls battle sexual harassment and helps them develop a sense of loyalty to one another through their membership in the girl gang called Foxfire (based on the phrase "Foxes of Fairfax Avenue," which was transformed into Foxfire in Legs' dream) (43). However, her combative spirit results in her imprisonment at a detention center or facility called Red Bank. After her release from youth detention, she becomes involved in another dangerous episode when she shoots a wealthy man; immediately thereafter, she disappears along with her car and is never heard from again. She has achieved a kind of mythical status in the mind of the narrator as someone who may have resurfaced elsewhere when Maddy sees a woman resembling Legs in a picture of a large crowd of people in Cuba.

Legs' image as a dynamic and unpredictable force leads her to found a female gang. In order to prove their allegiance to the concept of the gang, Legs and the other young women participate in a tattooing ritual. This act may not seem too extraordinary because male gangs, after all, frequently sport tattoos as a sign of commitment to the gang. However, because the novel depicts young women in the 1950s, this act of collective tattooing is definitely extreme since it reinforces the image of these women as forces of resistance to authority and to the 1950s' aesthetic of feminine beauty. Such an aesthetic would hardly have embraced the art of tattooing on women's bodies. The tattoo ritual and the symbol of the tattoo itself suggest the importance of desire and violence in the novel. Legs chooses the symbol of the flame as the group's "sacred emblem, red-stippled dots defining themselves into the shape of a tall erect flame" (41). The fire symbolizes a kind of rebirth for these women as gang members; the red color and the heat of the fire suggests anger and the potential to do harm, as well as the fire of sexual desire. In the novel Legs uses a silver ice pick to tattoo the other girls, and the girls then use red vegetable dye used for Easter eggs to inject color into the flame. They also mingle their blood to seal their allegiance to one another.

Like the representation of tattoo rituals in other texts and films, (e.g., *Tattoo, Never Again*[12]), the discourse and actions accompanying the tattooing focus not only on the painful aspect of the tattooing but on the sexuality of tattooing. For example, Maddy tells Legs, "... do it to me" (41) before Legs begins the tattooing process. After the ritual, the girls play in a sexually charged manner, emphasizing a lesbian eroticism combined with the visceral nature of the tattoo experience. The young women engage in a kind of group orgy displaying behavior reminiscent of the maenads or bacchantes from classical mythology. "[...] Rita shrieking smearing blood on Goldie pressing her grapefruit-sized

111

bare breasts against Goldie's smaller taut breasts and someone dribbled whiskey on Rita's breasts and licked it off, whiskey and blood and Rita was in a fever her hair in her face red-flaming and electric and Maddy's chest was bare her tiny breasts bare and the tiny nipples frightened and erect..." (42). The difference between the maenads and these gang members, however, is that the former were inspired by and worshipped the male god Dionysos (Chevalier and Gheerbrant 64) while the latter are inspired by the god- or goddess-like presence of Legs Sadovsky.

Even though the flame tattoo is a symbol of resistance for these young women, four of the girls make an effort to conceal it. Perhaps they do so because of the taboos surrounding body art in the 1950s, especially in under-aged women, or because they wanted to keep certain aspects of Foxfire a secret. Legs, on the other hand, "was the most careless about hiding her tattoo, or maybe defiant, why should I hide it, it's beautiful" (Oates 83). Yet while the other gang members are more careful to conceal their tattooed bodies, they still draw or paint the sign of the flame in "red crayon or ink or nail polish" (80) all over the school and the neighborhood as an act of resistance. In a society which does not permit women to form an identity outside a conventional, patriarchal, and heterosexual context, the reproduction of the flame tattoo validates the alternative identities of these young women, since they see an extension of themselves in the distribution of the symbol. It is a form of distribution that falls outside the closed and rather sinister system of exchange created by Wimpy Wirtz, who promises Maddy a typewriter in exchange for sexual favors. Oates indicates just how difficult it is for women to express their sense of self in a scene narrated by Maddy in a stream of consciousness style. It is a narration that describes an officer searching Legs before she is placed in a detention facility. The officer notices her tattoo and says "'it's a homemade tattoo, honey, isn't it?— your boy friend done it to you, huh?'" (145–6). Now this "memory" may be Maddy's imaginative re-creation of an event in Legs' life, but it still suggests the influence of the male involvement in a woman's life, even if Maddy is merely projecting her sense of what may have happened to Legs. In this reconstruction, the officer assumes that a boyfriend must have been involved in the creation of the tattoo and that this must have been an example of violation ["'your boy friend done it to you'" (146)] instead of a woman's voluntary act of self-expression. The assumption that Legs has been bullied by a boyfriend is not an unusual one in the context of the novel since the tattoo is not just connected to the desire for self-expression but is also compared to the bruised body. For example, Maddy describes a scene when she was exhibiting herself in the bathroom to contemplate her "beautiful FOXFIRE tattoo" (58) when her mother comes into the bathroom. In the mirror, Maddy sees her mother's "big purplish-orangish black eye as if a giant's fist had walloped her good" (58), perhaps the result of an encounter with a male companion. This section of the novel links two examples that suggest a voyeuristic contemplation of the marked body. Neither Maddy nor her mother knows whether the other saw the marked skin: "I shrank seeing and not seeing just as you saw my FOXFIRE birthmark and didn't see" (58). The secrecy and furtiveness associated with the gaze at the tattoo or the bruised face highlights the link between the mutilated body and desire.

In the mother's case, the desire to see and not see Maddy's tattoo is echoed in her own need to hide her evidence of a bruised body that may have been the result of a romantic encounter gone awry. In Maddy's case, the gaze at her mother's face through the mirror suggests an inability to communicate directly with her parent and that the only connection she can have to her mother is through the mediating influence of her tattoo and its similarity to another marked body. Near the beginning of the novel, Maddy makes it clear that she does not allow herself to think of her mother when she writes her notebook "except in specific terms of FOXFIRE" (20). Thus the tattoo and its connection to the gang Foxfire offers a mediated means of entering her mother's world.

The film adaptation of Oates' novel is similar to the novel in that it still depicts the girl gang members resisting various social structures or individuals, but there are some changes. For example, the historical period is the late twentieth century (the 1980s or '90s); this change in era may have been done to make the film appeal to a contemporary audience. The sexual harassment of the teenaged girls is carried out by a biology teacher instead of a math teacher; this particular change injects a more ironic note into the narrative, since this teacher of biology expresses his scientific curiosity or desire by trying to inspect women's bodies. Another example of heterosexual orientation is presented in the film through the opening scene, which reveals Maddy (or Madeleine) taking pictures of her nude boyfriend. In the film, Maddy is in a relationship with a young man, unlike Oates' character who is a less confident personality. However, this introduction of a boyfriend for Maddy does not merely function as a way of catering to a heterosexual audience. It shows how Maddy changes and how she is perceived as different by her boyfriend after Legs Sadovsky enters into her life. When her boyfriend sees Maddy's tattoo and discovers that she spent an evening acquiring a tattoo, he seems to sense that Maddy is distancing herself from him as she moves away from an exclusive relationship with a man and establishes a new-found interest in the company of young women. The image of the tattoo as a sign of difference and illicit desire is also presented through the interaction between the character Goldie (who appears to be Asian) and her white father.[13]

Despite the contemporary setting of the movie, some of the anxiety surrounding tattoos is still evident. Either this carries over from the sensibility of Oates' novel, or it is a further indication that tattoos are still not accepted by mainstream, patriarchal "authority" figures. For example, when Goldie's wealthy white father sees her tattoo, he says, "Why do you keep doing this? What are you, some kind of freak?" Of course, Goldie's tattoo is the least of her problems, since she is also a drug addict who feels alienated from her wealthy but busy white parents and who presumably turns to drugs as a way of filling this void in her life. Her addiction seems to wane as she becomes a member of a girl gang, especially since Legs discourages her from taking drugs. Thus the film suggests that the tattoo ritual or the sporting of tattoos should not necessarily be associated with other altered bodily states such as those achieved through substance abuse. Instead it offers Goldie a much needed sense of community since she feels alienated from her own family. When Legs, the leader of the group, is sent to a detention facility for breaking into the local high school after hours, Goldie actually reverts to her drug dependent state, perhaps because she once again feels abandoned in some way. Once Legs is released from confinement, she tries to help Goldie by asking Mr. Goldberg to give the girls $10,000 so that Goldie can get into rehab. The film changes a detail from Oates' novel in that the man who is accidentally shot by Legs is Goldie's father Mr. Goldberg instead of the wealthy Mr. Kellogg. This transformation may have been done to emphasize the alienation between child (Goldie) and parent (Mr. Goldberg), which is a common experience for teenagers.

Another change in the film is that Maddy is portrayed throughout as a photographer instead of a writer. While the novel indicates that she works with photographs as part of her job as an astronomer's assistant, it focuses more on her creative construction of the story of the girl gang.

In the film, the photographic connection may be the result of the visual emphasis, which tends to occur within the medium of film. Nevertheless, it also serves as a way of reinforcing the visual element of the tattoo and the theme of voyeurism that are also part of the girls' collective tattoo experience. In both the novel and the film, Maddy retains the important role as an artist who chronicles or records the experiences of others, albeit through different media.[14]

A rather significant change in the film's adaptation of Oates' *Foxfire* involves the treatment of tattoo imagery, even though the imagery still functions as a means of highlighting the outcast status of the girl gang members and the feelings of (illicit) lesbian desire. In keeping with the evolution of tattoo styles over the course of the twentieth century, the Foxfire gang's flame tattoo is somewhat more stylized than Oates' rather crude rendering of the image in the novel, and it includes both black and red dyes.

It is difficult to determine what kind of instrument is used in the film. It is a manual instrument or pin of some kind, but definitely not an ice pick. Another departure from the novel is the inclusion of multiple tattoos on Legs' body.[15] This reinforces her image as a female outlaw figure. These tattoos signify the unknown elements of Legs' past and contribute to her mystique as a girl who appeared out of nowhere, and who disappears just as suddenly in the film (or just as mysteriously in the novel). One of the tattoos that is actually decoded is dedicated to her mother, thus reinforcing the woman-centered focus of the film. It is an image of a broken and bleeding heart surrounding the name Audrey. Beneath the image is the inscription "1959–1994." This tattoo is a visual representation of Legs' narrative of her absent mother, who was killed while driving a car under the influence of alcohol. The tattoo re-inscribes but also re-constructs the convention of tattoos that serve as a tribute to mothers. The convention of the "I Love Mom" tattoo is firmly entrenched within a masculinist aesthetic — most men's mothers were supposedly paragons of motherhood; the tattoos suggested that the object of love was an image of perfection and that only the wearer of the tattoo would have had any rebellious tendencies. However, Legs' tattoo actually creates a feminist subversion of this masculinist aesthetic, since she as a woman is a figure of rebellion and so was the woman who was the reference point for her tattoo. The tattoo may also suggest her desire for a mother that left her too soon; the memory she has of her mother is quite different from her view of her dad who "is somewhere." Later in the film, Legs makes the statement that "fathers mean nothing," thus discounting the patriarchal influence in her life. However, her desire for an absent mother who died a violent death is articulated through her marked body. This desire and pain are then reproduced in another form through her tattooing of the Foxfire gang members. She figuratively gives birth to the gang known as Foxfire.

Like Oates' novel, the film emphasizes the woman-centered community developed between the five young women who are members of a girl gang. The tattoo is an emblem of desire, birth and endurance; it also symbolizes the excitement of being part of a resistance group. It is the flame that helps the girls battle injustice, but as Angelina Jolie's character Legs says in the film, the tattoo is also an image of destruction "if you don't respect it." The girl gang or community eventually dissolves with the "betrayal" of Legs at the end of the film. The girls abandon Legs as their leader when they panic during the hostage-taking of Goldie's father in the film, or the hostage taking of Mr. Kellogg in the novel; both men represent patriarchal authority. The film ends with the girls taking Mr. Goldberg to the hospital, and with Legs saying goodbye to Maddy and leaving town just as suddenly as she appeared.

In the novel, the image of the tattoo is once more evoked; this time the image of the flame tattoo suggests the correlation between desire and death: "[Maddy] 'So you don't believe we have souls I guess' and Legs laughed and said, 'Yeah probably we do but why's that mean we're gonna last forever? Like a flame is real enough, isn't it, while it's burning?—even if there's a time it goes out?'" (328). The passage describes the fact that the gang or communal experience will not necessarily last forever, but that this should not diminish the intensity of the experience while it lasts. The image also serves as a way of describing the intense feelings and desire Maddy harbored for Legs, even though Legs disappears near the end of the narrative. And finally, the tattoo also suggests the spiritual quality of the communal girl gang experience. This spirituality is based on a rejection of a patriarchal Christian perspective; it revolves around personal relations rather than institutional power.

Stories of Inmates

Gangs and prisoners share an experience of resistance to social systems. In fact the prison experience or incarceration may be the logical end for some gang members.[16] (Legs Sadovsky's detention time at Red Bank and the possibility that she would be imprisoned for kidnapping and attempted murder are two examples from *Foxfire*.) Like gang members, many prisoners are also the bearers of tattoos which symbolize a history, present, or future of violence and desire.

One of the earliest examples of a criminal whose mark defines him as a social outcast or prisoner is the Biblical figure of Cain. This son of Adam and Eve murdered his brother after God favored Abel's sacrifice of a lamb over Cain's offering of crops. The latter's violent actions were motivated by desire for God's approval. In his book *I Love Mom: An Irreverent History of the Tattoo,* John Gray identifies Cain as the bearer of the first tattoo: "And the Lord set a sign for Cain, lest any finding him should smite him" (Genesis 4:15). While one could argue with the interpretation of Cain as the *first* rebel, according to Gray, God's marking of Cain brands Cain as "the first rebel" (Gray 25). What is important about the marking of Cain is that the Biblical narrative links the concept of the tattoo to violence and to the marginalized status of the criminal. Cain's tattoo functions as a sign of difference and resistance to the Law. The narrative of Cain's murder and his ensuing outcast status are embedded in the visual power of the "sign," which Gray has chosen to call a tattoo. Yet Cain's tattoo also has an ambiguous, perhaps even a subversive, function, because when God the divine tattoo artist marked him, He not only marginalized him but also marked him as God's "property" to protect him from harm. Thus Cain is still branded as belonging to someone; while this does not have the same resonance for a gang member or a prisoner who might benefit from relations with another gang member or prisoner, the mark of identification serves as a way of signaling a kind of ownership. The subversive quality of tattoos, which depends on the relationship between containment and resistance, is also articulated in tattoo narratives about gang culture and prison culture. Like Cain, the gang member or prisoner articulates his or her resistance to an establishment, but in becoming part of a gang or group of like-minded prisoners, that individual may be shielded from not just harmful influences, but any outside influences that seek to infiltrate that individual's space.

Tattoos share a long history with resistance, violence, marginality and imprisonment. For example, the Persians, Greeks and Romans used tattooing for punitive purposes, "and delinquent slaves in late antiquity were tattooed, as were criminals, soldiers and prisoners of war" (Anderson, in Caplan 106). In pre-1600 Japan (the time before the famous Edo period) tattooing was used as a form of punishment.[17]

After 1797 in Bengal, individuals imprisoned for life had their name, crime and date of sentence tattooed on the forehead (108). In her study of the modern tattoo community, Margo DeMello describes prison tattooists and tattooed convicts as the most marginalized individuals within the tattoo community (DeMello 132). This is not surprising because, as a marginalized group, prisoners do not necessarily have access to sophisticated tattoo devices. Consequently the quality of their tattoos is in part a reflection of their lower status and the need to develop creative alternatives in tattooing, thereby resisting established and safe practices. The Tattoo Museum in Amsterdam (created by tattoo artist and historian Henk Schiffmacher, otherwise known as Hanky Panky) has a section dedicated to the materials used for tattoos by prisoners around the world. There are various jailhouse tattoo machines from Russian and American prisons. According to the Museum's Resource Guide, "[p]igment was and is made from all kinds of material: urine with burned men's papers, spit, semen, water, whiskey, doorpaint, shoepolish," thereby highlighting the alternative culture that is created in a prison environment — a place that demands resourcefulness. The innovative spirit of the prison tattooist is depicted in the *X-Files* television episode "Never Again" through the character of a Russian tattoo artist who concocted a striking red dye for tattooing while in a Russian prison. However, the dye had hallucinogenic properties, an unforeseen side effect of the resourcefulness of this particular prison tattooist. This prison narrative helps create the image of contamination by alien forces (in this case, Russian), thereby highlighting the questionable nature of the materials used for tattooing.

The red color of the tattoo ink mentioned in the *X-Files* episode also suggests a link to the concept of desire, which is an important part of the "Never Again" narrative that was examined in chapter two of this book. Thus, tattoos within a prison context are not only part of a narrative of violence but also impart a history, present, and future of various kinds of desire (sexual, religious, criminal). The connection between prisoners and desire may be less apparent than the history and continuation of violent behavior, but it is often intimately integrated into the character or community group of criminal minds, especially in artistic treatment of prison life in television.

Prison Television and Tattoos

Oz

Prison culture has always been popular subject material for television and film, but the American HBO prison drama *Oz* was the first series to be entirely set in a correctional facility, thus breaking new ground. The drama portrays the lives of prisoners (many of whom are tattooed) and guards within the walls of a prison called Oz, the abbreviation for Oswald Maximum Security Prison. The series, which debuted in July 1997, is the brainchild of Tom Fontana, whose dedication to his project is symbolized by his decision to acquire a tattoo of the word Oz on his own arm.[18] The process of tattooing the word Oz in red ink on an arm is depicted in the opening credits of the series and highlights the blood and violence that characterize this prison world. However, this opening scene also draws attention to the subversive function of the tattoo or its power of resisting a traditional narrative. The title of the series, *Oz,* is a subversive recontextualization of the fantasyland associated with the children's story and film *The Wizard of Oz*. During the opening credits, the tattooing of the arm with the word Oz alternates with scenes of prison violence, thus forming a kind of visual narrative (the process of completing the tattooing design) which accompanies the visual image of the tattoo. A further parody of Dorothy's world of Oz is established through the name of the experimental unit of the prison called Emerald City. The Emerald City in the television series Oz does have something in common with the Emerald City in the *Wizard of Oz,* since both are sites of disillusionment for the prisoners and for Dorothy respectively. Dorothy learns that the powerful wizard is just an ordinary man, and the prisoners in Oz learn all too quickly that they live in a world of chaos that cannot easily be controlled by their version of the wizard: the prison warden.

While *The Wizard of Oz* does have episodes of violence, the terrors of this children's book and film clearly pale in comparison to Fontana's stark drama. A poster for the series also parodies Dorothy's line in the children's narrative: "There's no place like home." A line on the poster reads: "Oz: It's no place like home." The negative simile is based on the transformed world of the prisoners in Oz, which no longer resembles a home environment. This is not to say that many of the prisoners, like Dorothy in the *Wizard of Oz*, do not have a desire to return home; on the contrary, many do express this wish, and yet the prison environment becomes a self-enclosed world in which other less pleasant desires, usually linked to an inevitably violent outcome, are expressed. In fact, the prison environment becomes a new kind of society that generates images of resistance or exclusion and belonging, since it includes the formation of discrete gang units that create different communities[19] within the prison environment.

On an extra-textual level, or on a level outside the context of the series itself, the promoters of the series have tried to foster a spirit of community among its viewers by holding a tattoo contest and by creating a "community" section on the Internet with a bulletin board for messages from fans.[20] Critics of violence in media art might argue that the series was condoning an aesthetic of violence by holding a tattoo contest and indirectly glamorizing prison tattoos. However, despite these kinds of objections, it is interesting to observe how tattoos in a television series can create a new narrative and community both within and outside the fictional boundaries of the program.

Like the members of a gang culture which is often comprised of individuals or groups that occupy the margins of mainstream society, the individuals and groups in *Oz* are also marginalized with respect to outside culture. Their tattoos often indicate this image of marginalization and resistance to some form of establishment; yet, at the same time, the tattoos of *Oz* inmates also serve as signifiers of inclusion in specific communities and reflect some of their strongest beliefs or desires, albeit somewhat dysfunctional ones. The heavily tattooed biker prisoners form a distinct group and seem almost a cliché of the tattooed biker; they serve as much of the muscle in the series, and they are rarely developed into strong, individual characters except for the character of Jaz Hoyt. Nevertheless, their heavily tattooed bodies often serve as the most colorful depiction of the tattoo and its link to the image of the tough guy — a tough "skin" that is so necessary in a prison environment. The Aryans or neo-Nazis constitute another tattooed faction. The Aryans, for obvious reasons, find themselves in conflict with a number of the other groups including the Muslims. Their leader, Vern Schillinger, sports a swastika tattoo among other tattoos which define his fascist tendencies. The O'Reilly brothers, Ryan and Cecil, are a gang of two and are identified according to their Irish heritage and by their dedication to sports. The two brothers have matching shamrock tattoos, and Ryan O'Reilly is a sports fanatic who supports his brother Cecil's boxing activities; he bears a Chicago Bulls basketball tattoo which reinforces his Irish heritage since Chicago is known for its Irish immigrants. While Beecher's swastika tattoo serves as a negative reminder of Schillinger's sexual violation of Beecher in the first episode of season one, many other tattoos in *Oz* do support Henk Schiffmacher's contention that the tattoo is a sign of "rebellion to show that the prisoner has not given up, has not been conquered or broken, proving the spirit in an imprisoned body" (Schiffmacher 18). By identifying the tattooed prisoners with specific groups, the creators of *Oz* attempt to foster some sense of community or gang spirit, even though the prisoners' beliefs are often morally questionable.

The tattoos in *Oz* function as an aesthetic of violence and as a narrative device that also develops the *individual* characters and their unusual desires, even though many seem to be part of an easily recognizable *group*. In terms of their aesthetic presentation, some of the tattoos are quite crudely fashioned because of the unavailability of proper tattooing instruments in a prison environment. For example, one prisoner by the name of Donald Groves, who harbored a desire for violence and cannibalism, killed and ate his mother and his father. He is depicted tattooing the word MOM on his hand with the help of a pen and a lighter.[21] The character is clearly a figure of resistance because of his aberrant criminal behavior, and yet he draws on the common tattoo convention of tough men tattooing the word "Mom" or the phrase "I love Mom" on their bodies, perhaps as a way of subverting this convention which usually does suggest some sincere feelings on the part of the sons for their mothers. In this prisoner's case, however, the love for his mother is an ironic tribute, since he is a cannibal who apparently "loved" his mother so much that he had to consume or absorb her presence.[22] As the California tattoo artist Madame Chinchilla points out, in Russia, tattoos often match the crimes or "sins" of the tattooed individual (Chinchilla 69). This also appears to be the case for this Oz prisoner. Ironically, the word MOM in red does not signify true love for the prisoner's mother; instead it signifies the blood associated with matricide and the desire to absorb the mother into his body and being, thus reversing the process whereby a mother gives birth to the child.

While Donald Groves does not appear to have an affiliation with a gang within the prison, his group affiliation might be with other prisoners who committed violent crimes against family members. The aesthetic of violence as symbolized by Groves' "MOM" tattoo is a key component of many of the tattoos in the series. This connection between violence and the tattoo is further evoked through the words of Augustus Hill, the black narrator, who takes issue with people who call Oz "Emerald City": "To me, it's a concentration camp,"[23] thereby highlighting the image of the prisoners as victims. The analogy between prison and the concentration camp experience not only emphasizes that the prisoners belong to groups considered socially or morally questionable, but that they are deprived of their individuality through their assigned numbers. Just like Jews who were given numerical tattoos in concentration camps, the prisoners in Oz are also referred to by a number. For example, Vern Schillinger is Prisoner 92S110 (*Oz* 1.1). However, as with so many of the incidents or images in Oz, even this parallel is subverted or inverted. In the case of Vern Schillinger and another prisoner, Beecher, this subversion is facilitated through the image of the tattoo and the theme of homosexual desire. Vern Schillinger is an Aryan or a neo-Nazi in the concentration camp known as Oz. He sports tattoos that are emblematic of Nazi ideology and German identity — a lightning bolt on each arm that is reminiscent of the SS insignia as well as the image of an eagle, a symbol of the German Reich. The irony of a neo-Nazi engaging in homosexual acts is not lost on members of the viewing audience who would be familiar with the Nazi policy of placing homosexuals into concentration camps. The concepts of a concentration camp tattoo and the fascist subjugation of the Jews are also

Oz 3.1: "The Truth and Nothing But..." (1999). Jaz Hoyt (played by Evan Seinfeld) is a heavily tattooed prisoner who belongs to the biker gang in the prison called Oz. In this scene, he fights Vern Schillinger (J. K. Simmons), the leader of the Aryans. Schillinger's lightning bolt tattoo (suggestive of the German SS) can be seen on his left arm, and his right arm shows the image of barbed wire. The latter tattoo suggests that Schillinger inflicts and experiences pain. In "The Routine" (1.1) he tattoos a swastika on Tobias Beecher's posterior. The bikers and the Aryans are just two clearly identifiable groups or units with the prison and serve as different illustrations of violence.

visually and narratively represented in Schillinger's relationship with his prison mate Tobias Beecher. The latter is a lawyer who is imprisoned for vehicular homicide, and who has the misfortune of becoming Schillinger's unwilling sexual partner or slave. In the first episode of the series, Schillinger engraves a swastika tattoo on Beecher's buttock and informs Beecher that he now belongs to Schillinger. Thus, even though Beecher was not previously part of a specific gang within *Oz*, Schillinger's branding of Beecher makes him the property of Schillinger and, by extension, of the Aryans. The swastika tattoo furthermore evokes an aesthetic of violation that in turn disrupts Beecher's relations with his wife. Beecher attempts to maintain a relationship with his wife based on mutual desire become more and more difficult. Apparently Beecher's wife cannot stomach the violent environment of the prison and, according to Tobias, she decides to divorce him after seeing the swastika on his behind (*Oz* 1.3), thus suggesting her rejection of Beecher based on his homosexual encounter.

As Schillinger's tattoos and his act of tattooing another prisoner demonstrate, the tattoos in *Oz* do not only serve as visual devices in this television series, they also function as visual entry points into the narratives and bodies of the individual prisoners. Schillinger's fascist tendencies are emphasized, and Beecher's future homosexual desire for the inmate Chris Keller, and his continuing role as a victim figure, are also foreshadowed in the tattooing scene. Another primary character whose storyline is enhanced through his tattoos is the character Miguel Alvarez, who is part of the group known as the Latinos. His tattoos are a part of the religious imagery and messages in the series and serve as a form of resistance to traditional images of Christianity. Alvarez was imprisoned for assault, but the series suggests that he is also guilty in a religious context — he commits the sin of pride, an ultimate desire to define oneself as infallible (or not subject to the law of a supreme being). Alvarez has several tattoos: an elaborate cross on his right arm, a naked woman on his left arm, a spider on his back and an unidentifiable design on his left hand which resembles a cracked object. (This could represent the shards of glass from the car windows that he demolished before assaulting a man.) He is presented as a figure of resistance, perhaps in keeping with a Satan figure who was also guilty of the sin of pride. Even Alvarez's tattoo of a cross is not the usual kind of cross; it consists of a pattern of circles that are shaped to form a cross, thus suggesting a departure from tradition. His resistance to God is demonstrated in the scene with Father Ray Mukada, the prison priest, when he asks the priest to pray for the health of his newborn baby boy. He refuses to ask God for forgiveness for his own sins and wants only to focus on his immediate desire to acquire help for his son. As Augustus, the Oz narrator, says: "God is one tough motherfucker. We have to give up what we want most." In other words, in the context of this

Oz **1.3: "God's Chillin" (1997). The prisoner Alvarez (played by Kirk Acevedo) has a tattooed cross on the right arm and an image of a nude woman on the other, thus suggesting an interplay between religion and desire. In the episode called "God's Chillin" he demonstrates the sin of pride when he refuses to ask God for forgiveness for his own sins or past crimes; instead, he wants a priest to focus on his immediate desire to acquire help for his baby boy. Unfortunately, Alvarez's son dies. Augustus, the Oz narrator, summarizes the interplay between desire and resistance in this episode when he says that God is tough and demands that we give up "what we want most."**

Oz episode, God would seem to demand the suppression of individual desire in order to be at peace with oneself and with the world. In Alvarez's case, this sacrifice could be his only son or his pride in believing that he can control his life. In the episode called "God's Chillin'" (Oz 3.1) Alvarez reveals his desire to create his own aesthetic of violence and suffering instead of yielding to God's will. He cuts his hand and his face with a knife as if to create another scar or tattoo of defiance.

While a character such as Alvarez appears to resist the traditional belief system of Christianity, the series also emphasizes how the rules or codes which were in place outside of prison are completely inverted within the prison environment. This applies to the image of God as well, who may initially be perceived as diametrically opposed to the morals of the prisoners. While the prison priest tries to present God as a loving figure, the prisoners think otherwise. The narrator, who is a kind of omniscient god-like presence in the series, states that "God is the ultimate gangster" (Oz 3). According to Augustus, the prisoners have to live by His code, and He never has to explain exactly why He does what He does. God is thus presented as a being with a loose moral code. Thus, paradoxically, the prisoners are closer to God than they may think because He too is associated with violence and suffering, both of which are also visually reinforced by tattoos or the act of tattooing. If God is a divine gangster figure or the "Godfather," then all of the prisoners, even the more independent inmates like Alvarez, are simply part of His gang and must figure out the mystery of what their leader wants.

Fictional tattoo narratives of prison culture and gang culture reveal how the tattoo is identified as a key symbol of resistance to various social structures or systems, depending on the nature of the gang or prison community. Usually some form of criminal activity defines a gang experience, even though in the case of Joyce Carol Oates' *Foxfire* (and the movie based on the novel) the concept of a gang is of a very different order than the yakuza in film and literature. Oates' female characters resist the structure of patriarchy, and their tattoos symbolize woman-centered desire and justice as an alternative to patriarchal power, masculine desire, and sexual violation. The tattoo's function in yakuza narratives is to highlight the joint images of beauty and violence that are often incorporated into the yakuza member's tattoo and into the narratives themselves. The painful tattoo sessions that are part of the tattoo's genesis emphasize the importance of enduring pain as a form of loyalty to the yakuza, an expectation that is reiterated through the finger mutilation ritual. Within the prison culture of *Oz*, tattoos reflect the personalities of violent, socially dysfunctional individuals, the narrative of homosexual desire, or the identity of different groups of tattooed prisoners, to name a few possibilities. The defining feature of all three groups — the yakuza in film and literature, Oates' female gang, and the prisoners in *Oz* — is how tattoos help carve out a sense of group identity or affiliation for their bearers while still acknowledging that these tattoos function as strong signs of resistance to what the individuals in these groups define as the Law.

CHAPTER FIVE

Scars of Imprisonment and Resistance: Marks of the Holocaust, Slavery and Colonization

There are stories of tattooed prisoners who committed crimes and become part of a narrative or cycle of violence that perpetuates their questionable moral beliefs and uncontrollable desires. However, there are other kinds of narratives which suggest another kind of restriction of freedom; these are narratives which focus on the marginalized individual who belongs to an oppressed group. In the prison series *Oz*, Tobias Beecher is the unwilling recipient of a tattoo, and his experience may be likened to that of a concentration camp prisoner, especially since the narrator in *Oz* refers to the prison as "a concentration camp" (*Oz* 1.1). In *Tattoo*, Maddy is also a prisoner violated by a social outcast who is a tattoo artist. Other tattoo narratives identify oppressed or marginalized cultures such as the Jewish victims of the Holocaust, African-American slaves, and colonized people like the Maori. While it may at first seem difficult to envision such narratives of violence in relation to "desire," the tattoos in these works still have some connection to different kinds of desire because the characters want to reproduce the suffering that has been inflicted on their ancestors either through domestic abuse or through the imitation of a tattoo. In some cases, these characters make others suffer for their own pain. In a more positive vein, a number of the characters in these narratives of suffering seek to reclaim the marginalized body in an act of resistance.

This chapter is therefore divided into three sections: 1) a discussion of concentration camp tattoo narratives; 2) an analysis of *Beloved*, a narrative of the slave's body; and 3) an examination of narratives about the New Zealand Maori. Stories that foreground the concentration camp tattoo are a form of prison narrative that highlights a painful history and present suffering for a character; in these stories the numerical tattoo inscribes the narrative of violence and pain, yet it also offers a unique way of resisting an established "story" or past. Toni Morrison's novel *Beloved* is a kind of captivity narrative about the scarred bodies of African-American slaves. Like the tattoos of Holocaust victims, their scars serve as sites of preservation and resistance. Stories of colonization contribute to yet another kind of scarring (both external and internal); New Zealand tattoo narratives that depict Maori culture show images of Maori resistance through tattoo imagery, but these stories also indicate how individuals within that culture express violent desires and perpetuate violence against their own people in a tragic imitation of colonial practices.

Tattooed Numbers: Concentration Camp Tattoos

One kind of narrative which foregrounds the oppression and imprisonment of innocent victims is literature about the Holocaust. There is a huge body of Holocaust narratives, including interviews, memoirs and fiction. Many of these texts mention the numerical concentration camp tattoos as one of the traumatic experiences endured by the victims and the survivors. Marianne Hirsch and Susan Rubin Suleiman indicate that "number tattooing was practiced only in Auschwitz and not in any of the other concentration or death camps, but Auschwitz itself has become a kind of shorthand to signify "the concentration camp" or "the Holocaust" (Epstein and Lefkovitz 103, Note 6). In *Sun Turned to Darkness: Memory and Recovery in the Holocaust Memoir*, David Patterson excerpts the comments of Holocaust survivors that pertain to their tattoos:

> "I became A-7713. After that I had no other name" [Wiesel 1960, 51].

> "Henceforth I would be, merely, KZ prisoner Number A 8450"]Myiszli 1960, 26].

> "Mine was 55091— my new name from now on" [Zyskind 1981, 211].

> "A filthy needle ... erased Natan Schapelski from the human race and brought into being Häftling 134138" [Shapell 1974, 116].

> [Patterson 165].

Patterson's listing of these common tattoo experiences reinforces the alienation and the marginalization experienced by these prisoners (as part of the Nazi desire to exterminate the Jewish race). However, as Hirsch and Suleiman point out, the danger of focusing on the commonality of the tattoo experience is that differences between survivors are erased. Thus any study of Holocaust narratives must take into account the particularity of the individual's experience while still recognizing the importance of the group experience.

Since an exhaustive overview of Holocaust texts falls outside the scope of this book, this chapter will focus on two short stories and two novels in which the concentration camp tattoo occupies a central role. "The Apostate's Tattoo" and "Weintraub's Education" by J. J. Steinfeld, Rochelle Krich's *Blood Money* and Emily Prager's *Eve's Tattoo* are texts that present the tattoo experience in the context of desire, pain and resistance. However, each text offers a different way of using the tattoo to "write" these narratives that attempt to reproduce the image of suffering.

"THE APOSTATE'S TATTOO"

J. J. Steinfeld is a Canadian writer who lives in Charlottetown, Prince Edward Island, Canada. He has written a number of short stories that deal with the topic of the Holocaust, including collections called *The Apostate's Tattoo* (1983) and *Dancing at the Club Holocaust* (1993). His story "The Apostate's Tattoo" appears in both collections and deals with Sam, a 36-year-old scholar of religious studies whose mother died in Auschwitz. His life has been marked by various acts of resistance, including his concealment of his Jewish identity from his fiancée until he and she "had begun to make marriage plans" (Steinfeld, *Apostate's Tattoo* 69). The story is referenced to the Holocaust experience as it is interlaced with desire, either in a sexual context or as a new obsession in life. In one example, the narrative of violence against Jews seems to interfere or conflict with the narrative of romantic desire and act of defiance that constitute his decision to marry a Gentile:

> Whenever the subject of religion came up he declared that he was an apostate and if he had had a few drinks, it was the quintessential apostate, the western world's consummate apostate, the Gordie Howe of apostasy (69).[1]

He continues his pattern of resistance by suddenly re-creating his life. He changes his area of study from Catholics in New France to Jewish life in Canada, an area that becomes a new obsession. This change results in his decision to take his wife, Sylvie, on a "mysterious trip" (68) and the shift in his perspective culminates with the decision to acquire a tattoo. As they arrive in an area of town that includes a tattoo shop, Sam describes the area as Gomorrah, the Biblical site of sexual excess and debauchery. Yet he also describes the streets as resembling the most "dreary, depressing parts of Poland" (69), thus suggesting a link to the Jewish ghettoes in Poland, and combining images of sexual desire with a violent past for Polish Jews.

As Sam and Sylvie enter the tattoo parlor, they also view "a framed photograph of a tattooed woman in a sideshow" (71). The image of the woman displays the connection between tattoos and circus or freak culture and the desire to gaze upon an oddity that signifies the public's interest in this kind of sideshow culture. At the same time the framed photograph is an interesting way of suggesting containment or imprisonment, an image that would have applied to Sam's tattooed mother, a prisoner in a concentration camp. His desire to obtain a tattoo to commemorate his mother would seem to fit the convention of the "I Love Mom" tattoos that men often sport; however, the tattoo he chooses is a very different kind.

As Steinfeld's narrative reveals, Sam's choice of tattoo does not meet with the approval of the tattoo artist: "the tattooist was amazed when his customer described what he wanted, and immediately tried to convince Sam to have a fancier, more aesthetic tattoo" (72). Sam's decision to have six blue numbers tattooed on his arm[2] (the reproduction of his mother's concentration camp tattoo) is an odd request which goes against the artistic sensibility of this tattooist. In the real world of tattooing, tattoo artists will sometimes discourage certain kinds of tattoos such as the names of current lovers, swastikas or other racist markers. While initially the reader may think that the tattooist is aware that Sam's tattoo is a concentration camp number, the narrative indicates that this is not the case since he refers to the tattoo as "a stupid number that made no sense" (73).

Sam's marking of his body with a numerical tattoo could be seen as an ultimate sign of disrespect or a kind of inappropriate appropriation, because he was not a concentration camp survivor. Yet, by choosing to have a concentration camp number inscribed in his flesh, Sam indicates that he has inherited the narratives of suffering and the memory of those Jews such as his mother who suffered and perished in the camps. He has an obsession and a strong desire to mimic the suffering that he can only imagine. As Marianne Hirsch and Susan Rubin Suleiman indicate in their analysis of Holocaust art and narrative, for an artist such as Tatana Kellner her visual narrative[3] *Fifty Years of Silence* reveals how the image of her parents' tattooed arms functions as a signifier of a child's absent memory of the parents' Holocaust experience (Epstein and Lefkovitz 97). In "The Apostate's Tattoo," Sam seems to be experiencing the same identification with the tattooed arm but takes the search for memory further by inscribing the narrative on his own arm.[4]

Sam's act of having himself tattooed is not merely an attempt at duplication or mimicry. It is subversive for two reasons; first, it undercuts the Jewish taboo of the "cuttings in the flesh" as outlined in Leviticus 19:20 ("Ye shall not make any cuttings in your flesh for the dead, nor print any marks upon you"). Secondly, it challenges the passivity associated with victims who were tattooed against their will with a voluntary act, thus emphasizing his powers of agency. Steinfeld, however, does not allow the subversive impact of Sam's tattoo to end here. In keeping with the common image of the tattoo's subversive power, Steinfeld draws attention to the possibility of a mistake in the tattooing process: "'We don't want any errors, do we?' the tattooist said as he underlined the number" (Steinfeld 72). The statement suggests the well known image of the incorrect tattoo that may include a missing letter or some other kind of error. The story ends with just this kind of ironic twist. While the actual tattoo itself is correct, Sam realizes — much to his horror — that he had told the tattooist to mark the wrong arm: "Sam, his face contorted, lay still, a hand clutching his forearm, attempting to cover the blue tattoo" (74). The effect of the misplaced tattoo conveys the message that complete identification with those who experienced the trauma of the Holocaust is not possible, and must remain part of a narrative of frustrated desire. Ironically, the ending of the narrative still reinforces Sam (or Shlomo) as a figure of resistance. His act of acquiring a tattoo (let alone a concentration camp tattoo) is presented as an act of apostasy, and his inability to successfully imitate the camp tattoo of his mother (assuming that these numbers were his mother's) also establishes that he falls outside the boundaries of a specific group consisting of those who actually experienced the Holocaust. What he does share with the victims and survivors of the concentration camps is suffering, even though his suffering is tied to the inadequate representation of a cultural memory through his tattoo. Thus, his desire to relive what his mother had experienced cannot be accurately reproduced through the mediated image of the tattoo. In this sense, the sign on the tattoo shop which read "TATTOOS, PAIN-LESS, REASONABLE RATES" (70) must also be read in an ironic way; most people would say that there is no such thing as a painless tattoo. Sam suffers from a pain even greater than that of a sore arm. The pain that he experiences after realizing that the tattoo has been placed on the incorrect arm is heartwrenching. His desire has been unfulfilled, and the story highlights this unfulfilled desire by linking it to Sylvie's frustration when her words "'I love you, I love you, Shlomo,'" (74) do not reach her husband. The final line of the story presents Sam "attempting to cover the blue tattoo" (74), quite a departure from his initial desire to reveal and display his marked body. (He used the word "Voilà!" (73) to indicate this act of exhibitionism.) Sam's reversal in attitude reinforces the subversive quality of the tattoo turned from an object of desire to an object of horror or an example of the abject.

In *The Marked Body: Domestic Violence in Mid-Nineteenth Century Literature,* Kate Lawson and Lynn Shakinovsky draw on Julia Kristeva's concept of the abject to discuss a relationship between the individual and the maternal body. They indicate that Kristeva defines abjection as the repulsion or horror experienced by an individual when a desired union with the mother cannot be fulfilled (Lawson and Shaki-novsky 51). The experience of abjection is described by Lawson and Shakinovsky as "a curious mixture of disgust and fascination ... sick-ening and desirable" (52). While these authors tend to focus on the violated female body, the concept of the abject also applies to Sam/Shlomo in "The Apostate's Tattoo." He desires a reunion with the mother through the reproduction of her tattoo onto his arm. The concentration camp tattoo is both disgusting yet fascinating for Sam. It evokes a painful memory of violence and imprisonment, yet it becomes his obsession to acquire a tattoo that is just like it. Steinfeld's narrative reveals, however, exactly how the tattoo, an image of the abject, becomes "the precondition for the experience of separation from the maternal" (52) or the inability to realize this desire to reunite with the mother's body. His attempt to cover the tattoo at the end of the story shows his realization that it is not the same as his mother's body and that he must remain separated from her unique experience of the Holocaust.

"WEINTRAUB'S EDUCATION"

Steinfeld's story "Weintraub's Education" also draws on a character's memory of his parent's concentration camp tattoo, but in this narrative the tattooed arm of the death camp survivor, an image of the abject, is juxtaposed against the tattoo of another marginalized figure, that of an ex-prostitute. Here the Holocaust victim's history of violence and suffering offers a somewhat unusual intersection with a former prostitute a narrative of desire. Like the fascination experienced by Sam for a tattoo in "The Apostate's Tattoo," the character Jonathan is also fascinated, but his desire is based on an interest in his student, an ex-prostitute, and her tattooed body. Jonathan Weintraub is a Jewish Ph.D. student writing a thesis about Elie Wiesel, who has written on the Holocaust. He has a conversation with an ex-prostitute who killed her pimp boyfriend while having sex with him and "got off with self-defence" (Steinfeld 76). Her past, which is a combination of violence and desire, is inscribed in her tattoos. These tattoos are linked to her former life as a hooker: "I would never have a tattoo done now, but in those days it was natural for me. My old man loved tattoos. I'm not the person I was six months ago. Or will be once I go through college and get a degree. But the tattoos are part of me" (83). The woman's tattoos signify an undesirable past, but she acknowledges that they are still a part of her identity. Her tattoos, however, also suggest the possibility of a sexual desire or voyeuristic experience for Weintraub, especially when he compares her to his future wife, Naomi, who "was thrust out of his thoughts, her image offering no more resistance than a feeble squatter" (83). She is, after all, an attractive woman, and her revelation of her checkered past presents her as an image of a forbidden fruit. Yet this ex-prostitute's tattoos serve as more than images that arouse Weintraub's sexual desire. They function as a site of mediation that permits a conversation to occur between two people. Weintraub feels the need to respond to the woman's candid sharing of her secret past by mentioning his mother's tattoo on her left forearm. This revelation on his part in turn allows the ex-prostitute a kind of voyeuristic access to Weintraub's past and his mother's past through the intermediary image of a tattoo. Even though Weintraub does not actually reveal what kind of tattoo his mother has, he has made some kind of breakthrough: "Of all the things in the world, why had he brought up his mother's concentration camp tattoo? He couldn't even discuss it with Naomi" (84). While Jonathan and the unnamed woman come from two entirely different worlds, the tattoo serves as a way of challenging the specificity of each person's individual experience and linking these two people in an interesting way. The tattoos function as signs of marginality and imprisonment: for the prostitute her tattoo serves as a reminder of her life as a prostitute and of her former pimp — a life bound up in sexuality and desire. For Weintraub, and even more for his mother, the concentration camp tattoo is a sign of imprisonment as well, albeit a kind of narrative which he is usually reluctant to share. Oddly enough, the prostitute's discussion and display of her own tattoos and her link to her own narrative of desire (to mark her past) have somehow subverted the narrative of silence that surrounded his mother's tattoo and allowed him to speak the unspoken. His desire to speak of his mother's tattoo is mediated through the exchange with a key representation of desire: a prostitute. Thus the tattooed body is transformed from a site of violence and violation (as in the case of the Holocaust victim's body or the prostitute's body) to a site of exchange, frank communication and transgressive desire. At the end of the story, Weintraub continues to look at the beautiful ex-prostitute even as he hugs his fiancée (84).

BLOOD MONEY

The experience of imitating a concentration camp survivor and his or her tattoo is also introduced in Rochelle Krich's murder mystery *Blood Money* (1999). Like other murder mysteries, including Takagi's *The Tattoo Murder Case,* it uses the tattoo as a device for identification purposes. However, Krich also employs the concentration camp tattoo in a subversive manner. The tattoo not only highlights a case of mistaken identity but also becomes part of a narrative of deception and the detective's desire to solve a concentration camp survivor's murder.

Like other tattoo murder mysteries (*The Tattoo Murder Case* or *The Snake Tattoo*) or examples of detective fiction in general, this novel emphasizes the connection between the tattoo and the reconstruction of the self. The plot involves a Los Angeles homicide detective, Jessica Drake, who tries to solve the mystery surrounding the death of Norman Pomerantz, an elderly concentration camp survivor in an old-age home. On his arm, the police find evidence of a numerical tattoo that had been partially removed, which turns out to be a concentration camp tattoo. Jessica's interest in the case also stems from the fact that she has recently learned that her mother was Jewish and had denied her Jewish past. Jessica finds out that her mother's entire family had perished in the war. Not surprisingly Jessica feels that she needs to explore this side of her cultural heritage, and she wonders whether her maternal grandfather "had numbers on his arm, too" (Krich 12). Thus her desire to solve the case of a murder in a nursing home becomes linked to her desire to discover more about her own past or Jewish culture in general. As she reviews a videotape made by Pomerantz, she learns that he had a brother called Moshe, who was sent to a different camp. According to Pomerantz, who had had his tattoo partially removed by an unskilled doctor when he emigrated to America, his brother "Moshe wouldn't have gotten rid of the numbers" (198). This statement becomes a crucial point in Jessica's ability to solve the case because she remembers that the man who has presented himself as Pomerantz's brother Moshe does not have a tattoo. This leads her to the conclusion that he may have been masquerading as the brother in order to acquire Norman Pomerantz's money. Thus the concentration camp tattoo and the words of a dead man work together to subvert the narrative of deception and the desire for money that are associated with Pomerantz's phony brother.

Clearly, the role of the concentration camp tattoo in *Blood Money* is not merely limited to an image of authenticity; it reflects a desire to imitate. Like Sam's concentration camp numbers in "The Apostate's Tattoo," the tattoo in Krich's novel serves as a sign that attempts to imitate an original tattoo, but ends up resisting representation. For example, in *Blood Money* the tattoo is used as a sign of deception to paradoxically solve at least some of the murder cases in the retirement home where Pomerantz and other elderly residents were found dead. Jessica, the detective, disguises herself as one of the residents, who was also an Auschwitz survivor, and who has a tattoo on her arm. She dresses like an 80-year-old resident and is given a temporary pale blue concentration camp number in order to deceive the man who is suspected of murdering the elderly. In this case a tattoo (albeit a fake tattoo) acquires a capricious quality in the context of death: while Jessica is not a concentration camp survivor and does not actually have a permanent tattoo, she is of Jewish extraction, and she narrowly escapes death. Thus her connection to these survivors is strengthened through the art of deception. Jessica's "fake" tattoo leads to a kind of revelation. However, this tattoo narrative suggests that, while the marked body can be the means to one kind of truth, many gaps remain in the history of the Holocaust or in other murder cases. At the end of *Blood Money* Jessica must accept that life does not hold all the answers: "If life were tidy, she thought ... there would be no unsolved murders" (337).

EVE'S TATTOO

Another work of fiction that highlights the numerical concentration camp tattoo and places it within narratives of desire is Emily Prager's novel *Eve's Tattoo* (1991). This link between the tattoo and the character Eve is visually represented on the inside cover of the novel, with the tattoo number 500123 written diagonally across the name Eve in the title *Eve's Tattoo*. This visual presentation of the superimposition of the number onto Eve reflects her desire to identify with the experience of a Holocaust victim. Eve is a woman of German ancestry who voluntarily acquires a tattoo of the numbers 500123. This is a number that belongs to a woman in a photograph of concentration camp victims. Eve is a writer engaged in research on a book dealing with women during the Nazi era: "I'm telling the histories of women who resisted and women who didn't and why" (Prager 144).[5] The novel includes Eve's re-construction of history from photographs and records of women who lived during the Second World War. The text acknowledges that history is a slippery and dynamic area of study, because accounts change as new information is made available, and because gaps always remain. Thus her desire to identify completely with the woman in the photograph is frustrated or deferred because she cannot find closure by identifying the mystery woman.

Unlike Steinfeld's leading characters in "The Apostate's Tattoo" and "Weintraub's Education," or even the character of Jessica Drake in *Blood Money*, the title character in *Eve's Tattoo* is not Jewish. Nevertheless, she is motivated by a desire to inscribe another woman's history on her body as an act of remembrance in order to keep the woman in the photo (whom she believes to be Jewish) alive (11). This memorial is viewed as an affront by Eve's Jewish lover, Charles, and results in the erosion of Charles' desire for Eve until her tattoo is destroyed in an accident. Contrary to the pervasive image of tattoos as seductive and erotic, Eve's tattoo is largely devoid of any sexual allure.[6] The tattoo tends to function as a way of curtailing sexual desire, even as it continues to be linked to another form of desire: Eve's ongoing thirst for knowledge concerning the identity of the woman in the photograph. For Charles, the tattoo does not serve as a mysterious mark that holds the key to a hidden identity. Instead, it functions exclusively as a marker of suffering and imprisonment, and his reaction to Eve's tattoo suggests that he feels the tattoo's meaning should be contained within the narrative of violence that is part of Jewish history.

For other people, however, Eve's tattoo is not an example of limited meaning, but an example of excess. It transcends the boundaries of a camp or prison experience and generates numerous interpretations or stories. Someone thinks that the tattoo is a Social Security number, another person believes that it might be a PIN (a personal code or number for financial transactions). These interpretations clearly devalue the original association of the tattoo with the imprisonment of a woman during the Second World War; however, they do demonstrate how tattoos suggest different things to different people, especially if they are not familiar with the specific cultural context of a tattoo. Eve also seizes upon the ignorance of people and changes the truth about her tattoo's origins when she discusses the source of the tattoo with some young musicians. She tells them that she was in a death camp, and they believe her, not realizing that she is too young to have been a tattooed Holocaust victim. Clearly her desire to find someone who might be fascinated with her tattoo (unlike Charles, who is disgusted by it) overrides her sense of loyalty to what she perceives to be the tattoo's true meaning: its role as a concentration camp number assigned to a Jewish prisoner. Her desire to create new stories for the woman in the photograph whom she has named Eva, including the act of appropriating what she thought might be Eva's story for herself, shows how Eve loses respect for the narratives that belong to Holocaust victims.

The turning point for Eve in the novel occurs when she sees an old man with a number tattooed on his arm, and becomes immediately ashamed of her own tattoo. She is clearly shocked when she sees a "real" concentration camp tattoo and seems to realize that her own tattoo somehow devalues the experience of an authentic Holocaust survivor. The man in question is Mr. Schlaren, a Yiddish transvestite whose sexuality seems indeterminate; Eve thinks that he could have been a woman. He tells her how he worked in the theater, and then begins to recount his own history of appropriation. He changed his gender, but unlike Eve, who appropriated a tattoo as part of a desire to make herself more fascinating and perhaps appealing to her Jewish lover Charles, he engaged in this transformation in order to survive. Mr. Schlaren's narrative is a story about the necessity of reinvention through gender affiliation. During the Nazi era, his mother instructed her son, who had been captured by the Nazis, to pretend that he was a girl so that his circumcised penis would not give away his gender or his cultural identity as a Jewish boy. He managed to deceive an SS man and feigned weakness so he would be released. Mr. Schlaren later narrates how he was captured a second time, and how he had to change back to being a boy, because at that time strong boys who could work were more desirable than girls (155).

This unusual encounter with Mr. Schlaren and his changing identity results in Eve's re-assessment of how she views her appropriation of Eva's tattoo, and she finally questions her desire to imitate or preserve the history of a Holocaust victim on her own body. This encounter with an actual death-camp survivor drives Eve to abandon her self-serving imaginary narratives or creative histories about "Eva," the mysterious woman in the photograph; instead she intends to find out the "real" identity of the woman in the photo. Her decision to find out the truth is dramatically underscored through an accident. She is run over by a van, and her tattooed arm is mutilated. When the arm is reconstructed, her tattoo has miraculously disappeared. She then phones the Yiddish Scientific Institute to trace the tattoo number. The novel nears its conclusion with a final narrative of the woman in the photo. This is presumably *the* authentic story, although the reader cannot be completely sure that it really is the definitive version, given the ambiguity surrounding previous narratives about "Eva." According to Eve's narrative, the woman in the photo was called Leni Essen, and she did not resist Nazism like her sons: "She was tattooed by mistake" (186) and murdered in a fight over some bread. The defiance in her eyes, which Eve had misread as resistance to Nazi ideology, was actually contempt for those who tattooed her by mistake. This incredible conclusion indicates that Eve had identified with a woman who had not even been Jewish. Like Steinfeld's character Sam in "The Apostate's Tattoo," whose number was tattooed on the wrong arm, the tattoo which Eve had acquired is associated with an error — a case of mistaken cultural affiliation. Furthermore, as in Takagi's *The Tattoo Murder Case* (chapter four of this book), photographs of a tattoo assist in the art of deception; they present a lie as a truth that is in turn misinterpreted by those who view the image. In Takagi's text, the tattoo in the photograph is misconstrued as a real tattoo, when in fact it is a pseudo-tattoo or a painted image. Similarly, in Prager's novel, Eve creates multiple identities and stories for the woman in the photo, which depict her as a force of resistance, yet when the final narrative is disclosed, the resistance ends up being a very different kind of defiance. With the revelation that the woman in the photograph was not Jewish, Eve's desire to identify with the oppressed has been diffused. The disappearance of her tattoo after the injury she suffered in her car accident is a convenient intersection with this revelation in the novel. Since she no longer has the desire to identify with the woman in the photo, she no longer requires her tattoo. In Prager's novel, the removal or disappearance of the tattoo allows Eve to discover the truth about the woman in the picture. Thus Eve's tattoo functions in a diametrically opposed manner to the way the tattoo is used in Rochelle Krich's detective novel *Blood Money*. In the latter, the "fake" tattoo paradoxically reveals "the truth" about the murder Jessica is trying to solve, whereas in the former, the presence of Eve's tattoo impedes or postpones the revelation of the identity of the mystery woman in the World War II photograph.

Prager continues the art of subversion in *Eve's Tattoo* through the revelation at the end of the novel of the secret reason behind Eve's decision to acquire the tattoo. She apparently acquired the tattoo because she found a Star of David in Charlie's closet and was hoping to find out the secrets of Judaism so that she could develop a stronger bond with him (194). However, as *Eve's Tattoo* reveals, the secrets of being Jewish cannot be accessed simply by a non-Jew's decision to acquire a tattoo. Even for Jews like Sam/Shlomo in "The Apostate's Tattoo" the desire to imitate or mimic the Holocaust experience can never be fulfilled, since it is an absent memory for the children of Holocaust survivors or victims. It is therefore not surprising that a Gentile should experience an even greater difficulty trying to identify with the experience of violence and suffering that is so particular to a generation of Jews.

Scars as Tattoos

BELOVED

The relationship between tattoos and scars (both physical and psychological) is present in fiction about concentration camp tattoos. This correlation is not surprising because of the trauma associated with the Holocaust. The concentration camp tattoo serves as a permanent reminder of the conflicting desires survivors and their descendents may have with respect to remembering and erasing the pain of this historical violence. All kinds of tattoos, but the concentration camp tattoo in particular, are visual reminders of some form of suffering, since the tattoo is, after all, the result of the skin's being cut, pierced or hammered, depending on the tattooist's technique. The tattoo is often viewed as an art form; however, in the case of the concentration camp tattoo, this aesthetic dimension seems to be rejected or at least minimized. In Steinfeld's "The Apostate's Tattoo," the tattoo artist sees nothing aesthetically pleasing about Sam's decision to tattoo his arm with uniform colored numbers. One could argue that in *Blood Money* and in *Eve's Tattoo* the tattoo can be linked to artifice and to the art of deception. However, by and large, the concentration camp tattoo in the works examined here is viewed more as a scar than a work of art.

A story which includes another depiction of the scarred body in conjunction with imprisonment is Toni Morrison's *Beloved*. Morrison's novel focuses on the slavery of African-Americans and the image of suffering. However, she also presents the scars as if they are also images of art and artistic creativity. The film *Skin Art* established this connection between an American soldier/tattoo artist's scars from torture in Vietnam and the tattoos that prostitutes bear as a mark of their suffering at the hands of a pimp. Marian Engel's "tattooed woman" (discussed in chapter two) engraves scars in her body as a way of resisting a masculine-determined aesthetic of feminine beauty. In her novel, Morrison's characters go through the process of reclaiming their broken bodies by viewing and describing the scars on their bodies in a creative way.

Toni Morrison's *Beloved* presents the scarred, branded or "tattooed" body in the context of a specific kind of cultural imprisonment: the slavery of African-Americans. The main character, Sethe, bears the scar on her back from a beating. It resembles the sculpture of a tree. Sethe's own mother bore the brand of a circle and cross, presumably the mark used to identify her as a slave. Yet, while these marks are presented in the context of slavery and broken bodies, Morrison also uses these images to write a narrative of reclaiming the body. In a sense Morrison's narrative of "skin and ink" is a kind of tattoo because it preserves a cultural memory of pain and resistance. Her characters' bodies also suggest these narrative and visual possibilities, and they become associated with another dimension of the tattoo, the link to desire. Sethe's lover, Paul D, kisses her scarred back, and it is Sethe who continues to use the description of a tree and the imagery of growth to talk about dead scar tissue, perhaps as a way of restoring her body: "Could have cherries too now for all I know" (Morrison 16). This way of reconsidering her body is similar to the healing experienced by breast cancer survivors who mark their bodies with tattoos as a way of over-writing the scars from the removal of a breast.[7] She also views this "tree" as an extension of the "mark" her mother bore. As a child she did not understand the brutality associated with the mark; she only wanted to have something to connect her to her largely absent mother:

> Back there she opened up her dress front and lifted her breast and pointed under it. Right on her rib was a circle and a cross burnt right in the skin. She said, 'This is your ma'am. This,' and she pointed. 'I am the only one got this mark now. The rest dead. If something happens to me and you can't tell me by my face, you can know me by this mark' [61].

This passage reveals Sethe's desire to reproduce her mother's body, which was marked or branded by violence, much in the same way that the characters in Holocaust fiction seek to reproduce the pain of the Holocaust victim or survivor by acquiring a concentration camp tattoo. Sethe therefore asks her mother to mark her too so that she can be like her. Her mother responds by slapping her, and, as Sethe tells her daughter Denver, she did not understand why until she had a mark of her own. This brief story of Sethe's reveals how the body can function not only as a site of violence, but also as a way of restoring the self by engaging in an act of remembrance. The final section of the novel presents Paul D's own scars from the collars slaves were forced to wear. His scars are reinterpreted by Sethe in a creative way as a kind of "neck jewelry"—"its three wands, like attentive baby rattlers, curving two feet into the air" (273). His body becomes a work of art just like hers; Sethe's tree and Paul D's neck scar are thus linked through their visual impact and through the form of narrative as Paul D "wants to put his story next to hers" (273). Their desire for one another continues despite the violence both of them endured.

Hirsch and Suleiman have addressed the imprisonment and resistance elements in Morrison's text by comparing it to Jewish Holocaust art. They establish a parallel between the narrative that accompanies Sethe's and Paul D's scars and Tatana Kellner's placement of her parents' Holocaust survival stories next to each other (Epstein and Lefkovitz 101).

The work of art that Kellner creates combines the visual image of a tattooed forearm with the stories of her parents' experiences in a concentration camp. In a similar fashion, Morrison interweaves image with story in order to show the signifying power of the scar or pseudo-tattoo in a narrative of blood and ink. While Holocaust fictions and Morrison's novel are stories of suffering, they are also stories of resistance which attempt to transform the violence of the past into a visual and narrative record for future generations. Art can record but also transform and thus empower those who were once victims, whether these individuals were Jews imprisoned in concentration camps or African-Americans sold into slavery.

Oddly enough, Sethe's and Paul D's scars or "tattooed bodies" serve as signs of empowerment as well as a sign of suffering and have some parallels with the experience of the Old Testament figure of Cain, the bearer of the first tattoo. Even though Cain was a murderer and remained a social outcast because of his crime and because of the sign that identified him as a criminal, his tattoo or mark protected him from further harm. Like Cain, Sethe also committed an act of murder (she killed her daughter); however, unlike Cain, who committed an act of revenge because he did not receive God's love in the form of approval for his offering, hers was an act of love. She killed her daughter to protect her from suffering the violence and violation experienced by African-American slaves. Morrison illustrates the suffering that Sethe and others experience as a result of horrific acts; however, she also shows how these physical and psychological scars or "tattoos" must be remembered as the subject of a culture's history and as an expression of resistance.

Tattoos, Tradition, Colonization and Violence

Toni Morrison's narrative about slavery highlights the scarred body that has been enslaved and violated; its intersections with Holocaust narratives include the focus on psychological as well as emotional scarring. Sexual desire plays a role in some of these narratives of oppression as a way of liberating the broken body. The individual's desire to imitate or reproduce the tattooed or scarred body and what that represents (identification with the original marked body and the preservation of a memory) seems to characterize all of the fictional narratives examined in this chapter. Another kind of marked body is presented through images of the aboriginal[8] body and their relationship to violent desires and the violence of colonization.

Tattooing among aboriginal peoples has been a way of preserving traditional ways. In many aboriginal societies, including Native American, Maori, and Hawaiian cultures, tattoos have been associated with genealogical commemoration or links to a mythical past.[9] However, the native body has also been constructed by the non-native as an image of resistance to European values, as a cultural Other. For some Westerners, this interest in cultural Otherness took the form of desiring the cultural Other by depicting exotic natives in European adventure fiction. However, by far the most common response to the tattooed native body has been one of fear or disapproval. Even the famous John Rutherford, who apparently acquired a Maori moko tattoo voluntarily, created a false narrative of how "he had been taken captive by Maoris in New Zealand in 1816 and forcibly tattooed" (Oettermann 198).[10] Western colonizers often viewed tattooing as an uncivilized, un-Christian practice, and as an affront to the concept of the pristine, undecorated body. As Terry Goldie points out in *Fear and Temptation*, nineteenth- and early-twentieth-century travellers to New Zealand argued in favor of the untattooed skin: "The mind revolts at the idea of seeing a fine manly race as any in the universe, thus shakingly disfigured; and producing associations similar to what may be imagined of so many fiends" (John Liddiard Nicholas, quoted in Goldie 38).

The tattooed aboriginal body has thus been inscribed within a context of violence and desire for the colonizer, who seems to have a paradoxical fear of and fascination with the colonized Other (not unlike the attitude towards the abject discussed in the view of the Holocaust tattoo). For the aboriginal individual, desire and violence are not only linked to the tattoo as part of a traditional system of values (as in the meaning of specific tattoo images); tattooed and non-tattooed natives have viewed their bodies with shame, thus internalizing the colonial perspective. As history has shown, this contempt for the aboriginal body or identity has had an impact on indigenous people who have absorbed colonial values and perpetuated a cycle of self-hatred and abuse within their own cultural circles.

Thus, within the context of encounters with Westerners, the tattooed aboriginal body functions in a dual capacity. It not only becomes a marker of tradition and a way of resisting colonial perspectives, but it may reproduce the violence of colonization. Post-colonial or contemporary narratives about aboriginal culture illustrate how the tattoo continues to serve in this dual capacity. Furthermore, these contemporary tattoo narratives often illustrate how the concepts of hybridity or mediation may operate in conjunction with the tattooed individual. In tattoo narratives which focus on aboriginal culture and the impact of colonization, the tattooed individual may be a mediator figure or an outcast because he is a kind of hybrid character aware of aboriginal culture. While some tattooed individuals continue to be demonized in accordance with historical colonial prejudice against the tattooed body (*Utu*), other individuals use the tattoo to transcend the limitations of colonization in order to create an alter(native) narrative about aboriginal culture (e.g., Nig in the film version of *Once Were Warriors*).

UTU

The 1988 film *Utu* is set in the New Zealand of the 1870s and depicts the Maori[11] uprisings against the British settlers, while presenting the tattooed and non-tattooed Maori in various acts of violence and resistance. The word *utu* as described in the film means "blood for blood" and refers to the Maori practice of seeking vengeance on their enemies. The concept was part of traditional Maori law and involved specific rules concerning who could seek vengeance for the death of a loved one.[12] The film also presents various kinds of desire, including one Maori's desire to return to a pre-colonial past, a desire to break the hold of the colonizer on the aboriginal body, as well as a cross-cultural love relationship between a Maori woman and an Englishman. It won international acclaim at the Cannes Film Festival during its presentation in 1983. The story deals with a Maori by the name of Te Wheke, who is a guide for a British regiment. He is presented in Western dress. He witnesses the slaughter of his village by soldiers and promises to avenge the deaths of his people, including his uncle. This decision to avenge the deaths of other Maori is marked by his acquisition of a Maori tattoo or moko.[13] His face is ceremonially tattooed in the painful, traditional Maori fashion[14] and signifies a desire to return to a pre-colonial state. This visual transformation mirrors his transformation into a dual image of tradition and rebellion much like the full body tattoo of the yakuza in Japanese culture. His moko includes all of the spirals that are typical of a Maori facial tattoo, including lines on the forehead, chin, nose, and cheekbone.[15] The tattoo also serves as a reminder of the other Maori who perished at the hands of colonial violence and as a reflection of his resistance to the image of the non-tattooed face that characterizes the image of the white colonizers for Te Wheke.

However, despite the obvious functions of the moko as a key sign of the desire to return to a pre-colonial past, Te Wheke reveals that it is impossible to ignore the influence of the colonizer. Even when he declares war on the white New Zealanders, he uses the words of a colonial religious text, the Bible. Before he kills white New Zealanders, including a priest, he turns the words which were levied against the Maori for their primitive ways, "he who lives by the sword shall die by the sword," against the colonizers. Thus he implies that they have used the sword or, in some cases, guns to kill his people, and they shall die as well. While one can interpret Te Wheke's quoting from the Bible as

an act of resistance that simply uses the "weapon" or words of the colonizers against them, this scene also draws attention to the fact that Te Wheke is a cultural hybrid even if he changes the appearance of his face with the moko. The use of the Biblical text combined with the traditional Maori tattoo indicates that Te Wheke must be viewed as an example of cultural hybridity. In a sense, he cannot completely shed his colonized skin despite his desire to do so through the act of receiving a moko.

Utu reveals other Maori characters who have been influenced by interaction with non-Maoris and how, in a colonized society, the neat separation into Maori and non-Maori or tattooed and non-tattooed does not necessarily work. The film shows that loyalties or alliances are complex and not merely a function of white-versus-Maori principles. A Maori woman loves a colonial soldier by the name of Mr. Scott, yet despite her Maori heritage Te Wheke does not hesitate to kill her, because she has betrayed the Maori rebellion by divulging part of the battle plan to the enemy. In this sense her identity as a Maori does not compensate for her betrayal of the greater Maori cause. Similarly, the fact that her aunt is a tattooed Maori (hers is the typical chin and lip tattoo of Maori women) does not imply that the woman will support Te Wheke, another tattooed Maori. Instead, she intends to avenge her niece's death. Like Te Wheke she bears a tattoo and intends to kill the rebel leader: "I have watched this man murder my cousin, beat my niece to death. For me it is blood for blood. *Utu*." The linking of these two figures through their facial tattoos indicates the different kinds of resistance presented in the film, based on the complicated loyalties that are created in a colonial context. As a result the traditional concept of

Opposite page: *Utu* (1983). Utu Productions. Anzac Williams is the Maori rebel Te Wheke, who acquires a *moko* or facial tattoo after a village of Maori are killed by colonial forces. The photograph is a composite of the Maori and the colonial conflict. In the lower left, one can see the profile of a Maori woman with the traditional chin and lip tattoo; in the center is the imposing presence of the colonial military force. Te Wheke's head towers above the other images, yet the images below appear to become part of his body, thus representing the colonial presence and Maori tradition which are an undeniable part of his past and present.

utu is also altered so that it translates into a seemingly endless perpetuation of violence.

The cross-cultural conflicts are also reinforced through the use of face imagery in the film. The concept of a false face serves as the reason for Te Wheke's murder of this woman's cousin. For example, in one scene, Te Wheke dips the cousin's head into a bag of flour and calls him a *pakeha* (a white man). Te Wheke tells him to remember what side he is on. In a later scene he kills this man, perhaps because of the man's wounds (to put him out of his misery), or perhaps to extinguish the life of a man with a pseudo-white face (he still had the flour on his face as he was killed). Again, for Te Wheke, Maori identity is less important than the demonstration of loyalty to his cause. In a sense the flour echoes the visual transformation that Te Wheke underwent when he acquired the facial tattoo; however, there is an important difference. Unlike the moko, which is permanent, flour can simply be washed or wiped off, thus suggesting an individual's ability to change his or her affiliation when convenient.

Te Wheke's power as a figure of resistance to the authority of the colonizer in New Zealand comes to an end when the rebel leader eventually faces his own death. However, his death does not occur through *utu* at the hands of his tattooed female opponent. If this kind of closure had been offered, the film could have been advocating the preservation of some element of a pre-colonial tradition. Moreover, Te Wheke is not killed by the colonial lover of the woman he murdered. If the film's audience had been presented with this conclusion, then the film might be interpreted as reinforcing the colonial perspective. Instead, the Maori rebel is killed in a less dramatic manner by the impersonal gun of another Maori character, who functions as a cultural mediator.

The character who kills Te Wheke reveals that he is Te Wheke's brother, but he serves an important role in the film's narrative for another reason. He acts as Te Wheke's double and brings the narrative full circle. At the beginning of the film, Te Wheke was a guide before he decided to wage war against the British and tattoo his face. Wiremu is also a guide for the British or white New Zealanders. Yet Wiremu, Te Wheke's double, differs from the latter in an important way. Wiremu claims that he has no desire for *utu*, and in a sense his disinterested or dispassionate murder of Te Wheke breaks the cycle of revenge that dominates the film. This desire for revenge was reinforced through the image of the tattoo as a sign of traditional warrior activity and resistance to colonization. This guide is Te Wheke's alter-ego, minus the tattoo, and perhaps represents a return to Te Wheke's self before he turned to the slaughter of others. Since the tattooed warrior is demonized in *Utu*, the film's moral position is rather contentious. While it does offer a way out of a cycle of revenge through the intercession of Te Wheke's double, it also suggests that the non-tattooed Maori is the voice of reason and that the tattooed Maori can only be associated with brutal actions. The film may be using this depiction of nineteenth-century New Zealand to suggest an ongoing anxiety among contemporary non-Maori New Zealanders about the image of the marked native body. Thus there is the danger that the film may simply be re-creating or re-inscribing the colonial fear or demonization of cultural Otherness (Goldie 87), at least in its masculine manifestation,[16] through the tattooed body of Te Wheke.

ONCE WERE WARRIORS

Alan Duff's disturbing novel *Once Were Warriors* (1990) and the film adaptation (1994) of this work present the impact of colonization on the Maori people in its frank and graphic depiction of modern Maori culture. Tattoos appear in both the novel and film and are part of the narratives of desire, violence and resistance that characterize the post-colonial world of the characters. The tattoos in question are predominantly Maori tattoos, including the moko, or facial tattoo, but non-Maori designs are also represented in the film, perhaps as a way of reinforcing the hybrid nature of post-colonial Maori society in New Zealand.

While there are a few variations between the plot of the novel and that of the film, the story focuses on the issues of frustrated or displaced desire, violence and abuse within the Heke household, a Maori family in contemporary New Zealand. The father, Jake, has lost his job and has turned to drinking; his wife, Beth, also drinks. One of their children, Nig, joins a tough gang, and the younger son, Boogie, is sent to a Social Welfare Institution. Tragically, their daughter Grace is raped (in the novel the aggressor is the Jake, the father, while in the film, it is Jake's friend) and hangs herself.[17]

Because of the visual nature of the film medium, tattoos are much more ubiquitous in the film adaptation than in the novel; however, Duff's text does include a number of key scenes and descriptions where tattoos reinforce the presentation of Maori warrior culture and the post-colonial transformation of this culture in the context of contemporary family and gang violence. Duff suggests that this culture of violence among the modern Maori is a distortion of a noble warrior culture which has degenerated into a culture of abuse and self-abuse, the direct result of the violence and violation inherent in the colonization process. The presence of the colonizer is more apparent in the book than in the film reflected in passages which are addressed to a white narratee: "Good luck to you, white man, for being born into your sweet world" (Duff 1). The white world is less prominent in the film version and only hinted at through a term such as "Royal," the name of the bar where the leading male character Jake drinks with his "mates." The word "Royal" draws attention to the disparity between an image of royalty and the reality of the Maori men engaged in excessive drinking. The name of the bar fosters the desire for a better life, but it actually creates the conditions for self-abuse and the abuse of others.

Beth, the mother of five, is one of the few characters who tries to rise above the violent environment that is created within and outside the family circle. She comments on the link between tattoos and the warrior past in order to remember the nobility of a people before their destruction by colonization:

> We used to be a race of warriors, O audience out there....
> And our men used to have full tattoos all over their ferocious faces, and it was *chiselled* in and they were not to utter a sound.... The women, too, they had tats on their chins and their lips were black with tattooing (41).

Tattoos are presented as a symbol of cultural affirmation, and the suffering of the Maori men in a pre-colonial past was linked to an ability to endure the pain of receiving a facial tattoo. The women also wore tattoos as a sign of cultural pride. In Duff's text and the film, tattoos are often used to show how some Maori individuals have moved away from a proud warrior tradition to a culture that sanctions domestic violence. While Beth does not have a lip tattoo, her lips are bruised from beatings. Her face bears is an ironic imitation of the Maori lip tattoo: her "lower lip swollen with a deep cut about midway and leaking blood. Bruises all over" (32). This bruising of the body replaces the traditional Maori tattoo and signifies the need for a new kind of resistance to pain that is not related to enduring the pain of the tattooing process. In the film *Once Were Warriors*, Beth has a tattoo of a bird resembling a swallow on her left breast. The placement of the tattoo on her breast suggests a highly sexualized site, which may suggest the desire for women that is part of the narrative.

The style of the bird tattoo is an interesting choice because it is not a typical Maori tattoo. Instead, it resembles the style of the bird image used by American tattoo artist Jerry Collins and continued by Jerry Swallow, whose flash follows the "traditional style" of tattoos that were common forty years ago (Swallow 14–15). As a "foreign" symbol on a Maori woman's body, the tattoo has a conflicting set of meanings. It may represent the negative impact of white culture on Maori communities and the loss of Maori tradition; yet, at the same time, a bird represents Beth's desire to liberate herself from the violence she and her family have endured.

Just as Lee Tamahori's film *Once Were Warriors* presents Beth with tattoos that are not mentioned in the novel, the film also presents a profusion of tattoos on the bodies of Maori men, some of which are Maori-style tattoos and others of which are designs from other cultures. The mixture of Maori and no–Maori designs contributes to the intersection of desire and violence in both the novel and the film. The cultural hybridity of Maori culture is also emphasized, since the Maori are presented as a people who cannot return to an idealized pre-colonial state. Jake's tattoos are particularly symbolic in terms of defining

Once Were Warriors (1995). New Line Home Video. Jake Heke (Temuara Morrison) and Beth Heke (Rena Owern) in *Once Were Warriors*. Jake's poisonous and violent character is illustrated through the image of the scorpion which is tattooed on his right shoulder and the barbed wire tattoos on his left arm. While Beth does not have the traditional lip and chin tattoos of Maori women, her lips are often bruised from beatings. Her lip is an ironic imitation of the Maori lip tattoo with her "lower lip swollen with a deep cut about midway and leaking blood. Bruises all over" (Duff 32).

his role as an outsider. He is the man who was not considered a desirable husband for his wife, so she became his illegitimate companion without the approval of her family (who appear to have some significant status in the Maori community). Even though he sings Maori songs, he is a man who has lost meaningful ties to traditional Maori culture. The assortment of tattoos on his body suggests his violent, poisonous character, even though he is a less disagreeable character in the movie than in the novel. Jake's body is, fittingly, adorned with a scorpion on his collarbone area and a scale-like lizard skin tattoo on his right fore-

Once Were Warriors (1995). New Line Video. Jake Heke (Temuara Morrison) and Beth Heke (Rena Owern) illustrate the intimate relationship between desire and violence in this film about the Maori in contemporary New Zealand. Jake's barbed wire tattoo on his left arm also represents the self-abuse and suffering of the Maori as a colonized people.

arm. The lizard skin tattoo does not appear in catalogues of traditional Maori designs; however, the symbolism of the lizard is significant in the context of a cyclical activity. As Peter Gathercole points out, the word moko also means lizard (Gathercole 176). Lizards such as the New Zealand tuatara shed their skins and "enact a metaphor, whereby they continually cycle from life to death to life, and so on, dropping one 'mask,' one might say, in order to assume another" (176). Jake's life mimics this cycle in a post-colonial fashion; he has rewritten the traditional Maori narrative of the noble warrior by engaging in a seemingly endless cycle of desire, violence and self-abuse.

The barbed wire on Jake's upper left arm and the image of the scorpion continue this emphasis on violence. The scorpion and the barbed wire are not Maori designs, but perhaps that is just the point. He has broken away from his roots. The scorpion is a poisonous creature symbolizing his image as a dangerous man. The barbed wire tattoo which encircles his arm suggests that, in hurting others, he is also destroying a part of himself. Another arm tattoo is an image of a knife going through a heart with the words "Jake Loves Beth" running down the arm. Like Beth's bird tattoo, this design is a highly conventional design from 1950s' American tattoo culture signifying the fusion of love and violence in their relationship as well as a symbolic dislocation from Maori culture, since the design is American. The reptilian-like scales on his arm do not seem to be a Maori design either, yet in this case there is some relevant symbolism associated with the lizard in Maori culture: lizards "were feared by the Maoris, and were linked with both the dreaded mythical dragonlike *taniwha* and the very real *tuatara* (*Sphenodon punctatus*)" (176). While in many different cultures the bearer of a tattoo will often wear the symbol of that which he or she fears (e.g., demons) as a sign of courage or as a talisman, it appears that in Jake's case the image primarily reinforces his self-destruction.

The facial moko serves as the most graphic indication of various kinds of tradition and resistance among Maori men. As a feature of post-colonial (rather than pre-colonial) Maori society, it is both an expression of Maori identity as well as a promotion of the spirit of rebellion associated with gang membership. Contemporary tattooing among Maori reflects the influence of Maori gangs such as Black Power and the Mongrel Mob "that spearheaded a late 1970s revival of the *moko* in a more modern guise" (Pfouts 58). One of the more modern elements in the film *Once Were Warriors* is the inclusion of a word as a tattoo on the body of a gang member. One gang member bears the word TOA, which is also emblazoned on the gang members' jackets as part of the phrase *Toa Aotearoa*. The latter term translates roughly as "New Zealand warrior." Nig, the oldest son of Beth and Jake, joins this gang and acquires a moko to show his resistance to pain and express his manhood, an extension of the traditional Maori practice. This tattoo is viewed as a requirement for membership in the Brown Fist gang. However, both the novel and the film indicate that there has been a change in the signification of the moko for a new generation of Maori youth. This change is the result of different tattooing techniques as well as a dislocation from a cultural context. Nig's moko is not "chiselled in" according to the practices of his ancestors by a Maori tattooist known as the *tohungata-moko* (Gathercole 171); instead, he is tattooed by a white man who is paid by the Maori gang members to tattoo their initiates. This insertion of the white man's economy into the Maori community distances the Maori men from the ritualistic tattooing process. Instead of having a specialist apply the design, the gang members receive a design several times removed from the hands of a Maori tattooist. In presenting a white tattoo artist to produce a Maori design on the bodies of these men, Duff is suggesting that these Maori may have internalized feelings of inferiority about their culture which were part of the colonizing mission. Instead of turning to one of their own to obtain a Maori tattoo, they rely on the "authority" of the white man. As Duff points out, however, the white tattooist had copied a design "out of a book from a photograph of a real tattooed Maori head" (Duff 175). Thus Maori culture is mediated by a white man's duplication of their traditional tattoos; the Maori men have become so distanced from their pre-colonial traditions that they can access their tradition only in an altered fashion mediated by the colonizer's perspective.

In Duff's novel, Nig's tattoo does not protect him from death, one of the key functions of tattoos in tribal societies.[18] Instead, the tattoo seems to ensure that he will be led down a violent path; he is killed in a brawl with another gang, the Black Hawks. However, in the film version of *Once Were Warriors* (which tries to avoid the heartwrenching despair of the text), Nig survives, and his tattoo may be the chief indicator of this. He also acquires a facial moko in the film, but it is only a partial one on the left side of his face. According to Sir Peter Buck, the wearing of *moko* on only one side of the face was sufficently distinctive to bear a particular name —*papatabi*, meaning "one side" (Buck as cited in Gathercole 175). Despite the existence of a partial facial moko, Gathercole notes that there are numerous "recorded instances in the literature of Maori men saying that without complete *moko* they are not complete persons" (175). If Maori culture prized the complete moko, then what signficance does the partial moko of Nig in the film version of *Once Were Warriors* carry? It could signify that he is somehow incomplete, perhaps as a result of the impact of colonization on the Maori. This loss of tradition was strongly associated with the incomplete facial moko during the nineteenth century, when Christian negativity towards tattooing also influenced Maori men to refrain from completing their moko. Men were also encouraged to grow beards and moustaches to cover some of their facial tattoo: "Such of the natives as were converted before their moko was complete discontinued the task and remained as they were, moko being incapable of obliteration. The effect is curious, not to say ludicrous, when they appeared partly tattooed and partly plain" (Robley 123–124). Robley's observations demonstrate how the Maori were marginalized when they were completely tattooed and how they continued to be marginalized even when they attempted to conform to the dominant ideology. In Nig's case, the partial moko could be viewed as a negative element if it represents the loss of traditional Maori culture. Nig's partial moko and his Brown Fist gang vest (which has a design that resembles a tattoo pattern) may signify how the modern Maori have distorted their original warrior heritage and become disconnected from their traditions.

However, since Nig does not die in the film version of *Once Were Warriors*, the partial moko may have an alternate meaning that is more positive.[19] While it still reinforces his image as a cultural hybrid (due to the impact of colonization on Maori culture), Nig's partial moko or difference may be viewed as an extension of a decision to set himself apart from others, whether white or Maori. In the film, he is presented as a survivor, and he takes on the male leadership role when his mother breaks the cycle of violence in her family and decides to leave Jake. There is even the possibility that he could leave his gang, although it is difficult to ascertain how likely this will be. In the world of late-twentieth-century New Zealand, the partial moko as depicted in the film may also be "read" or viewed in a more positive manner. This is in contrast to the nineteenth century, when an unfinished moko usually signified a Maori's assimilation of colonial values. In the film, the partial moko may well carry a message of hope (a message which is not easily gleaned from the novel). This message is that, despite their separation from the world of their ancestors, the Maori will be able to renew their identity, albeit in a changed form, given the colonial disturbance of their way of life. [20] The final exchange between Nig and his brother Mark in the film suggests that the desire to acquire a visible moko of any kind is not even necessary to have the heart of a warrior:

> Good look there bro.
> Would you like one then?
> No thanks. I wear mine on the other side.

Once Were Warriors includes numerous images of or references to tattoos on male bodies; however, relatively little attention is paid to the tattoos of women in either the film or the novel. One could argue that this may be a logical extension of the traditional moko on Maori women, which tended to be limited as well; the tattoos were much less dramatic since they were generally placed on the lips and the chin. In the film *Once Were Warriors*, a young woman bears a black chin and lip tattoo, perhaps as a way of honoring her Maori culture, but her character is not developed, so perhaps this tattooed woman serves primarily a decorative purpose. In the novel, on the other hand, women's tattoos highlight the problematic relationships between Maori men and women that are often characterized by violence, pain, inappropriate expressions of desire and the absorption of colonial values that denigrate Maori culture. Tania (Nig's girlfriend) has tattoos, and while they are not described in detail, they are significant in how they reveal Nig's attitudes about women. For example, before Nig's sexual encounter with Tania he notices her tattoos and thinks, "Pity about them tats: can't stand a tat on a woman. Make em look cheap. Like they're a slut" (Duff 143–144). His view of her tattoos reflects colonial attitudes about a pristine body, especially in the case of women. This view falls outside the realm of traditional Maori culture, since, as H. G. Robley mentions in *Moko: The Art and History of Maori Tattooing* (originally published in 1896), "fashion and custom required among the Maoris that their women should also receive certain marks of moko.... The lips and chin were the chief objects of attention" (Robley 33). A photograph of a Maori woman taken around 1900 also displays a tattoo consisting of the word KOTIKAWETAUA on her left arm (Schiffmacher 80–81), thus illustrating that Maori women also had tattoos other than facial markings. However, Nig does not seem to wish to see the continuation of the tattoo tradition on the female form, and thus he reflects a changing aesthetic value among modern Maori men. This is probably the result of his colonial heritage as a Maori man who may have absorbed some of the masculinist Western negativity towards tattoos on the female body.[21] This marginalization of women evident in Nig's perception of Tania's tattoos is articulated in an even more damaging way when he slaps her (Duff 145), thus attempting to mark her body in another manner. In an eerie way, Nig reproduces the actions of his abusive father, Jake, who beat his wife and sexually assaulted his daughter Grace. Nig's perception of feminine beauty and his willingness to engage in physical abuse of his girlfriend contribute to the continual self-effacement of cultural pride. In destroying or diminishing the status of Maori woman, Duff suggests that the Maori men turn themselves into slaves. Nig's debasement of the tattooed woman is a far cry from a traditional Maori song that praises the beautiful lips and chin of a tattooed Maori woman (Robley 118).

It is telling that the only positive presentation of the tattoo on a woman's body is Beth's American-style tattoo of a bird as it appears in the film version of *Once Were Warriors*. While this could simply be a way of appealing to non-Maori viewers who might prefer the appearance of North American-style tattoos, another possibility is that the film is suggesting that contemporary Maori are cultural hybrids. If this is the case, then they must redefine themselves since it is impossible to live in a pre-colonial past. Perhaps the creators of the film felt that authentic tattoos or moko from Maori culture were too closely identified with a pre-colonial past that cannot be recaptured because the context for the reception or interpretation of these tattoos has radically changed. The film's references to the moko which is worn "on the other side" or inside and to the spear which is carried inside[22] also highlight the image of the psychologically tattooed Maori warrior who must fight a different kind of battle in a post-colonial world. As a woman, Beth does not have a moko, and she does not have a lip or chin tattoo, but as the film indicates this is not because she lacks courage; she has the strength to survive spousal abuse and the loss of her daughter. Her bird tattoo, while not a Maori design, therefore still serves as an important symbol of her cultural hybridity as a Maori living in a post-colonial world and of her desire to escape the prison or confines of her former life.

Contemporary tattoo narratives about the Jewish concentration camp experience, African-American slaves and New Zealand Maori culture illustrate the different kinds of imprisonment and pain that are conveyed through the imagery of tattoos, scars or bruises. The numerical concentration camp tattoo and the scarred and branded bodies of slaves reveal the evidence of an oppressor's desire to mark a body as cultural Other. In the case of *Once Were Warriors,* the tattoo functions as a marker of tradition, but it is a mark that has been mediated by a history of colonial violence, and so it is not an uncontaminated image of cultural pride. It too becomes associated with revenge or with the infliction of pain onto others (even if they are members of Maori culture). The images of sexual violation, domestic violence and self-abuse that permeate Duff's narrative and the film reflect the Maori desire to reproduce or multiply the pain of colonization because of the internalization of colonial or racist attitudes. Characters in texts which focus on the concentration camp tattoo also seek to reproduce the pain of the Jewish past. By reproducing the concentration camp tattoo onto their bodies, they reflect a desire to create a permanent memory or record of a victim's pain onto their own body. When these characters are the children of Jews who experienced the Holocaust first-hand, the desire to duplicate this pain is usually subverted by the tattoo, thus indicating that this desire cannot be fulfilled. However, in Steinfeld's story "Weintraub's Education," tattoos, including the concentration camp tattoo, are mentioned in the context of other kinds of desire — sexual interest and the wish to communicate with a member of the opposite sex. This view of the marked body as a way of subverting earlier contexts of unutterable suffering is also articulated in Toni Morrison's

Beloved when she presents a scarred or beaten body as a work of art. *Beloved* articulates the beginning of a healing process for African-Americans through a former slave's desire to embrace a broken body. Although all of these stories of trauma include very different kinds of tattoos and very different kinds of cultural contexts, these texts of psychological scarring and imprisonment reveal how the tattoo functions as a marker of cultural history and as a way of subverting the desire to merely mimic the past.

CHAPTER SIX

What's Normal? Tattoos, Dangerous Freaks, Dangerous Desires[1]

> We all know that bad guys are identified by their tattoos. Every time we watch "America's Most Wanted," we see tattoos as part of the description of the convict. In the movies, most criminals have one or more tattoos. In the movie Cape Fear [sic], Robert De Niro was covered with them. Tattooed mavericks are part of the bad scene and traditionally carry with them the socialized images of the 'bad guy.' Rarely does one see a tattooed 'normal' person on the big screen. They are usually anti-social ... either outlaws or outcasts [Chinchilla 18].

The tattooed body may generate an image of otherness, as numerous examples from fiction, television and film have shown. Because this image often violates the social "norm," it is often viewed as a sign of resistance by members of mainstream society; yet the tattoo also has the power to inspire the viewer with the desire to possess one just like it. In "Eric's Drunken Tattoo,"[2] an episode of the popular television series *That '70s Show,* the generally conservative character Eric tries to re-create himself as a more dangerous type by acquiring a tattoo. In other words, he reinscribes the link between the tattoo and the bad guy as depicted in fictional narratives, thus reinforcing the image of the tattooed individual as someone who falls outside the realm of the "normal." He desires this symbol of the individual who goes against the grain. However, in keeping with the tattoo's subversive potential or its image of resistance, Eric's tattoo ends up being anything but dangerous. It turns out to be a tattoo of the "Peanuts" character Woodstock, a goofy-looking bird. Yet, while Eric's tattoo falls outside the category of dangerous abnormality, it still upholds the image of the tattoo as a sign of otherness — only in this case the otherness is not equated with being cool or dangerous. For Eric, the tattoo reinforces his image as a kind of tattooed "other," but in a comical light. Eric's tattoo upholds the association of tattooed individuals with falling outside the "norm," but in this comic plot he becomes associated with the image of a freak.[3]

The term freak has often been used in conjunction with tattoos to marginalize those who are marked or to marginalize people whose lifestyles distinguish them from the mainstream. Rachel Adams indicates that "*freak* is not an inherent quality but an identity realized through gesture, costume, and staging" (Adams 6). It is also a term that has traditionally been used to designate the excesses or indeterminacy of the body, spanning definitions such as the heavily tattooed individual, the dog-faced boy, or the half-man, half woman sideshow oddity. However, there is also an important narrative component in the construction of the freak as a figure of resistance and desire. Historically the term was applied to human oddities who often had their own narratives to explain their appearance as circus or sideshow performers with bizarre acts. For example, W. L. Alden, a nineteenth century author on freak culture, mentioned how "every museum was bound to have a Tattooed Girl, with a yarn about her having been captured by the Indians and tattooed when she was a little girl" (Alden as cited in Oettermann 200). Other tattooed individuals were sideshow performers who told stories of their tattoos. John Hayes, an American performer in Barnum & Bailey's sideshow, created a narrative reminiscent of John Rutherford's fictionalized Maori tattoo odyssey and told of how his 780 tattoos had been "forced on him during a 154-day period of 'torture'" during the Indian Wars (Oettermann 200–201). Both stories of individuals being sadistically tattooed by Indians are

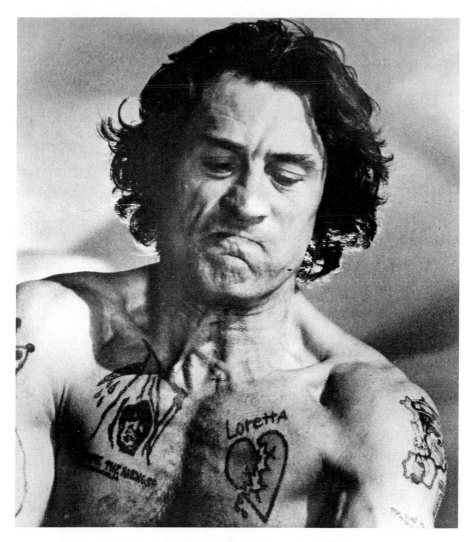

Cape Fear (1991). Universal City Studios and Amblin Entertainment. Robert De Niro plays Max Cady, a psychotic killer. He projects the image of the tattooed "bad guy," criminal or freak that is so pervasive in film, television and literature.

stories of violence and desire that were designed to appeal to an audience's craving to know more about the genesis of the freak. The emphasis on violation in these two examples creates a narrative of excess that enhances the voyeuristic experience of the spectator viewing a tattooed body. These stories also reveal white society's fear of racial intermingling and suggest that the audience may have had a desire to demonize the aboriginal Other, by viewing native people as sadistic tattooists marking the white body.

While tattooed individuals and circus culture share an interesting history and are occasionally depicted in fiction (e.g., "Humbug," an *X-Files* episode), these circus freaks are a rapidly disappearing phenomenon. When they do appear in narratives, they continue to be presented as marginalized characters who resist containment by the establishment or the mainstream. Beyond its specific association with circus or sideshow culture, the term freak has found its way into other kinds of social and performance contexts. These include contemporary performance art, images of mutants or genetic aberration in fiction, depictions of youth culture, and the discourse of sexual identity (drag queens, transgendered individuals, gay and lesbian experience). In contemporary tattoo narratives, the tattooed individual is presented in tandem with that which is alien and is therefore compatible with freak culture and constructions of otherness. Not surprisingly then, tattoo narratives which highlight the body as an alien form may be found in the genre of science fiction and in narratives which foreground teenage rebellion as well as in narratives of gender ambiguity and racial identity. Such stories present the body as a site of resistance to established or clear definitions of human identity, gender or race. The narrative of the tattooed freak is often one that is accompanied by silence, concealment; it is an alternative language to that of the perceived mainstream. At the same time, the term freak is shown to be a relative term, and even within freak culture it may be used to designate an individual who might not normally perceive himself or herself as such. It thus subverts the master narrative of those who seek to relegate the freaks to the margins through a centrist fear of otherness or difference: "freak ... is a frame of mind, a set of practices, a way of thinking about and presenting people" (Robert Bogdan as cited in Adams 6).

Because the tattoo or tattoo culture has often signaled difference, distinguishing the marked body from the unmarked, tattooed bodies are constructed as Other in certain stories. Twentieth-century or contemporary tattoo narratives present the freak in different forms, including the tattooed carnival worker or performer, the heavily tattooed girl, the transgendered person, and the tattooed ethnic rebel in search of self-definition. All of these individuals serve as emblems of resistance and marginality and reinforce the concept of an alternative aesthetic. The freaks in these narratives are usually involved in stories of desire and violence. These stories portray the dual emotions of fascination and fear that the freak body generates because of its difference. The examples of the freak in this chapter share some compelling similarities with historical circus freaks or performers, even though the concept of the freak changes according to specific cultural and gender contexts.

The Tattooed Circus or Sideshow Freak

Circus sideshows have been one of the domains where the tattooed individual could express his or her freakishness, both through the visual appearance of the tattoo and through the narratives which accompanied the genesis of these body markings. Margot Mifflin's study of "circus ladies" describes the participation of women in the tattoo culture of the nineteenth and early twentieth centuries. The origin of their "skin illustrations" was often enhanced through the fictions generated in stories told by the performers or through memoirs such as those of Nora Hildebrandt, "the mother of all tattooed circus women" (Mifflin 10). In the narrative that she sold at shows, she described how she and her widowed father had been kidnapped by Sitting Bull and his tribe, who directed Mr. Hildebrandt to tattoo his daughter from head to toe, for one year, "accomplishing three hundred and sixty five designs" (18) This narrative of violation was probably designed to enhance the already voyeuristic appeal of a tattooed woman's body that was such a rarity outside the context of circus culture. However, the heavily tattooed body seemed to warrant extensive narrative details even when it was male. Margot Mifflin indicates that "when commercial freak shows began to thrive, tattooed men were regularly introduced with far fetched fictions" (20); this narrative accompaniment to tattooed images continues to this day, as tattooed individuals often have stories leading up to the decision to acquire their tattoos. Despite the proliferation of tattoos in Western society, non-tattooed individuals will often display a keen fascination with the very idea of acquiring a tattoo, instead of asking about a particular design, thus constructing the tattooed individual as a kind of freak. As John Gray points out, the act of acquiring a tattoo is often more unsettling or significant for the uninitiated viewer than the designs themselves. He indicates that the content of the tattoo itself is less important than the *fact* of a tattoo: "the tattooee has chosen to have an image indelibly stamped on his or her hide for no apparent reason other than a desire to be different" (Gray 14). Non-tattooed individuals often ask why someone would get a tattoo (thus demanding an explanation that would delineate a process) instead of asking about the symbolic significance of the design. On the one hand, this human response may simply be an extension of humanity's interest in narrative or storytelling, which explains the creation of other narrative genres such as the etiological tale[4] or the murder mystery. However, it is more likely a reflection of the mixed fascination and fear or even disgust that characterize a non-tattooed person's reaction to a heavily tattooed body.

THE ILLUSTRATED MAN

A well-known depiction of the tattooed freak and the tattoo artist occurs in the prologue and epilogue of Ray Bradbury's *The Illustrated Man* and in the film adaptation of this science fiction text. While Bradbury's work was discussed in chapter two in terms of the female tattoo artist as a figure of resistance, it also lends itself to a discussion of tattoo culture in the context of the freak. Both the text and the film depict the interrelationship between image and narrative as well as the relationship between desire and violation in the context of a freak aesthetic. The first-person narrator in the prologue, and the character/observer in the film, are involuntarily engrossed in the tattoos on the

The Illustrated Man (1969). Warner Bros. Rod Steiger stars as "The Illustrated Man" in a film based on Ray Bradbury's novel. His tattoos reflect his freak status as a man tattooed all over his body by a mysterious woman. The heavily tattooed man fascinates and repulses; he is a symbol of desire and violence.

The Illustrated Man (1969). Warner Bros. Rod Steiger plays "The Illustrated Man," whose tattoos have the ability to move and captivate the viewer. In the case of the character who meets the Illustrated Man, his pleasure in viewing the images is undermined as he views or reads the narrative of his death on the back of this marked man. Thus desire = death.

172

body of this man who worked in a carnival and sideshows. While tattoos have a history of associations with circus freaks, the freakishness of the tattoos in Bradbury's texts is developed even further through their animated state. The images on the back of the "Illustrated Man" move and eventually turn into the image of the person who gazes upon the images. They also depict the entire life narrative of an individual and, in Bradbury's collection, form the 18 tales that make up the stories of the collection and the narratives that comprise the film version of the text.

The Illustrated Man's account of the origin of these images also serves as another narrative which contextualizes the tattooed images and introduces an element of otherworldliness or freakishness into the story. The female tattooist responsible for the generation of these images which compel others to gaze at them is described as a witch. She was apparently a time traveller from another world. Her alien character contributes to the supernatural quality of the images on the man's back and helps create a freakish element that is not unusual for the genres of fantastic or science fiction. In addition, the man with the narratives and images tattooed by an alien woman functions in a metafictional capacity; he may be viewed as the pages of the narrative which Bradbury's readers enjoy in order to satisfy their desire to read about strange and alternative worlds of experience. In the case of the character who meets the Illustrated Man, his pleasure in "reading" the "text" is undermined as he reads or views the visual narrative of his own death on the man's back: "The picture on his back showed the Illustrated Man himself, with his fingers about my neck, choking me to death" (Bradbury 186). Similarly, Bradbury's readers may have to prepare themselves for unsettling experiences as they become spectators in the author's narrative freak show. The reading experience is therefore analogous to the spectators' reactions at a freak show; it is a mixture of fascination and repulsion, desire and violence.

"HUMBUG" (THE X-FILES)

Like Bradbury's exploration of the freak through the genre of science fiction, the popular television series *The X-Files* has frequently showcased various kinds of freak identity, thus tapping into its audience's desire to view unusual or fantastic[5] occurrences. Chapter two of this book has examined the episode "Never Again" and its presentation of a seemingly supernatural tattoo that was part of a narrative of sexual desire and the violent consequences of this desire. The episode "Humbug" (1995) is another *X-Files* episode that presents the tattooed body in the context of desire, violence and the supernatural, but in this case the tattoo is on the body of a sideshow freak, and the kind of desire emphasized in the story is that of consumption or ingestion. The storyline involves FBI agents Dana Scully and Fox Mulder arriving in a small town to investigate the murders of various members of a sideshow who are killed by some mysterious creature. The murderer turns out to be Leonard, a mutant twin brother of a former sideshow performer. He lives in his brother's stomach cavity. When the brother is killed by this mutant, the latter seeks another host. His new abode becomes the tattooed man called the Conundrum, and the story ends with the Conundrum character suffering from indigestion and uttering the following words: "Probably something I ate."

While the Conundrum, the tattooed man who happens to eat raw fish, is not the only example of freak culture in this episode, his physical appearance and symbolic significance correspond to a number of other freaks in the program because of their "dangerous" qualities or unusual desires. The opening scene sets the tone for alternative individuals by presenting "the alligator man" in a pool with two boys. His condition is explained in scientific terms as the result of a skin disease, but his initial sudden appearance in the pool is horrific, and he appears to be a danger to the boys until the viewer realizes that he is a father figure and not a threat. His scarred body serves as an example of the freak whose body violates the norm of the unblemished face or the aesthetic of perfection that has dominated Western and other societies.[6] The host of freaks who appear at his funeral replicate the image of the freak body: little people, a giant man, a bearded lady, an amputee minister who gives the eulogy at the alligator man's funeral and turns the pages of his text with his foot, and finally the equivalent of a "sword swallower" character who emerges from the ground in a performance designed to upstage the dead man. Even the town's sheriff is not exempt from freak status. Scully's research indicates that he was an orphan in Albania who was known as the dog-faced boy. He could not speak, devoured chunks of raw meat and eventually ran away from the circus. Thus his status as an Other with an unusual desire to consume raw meat make him a likely suspect in the murder investigation as well, especially since the murders involved some form of ingestion.

All of these freak characters are in some way linked to the figure of the tattooed character called the Conundrum because they are conundrums of nature. Their bodies have been altered in some fashion, which indicates their otherness. Furthermore, like the Conundrum's body, their bodies and actions reflect the mysterious world of sideshow culture as well as the unusual events surrounding the murders. The Conundrum's own body consists of tattooed images of a jigsaw puzzle, some filled with blue ink and others left as blue outlines with blank spaces. He is both literally and emblematically a puzzle. His flesh represents the puzzling events or mystery that mark the storyline as well as the desire of the FBI agents to solve the case.

The Conundrum's desire for raw fish is another odd characteristic which further places him within the category of a freak in the context of the story. This unusual appetite aligns him with a sideshow exhibit known as the Fiji mermaid. This was a sideshow creature with the hybrid body of a monkey and the tail of a fish. The narrative of the Fiji mermaid serves as an interesting subtext in "Humbug" as well as a red herring for the primary narrative involving the malformed twin. However, this minor story still has parallels with the main narrative, since the Conundrum, another kind of fish monster (he eats raw fish), becomes a fitting choice as a host for the parasitic creature or malformed twin that has been murdering the other freaks. The fact that the Conundrum has ingested the mutant twin emphasizes a literal reading of the line uttered by the sheriff: "It's what's inside that counts." This statement has an interesting meta-narrative component because it suggests that the television viewer's voyeuristic desire to contemplate the tattooed body of the Conundrum or to read the Conundrum's body as a narrative of violence will not lead to any answers. Instead, viewers should focus on the inside in order to solve the mystery. The sentence also offers an an ironic twist on agent Mulder's recurring belief that "The Truth is out there."

In this case, the truth is not *out* there but *in* there — literally, within the confines of the Conundrum's body.[7] Thus the terrestrial body rather than the extra-terrestrial body becomes the source of the truth that Mulder and — presumably — the viewer of the television series so desire.

The narrative and meta-narrative play at work within *The X-Files* series highlights the relevance of the tattooed individual as a freak who resists mainstream views of the normal, including normal desires. However, there is also an interesting extra-textual (as opposed to extra-terrestrial!) fact that further enhances the "Humbug" story: the actor who plays the Conundrum is really a tattooed man by the name of the Enigma. His enigmatic name suggests that his identity still evades understanding, and thus he functions in an extra-textual or meta-narrative capacity as a way of highlighting the unknown. Furthermore, the Enigma's full facial tattoos also introduce a transgressive element, since full facial tattoos are still a relatively rare phenomenon and considered taboo in Western society. Thus the Enigma's tattoos introduce a substantial element of difference into the episode. Like the character he plays, the Enigma does not appear to answer questions; he merely poses them. His own appearance has often been the source of much questioning. Finally, like the Conundrum, the Enigma has been a consumer of violent "objects."

As a sideshow and tattoo convention performer, he has done violence to his own body by swallowing swords. In the role of the Conundrum in "Humbug," he consumes a violent creature and utters the words, "Probably something I ate." This line is therefore doubly ironic because of the Enigma's own ability to ingest an unusual substance outside the context of the show; the quotation highlights the freak status of both the actor and the character.

Another way that the tattooed individual and other freaks in "Humbug" challenge the order of the normal involves the episode's rel-

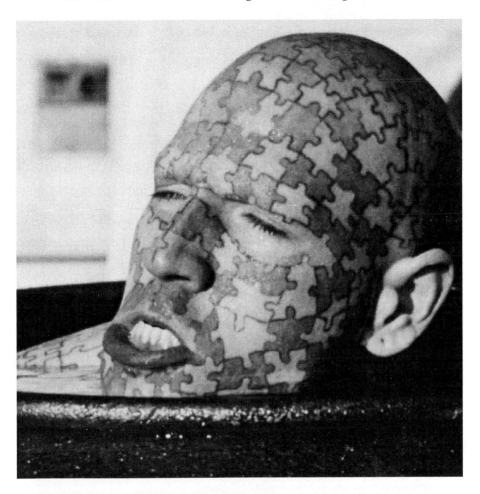

The X-Files 2.20: "Humbug" (1995). The Enigma, who actually has a tattoo of a puzzle on his face, plays the tattooed character "The Conundrum," who consumes or houses a mutant creature that murders circus freaks. The unusual expression or shape of the character's mouth highlights the theme of strange appetites in "Humbug."

ativization of the term freak. In "Humbug" the "normal" FBI agents, Scully and Mulder, are transformed into freaks or objects of curiosity in the context of the sideshow society that they enter. This is a reversal of the usual scenario where the "normal" person watches the circus freak and expresses a combination of fascination and disgust with the freak. In one scene, Scully is offered a bug by one of the sideshow performers, and she appears to swallow it, thus shocking Mulder and constructing herself as a freak with an unusual appetite for bugs. Even though the image of Scully is not sustained (she reveals she has made use of a magic trick), she is presented as someone who has dealings with the alternative culture of magicians. Scully's partner Mulder is also constructed as a freak in this episode of *The X-Files*. Dr. Blockhead, a swallower of strange objects, offers some significant commentary near the end of the television program by constructing Mulder as a freak. He criticizes science and genetic engineering for trying to eradicate freaks of nature in an attempt to create "perfect"-looking individuals such as Mulder; in making this statement his contempt for Mulder is obvious, and he actually manages to present this tall and handsome agent as a freak. He further indicates that Nature abhors normality and creates mutants. One has only to recall a poem by the nineteenth-century poet Gerard Manley Hopkins to see that there may be some truth in Dr. Blockhead's statement. In his poem "Pied Beauty," Hopkins credits God with the ability to create aberrations in nature: "All things, counter, original, spare, strange; / Whatever is fickle, freckled, who knows how?" (Satin 1324). Like Dr. Blockhead, Hopkins relativizes the term freak and indicates that these "dappled things" are beautiful. The suggestion in "Humbug" is that science seeks to artificially prevent mutations from occurring but that nature will resist this kind of hegemony and reappear in various forms. These aberrations may include sideshow freaks with genetic abnormalities, or tattooed individuals who resist the social mainstream with their strange desires or appetites. As he leaves town with another freak, the tattooed or marked Conundrum character, who also houses the body of a mutant twin, symbolizes this ability of nature to elude the controlling impulses of rational society. On a metafictional or metanarrative level, this *X-Files* episode may also be a comic critique of the cult of perfection that characterizes American television or movie stars — actors like David Duchovny and Gillian Anderson, whose perfect bodies and flawless complexions inundate us on a daily basis, inspiring us with the desire to be like them but all the time reminding us of our "mutant" selves.

TATTOO GIRL

A less comical treatment of the tattooed freak is presented in Brooke Stevens' novel *Tattoo Girl* (2001). This narrative is full of characters who are freaks because of their physical appearance and because of their unusual desires which are expressed through images of circus culture, religion or sexuality. The story revolves around a young girl called Emma who is found in a shopping mall. Her body is covered with fish-scale tattoos. She is eventually adopted by Lucy, a former circus fat lady, who feels some kind of rapport with Emma since she was also a freak and associated with other freaks. The story involves the mystery of how Emma obtained her tattoos; in the course of the narrative, her past becomes intertwined with Lucy's and that of the man who was a common denominator in both of their lives. An unusual combination of religious fanaticism, symbolism and the freak body are also introduced into this tattoo narrative. Eventually, it is revealed that Emma had been tattooed by a man who was a freak of nature; he was born with gills. He had abducted Emma in order to tattoo the image of a fish (a symbol of Christ[8]) onto her body in order to create an image of perfection and purify himself.

Like the freaks in historical sideshows or circuses, the tattooed freak in *Tattoo Girl* has the dual ability to fascinate and repulse; furthermore, as in "Humbug," the very definition of who is considered a freak is questioned, thus suggesting that the term freak is a slippery category. For example, when the religious fanatic known as Grecco (an interesting play on El Greco, a Spanish painter of Christian figures and scenes) abducts Emma and tattoos her, he believes that he is attempting to fulfill his desire to create a work of art that will undo other kinds of sin or imperfection: "*When Christ sees you, He shall anoint you and we shall be saved, we shall have eternal life*" (Stevens 262). He is convinced that he can fulfill his desire to save himself through this tattooed woman.

While Grecco, Emma's "maker," perceives her as an expression of the beautiful, another religious fanatic refers to her as a "Satan lover" (228) even before he sees her tattoo because of his own obsession with characterizing other people as being under the influence of Satan. When this man actually sees her scales, he views her as a freak and as the very incarnation of Satan: "Look at that! I knew it. Satan herself! Jesus, have mercy, Scales and all!" (228). In this scene, Emma's fish scale tattoos, which were supposed to be an image of perfection, an image of Christ, are transformed into a demonic association with Satan. This scene in the novel reinforces the shifting image and interpretation of a particular tattoo and how the interpretation of Emma's identity is a reflection of the desires of the individual spectator.

Other examples of how the novel depicts freak as a relative term include Pastor Joe's hatred of freaks as opposed to Lucy's and Emma's interest in them. Lucy claims that she likes freaks, and Emma is also drawn to the pictures of freaks in Lucy's circus photos. The dwarf Pidge, who helps Lucy escape and sacrifices his life for this, is an example of a good freak as opposed to Pastor Joe, the bad freak.

While others may view Emma as a freak because of her tattoo, Brooke Stevens suggests that it is even more damaging when an individual internalizes this label and identifies herself in this way. Emma is acutely aware of her identity as Other because of her visual difference and indicates that in revealing her tattooed skin, she would somehow be revealing who she really is, thus allowing others to engage in a kind of voyeuristic knowledge of her inner self: "*I'm physically different from them. By showing their skin, they're not exposing who they are at all, they're just showing how similar they are, whereas if I showed my skin, I'd reveal how different I am, who I really am. And that will always be a secret, always ...*" (202).

As John Gray has argued, the tattoo reinforces difference (Gray 14)[9]; it also invites a gaze in a way that unadorned skin does not and suggests that a spectator can assume knowledge of the inside by merely looking at the outside. This assumption that the external is a mirror of the internal is an assumption that is made in "Humbug," and it is upheld in an ironic way when the Conundrum, a man with a strange appetite for raw fish, ends up swallowing a mutant creature who has murdered circus freaks. Similarly, Emma fears that others will assume that her external ugliness is a sign of an inner deformed character.

In *Tattoo Girl* Emma's tattooed body and freak identity are related to a number of other freaks in the story. There is the dwarf Pidge, who is linked to Emma because he was a circus freak and she resembles one. Furthermore, like Emma, who lost her voice due to the trauma of her tattoo experience, "he wasn't much of a talker" (Stevens 38) according to Lucy, the woman who takes care of Emma and who used to be a circus fat lady. Because of her background in the circus, Lucy is familiar with the world of freaks. Her narrative intersects with Emma's even though she is not a tattooed freak near the beginning of the novel. As a fat lady called Mrs. Big in a circus, her circus act involved being paired with Pidge, the dwarf or Mr. Little. Their radically different appearances were used to illustrate the concept of a freaky married couple. This pairing of a freak fat lady with a dwarfish man undoubtedly created the titillating, voyeuristic effect that many spectators paid and pay to see at circuses or sideshows. It is even more telling when, years later, after Lucy has shed her weight, she still feels like a freak: " '*I'm* a freak myself [...] I was a fat lady'"(12). This perception of herself as a freak despite the fact that she is no longer "a fat lady" indicates that "it's what's inside that counts" ("Humbug"). Her feelings of self worth are tied into how others constructed her, and this negative image remains strong. Because of her past and her present sense of herself as Other, Lucy feels drawn to Emma, the tattooed circus girl who is found in the mall, and takes her into her own home.

Lucy's sense of herself as a freak, however, predates even her circus days as the storyline of *Tattoo Girl* unfolds. She had run away to the circus at the age of fourteen after being raped by a man called Pastor Joe,[10] and, as the novel reveals, this is the same man who tattooed the fish scales on Emma's body. Therefore both women are linked to the expression of different kinds of desire as expressed by the same man. In Lucy's case, he violated her sexually, calling her a "freak lover" (65), implying that she was to blame for his deviant act of raping her. She was only fourteen at the time, and she became pregnant with his child. In the case of Emma, his tattooing of her is similar to Karl's violation of Maddy in *Tattoo*. He imagines that he is engaging in some kind of purifying ritual and uses this as a way of displacing sexual desire for

The Night of the Hunter (1955). MGM Studios. Robert Mitchum plays the part of Harry Powell, a preacher gone bad much like the Pastor Joe/Grecco character in Brooke Stevens' novel *Tattoo Girl* (2001). The tattooed letters of "love" on Harry Powell's right hand are juxtaposed against the word "hate" which is tattooed on his left hand. The two tattoos illustrate his duplicity since he pretends to love a woman but then kills her. This love/hate relationship resembles the split in the Pastor Joe/Grecco character in *Tattoo Girl*. Pastor Joe claims to be a young girl's friend and then rapes her. He also kidnaps another young woman and believes that he is achieving a state of salvation and union with God by tattooing fish scales onto her body.

her. Sexual desire is transformed into a kind of religious ecstasy for Pastor Joe.

Emma's tattooed body thus becomes the site which articulates not only her secret story but Lucy's narrative[11] and Pastor Joe's or Grecco's as well. Emma's tattoo is the result of Grecco's or Pastor Joe's desire to purge himself of his previous violation of Lucy, but it is also linked to his own freak identity. He has gills on the side of his neck, and his comments about circus freaks (he has pictures of them in his household) indicate both a hatred of otherness and self-hatred. Pastor Joe calls freaks "aberrations" (57) and "God's dirtiest souls" (59). His tattooing of Emma is an ironic reflection of his desire to purify himself, even though in tattooing her body with fish scales he only draws attention to his own fish-like deviancy. This religious freak is killed at the end of the narrative when Lucy wrestles with him in the water during her attempt to escape from him after he had held both Lucy and Emma captive.

Brooke Stevens' novel highlights the connection between Lucy and Emma even further through Pastor Joe's or Grecco's joint abduction of these two women, and through the fact that Lucy also acquires a tattoo. The joint abduction is a reflection of how both women functioned as the objects of this man's desire. He raped Lucy when she was fourteen years old, and he tattooed Emma as a way of washing away his previous sin with Lucy. Thus the tattoo moves beyond its usual association with the visual realm and enters into the realm of narrative or story. By linking her narrative to Lucy's, Emma begins to recover her voice, which she had lost due to the trauma of her tattoo experience. As in the *Star Trek: Voyager* episode "Tattoo," when Chakotay uses the image of his tattoo to communicate with an alien race,[12] the tattoo in Brooke Stevens' novel is the unspoken narrative of Emma's past which speaks to Lucy in a way that it does not to "normal" individuals.

In this sense, the tattoo has an ambivalent status; it is both a site of resistance as well as a site of recovery. As a silent marker and a site of trauma, it has deprived Emma of memory and voice. Yet, at the same time, the tattoo's secret narrative must be told for healing to occur. In Lucy's case, there is a similar desire to communicate, and it is through Lucy's encounter with Emma that both can begin the process of healing and remembering. A doctor had told Lucy when she was still in the circus that she had to communicate with others: "You've got to tell someone your story" (107), because if she did not, she would not survive. Lucy benefits from her interaction with this tattooed girl, since Emma encourages Lucy to tell stories about her own life as a freak, a circus freak. Thus Emma's desire to communicate is mediated by Lucy, and Lucy's ability to forget some of the pain of her past is mediated by her contact with Emma. Eventually the two lives are bound even more closely together when Lucy is tattooed by the same man who tattooed Emma. Lucy's tattoo is that of Siamese twins "locked together at the hips in a bloody fight with each other, one with an axe raised in one hand, the other a hammer" (221). Her tattoo is a sign of duality, a sign of resistance or struggle, and a place of mediation for her pain and Emma's suffering. The image of the Siamese twins reinforces her connection to Emma, another tattooed woman, as well as symbolizing the dual image of Lucy as a woman who can never completely shed her past image as a circus fat lady despite her slimmer or "normal" appearance in her present life. Furthermore, it is only when Emma sees Lucy reliving the narrative of Emma's captivity (252) that Emma regains the use of her voice. The end of the novel indicates how Emma finally becomes one with her own tattooed skin, thus suggesting that she has reclaimed the term "freak." Instead of denying the existence of her fish tattoo, she sees herself as a fish swimming in the water.

Gender Bending, Cultural Others and Tattoos

In contemporary literature and film, the appellation "freak" surfaces in several contexts other than circus culture, especially since circuses do not have the same presence as they once had. Other kinds of freaks are presented in the context of transgendered identity, drag queens, or even in the relation to ethnic affiliation. For example, in *Eve's Tattoo* (discussed in chapter five), a story about a non-Jewish woman researching the Holocaust, an intriguing Jewish transvestite character with a concentration camp tattoo appears in the narrative. Mr. Schlaren is a Yiddish-speaking transvestite who works in the theatre. He tells Eve how changing his gender actually saved him from death; his mother instructed him to become a girl so that he would stand a better chance of survival. Then later, when he was captured a second time, he changed his identity back to that of a boy because in the second context rigor was important (Prager 155). Thus, while the numerical tattoo initially appears to signal the "common" or shared plight of concentration camp prisoners and survivors, the narrative of the text reveals how it remains a key indicator of difference.

A hybrid identity and the concepts of ethnic and gender difference also enter into the depiction of a tattooed character in the film version of Joyce Carol Oates' novel *Foxfire* (discussed in chapter four). In the film, the Asian character, Goldy Goldberg, is called a freak by her white father when he discovers the tattoo she acquired during an initiation ritual for the girl gang Foxfire. Her boyish appearance and dress challenge the boundaries of social acceptance and a feminine aesthetic associated with easily recognizable images of womanhood. In the film the tattoo symbolizes the bonds between women and the possibilities of lesbian desire which are perceived as a threat to the dominance of the heterosexual male value system. Even though the film is set in the 1980s or '90s, some of its attitudes echo those of the novel, which uses a 1950s time period. In her article on tattooed lesbian delinquents in the 1960s, Beckie Ross argues that even the 1960s still reflected 1950s values that presented homosexuality or lesbianism as a threat to the security of the family and the nation (Ross 569).[13] Not surprisingly, the tattooed body came to symbolize the freak body in need of repair. It was regulated and contained by a social system that perceived the marked body as a threat. "Tattoos were construed by authorities ... as antithetical to the performance of properly socialized femininity" (581) or the social norm. Thus Goldie's tattooed form and masculine appearance, suggestive of ambiguity or gender bending, offers an image of the freak that is not tolerated by her father.

Another Asian representation of the tattooed freak appears in the novel *Cover Me* (discussed in chapter two). Canadian writer Mariko Tamaki presents a Japanese-Canadian teenager who marks her body, first by cutting her flesh and then by acquiring tattoos. Interestingly enough, the author of this novel has self-identified with freak culture: "'I'm a freak at heart'" (Cole). She has tattoos, is a member of an alternative "girl band," she is concerned with the marginalization of other "freak" bodies, including those of overweight women. In a sense, the tattooed body in Tamaki's novel serves as a metaphor for many kinds of marginalized individuals — from the mentally ill to minority groups to teenagers trying to define themselves as something more than an extension of their family. The tattoo is also associated with a kind of deception and trickery an idea explored in the discussion of Takagi's *The Tattoo Murder Case* and Steinfeld's "The Apostate's Tattoo." For example, in *Cover Me,* the narrator transforms her identity by changing her name for a tattoo appointment. Like the author Tamaki, who changed her own name,[14] the narrator transforms herself by deliberately using a Chinese-sounding name (Tamara Chong) to book her tattoo appointment, thereby resisting the notion of identity as an unchanging or stable concept.

SKIN DEEP

The Canadian film *Skin Deep* (1997) offers an even more complex exploration of the image of the freak in conjunction with tattoos, sexual desire, violence, gender identity, and ethnicity. The film portrays a lesbian Japanese-Canadian director called Alex, who is making a movie about tattoos; the movie within the movie has sadomasochistic elements in order to highlight its alternative content. Alex's producer describes the plot as a story about a tattooed woman who goes crazy and kills her lover. Elements of this plot then enter into Alex's own life when she hires a person by the name of Chris Black, who responds to her intriguing ad:

> I want the real story. The bare tattooed truth. Tell me your
> wildest stories. You could end up in the movies.

The opening scene of the film depicts Chris writing a letter and sterilizing a device for tattooing with a lighter. Chris, who is a man trapped in a woman's body, accidentally spills ink over the advertisement, thus symbolically resisting Alex's quest for the "real" and the "tattooed truth." A flashback sequence indicates Chris' past narrative as a freak that is framed in the context of violence and desire. She was beaten by some men after her girlfriend discovered that "he" was a girl: "You're a girl; you fuckin' freak." Chris' resistance to her socially constructed identity as a woman is further indicated through her angry reaction to the comments of two drag queens who assume that she is a lesbian dressing in a masculine manner. One calls her "baby butch" and another tells her that Tuesday is dyke night at a club. Chris responds, "I don't dress this way because I'm some kind of freak." The film attempts to challenge the perception of individuals as freaks (even when they are called freaks by other freaks) by exploring the multifaceted aspect of relationships that transcend any simple kind of classification or easy categorization into one kind of sexual identity.

Rachel Adams develops the constructedness of the freak by indicating that "*freak* is not an inherent quality but an identity realized through gesture, costume, and staging" (Adams 6). This definition of the freak is evident in tattoo narratives about circus culture such as "Humbug" and *Tattoo Girl* and is also apparent in discussions of other performance cultures such as drag queen performances. "Freak" is a term that has traditionally been used to designate the excesses or indeterminacy of the body, spanning definitions such as the heavily tattooed individual, the dog-faced boy, or the half-man, half woman sideshow oddity. In *Skin Deep*, the term may be used in relation to otherness as it applies to racial minorities, to drag queen performers, to the character of Chris Black (a sexually ambiguous character who is not a drag queen), and to tattooed individuals. All of these individuals either view themselves as freaks or are viewed as freaks by others: "freak ... is a frame of mind, a set of practices, a way of thinking about and presenting people" (Bogdan cited in Adams 6).

While the film portrays the fluidity of gender identity, it also addresses the danger or consequences of imposing a sexual category on another. Perhaps not surprisingly, one of these dangerous individuals is also a tattooed character by the name of Chris (echoes of Eric's "drunken tattoo" in *That '70s Show*). Furthermore, this tattooed character is a transgendered individual determined to construct herself as a man. She convinces herself that Alex still likes men and not women despite her lesbian relationship with a Black woman called Montana.

Chris had based this belief on an old photograph of Alex with her former male lover. When Alex does not reciprocate these feelings despite Chris' determination to construct a heterosexual relationship for the two of them, Chris stabs herself in an effort to remove her breast, a sign of a woman's identity. Alex's producer views her act of mutilation as the act of a freak: "What kind of a freak tries to slice her own tit off?" Despite Chris' attempt to rid herself of what she considers to be alien to her sexual identity, she is still perceived by others as strange — not to mention dangerous.

In addition to highlighting the link between tattoos and sexual identity, Onodera's film also uses tattoo culture to present the ethnic facet of the multicultural experience. The opening credits reveal a number of multi-cultural elements, including Japanese style drumming and tattoo designs by American artist Don Hardy as well as Asian and First Nations tattoos. However, the film also uses the tattoo as a way of extending multiculturalism into the territory of sexual identity[15] and freak culture. *Skin Deep* encourages us to reevaluate our concept of multiculturalism as being limited to the notion of stable ethnic identities. The film presents alternative art (drag queen performances), ambiguous sexual identity and "tattooed individuals" who become images of otherness or freak culture in the film. *Skin Deep* furthermore establishes a link between multiculturalism and freak culture in order to explore shifting and relative concepts of normality and otherness.

The film appears to be set in a multicultural metropolis, probably Toronto. (While Toronto may be a multicultural Mecca, the centrist attitude often identified with this Canadian city is evident in an urban character's (Alex's) disparaging reference to Timmins, a smaller Ontario town. The subtext is that those who inhabit areas outside of an urban center may well be freaks.) Multi-ethnic elements as well as images of the freak abound in *Skin Deep*. For example, Alex's Japanese great-grandfather was an artist, Alex is fascinated with the Japanese art of tattooing, her female lover Montana also happens to speak Japanese, and Alex is called "Hong Kong" by one of her drag queen friends. However, other elements that fall outside the category of ethnic identity also contribute to the film's presentation of Canadian cultural alternatives. These include the film's depiction of freak culture in the form of ambiguous sexual identity. For example, there are performing drag queens, including an individual who sings a song in Spanish, another drag queen who is a woman playing a man playing a woman, and Chris Black—a man trapped in a woman's body. The film thus demonstrates the fluidity of ethnic and sexual identities and the pervasiveness of freak culture.

A club scene in the film shows the overlap between multi-ethnic individuals, sexually ambiguous individuals, and tattooed people as part of a multi-cultural world of freaks. Yet, unlike definitions of the freak which suggest that the freak is an essence, *Skin Deep* reveals how notions of normality and freakishness are relative and contextually constructed. For example, the "established" freaks or drag queens view Chris' sexually ambiguous identity with suspicion and also marginalize his/her tattoos, referring to them as "outlaw biker" tattoos and establishing a clichéd association between tattoos and violence. One would think that the tattoo's own historical associations with circus freak culture would establish some rapport between a drag queen and Chris. However, this scene in the film shows how the concept of the freak is a construction, a way of viewing another, rather than a stable, essentialist term.

Skin Deep demonstrates how multiculturalism consists of a complex series of relationships that involve shifting notions of desire, power, privilege and marginality, thus defying stability or unity. As Smaro Kamboureli points out, "the unity of Canadian identity is a cultural myth, a myth that can be sustained only by eclipsing the identities of others" (Kamboureli 10). In a sense this concept of unified identity also applies to a multicultural ideal of diversity that fails to acknowledge the presence of a power differential among minority groups. A scene that challenges the stability of identity while also incorporating the concept of freak identity involves Alex and her lesbian lover Montana, who is also her assistant on the film set. *Skin Deep* actually argues against an essentialist or privileged racial position for members of specific cultural communities. For example, Alex's inability to communicate with the Japanese tattoo master (despite her Japanese heritage) might make some view her as a freak. Similarly, Montana's effectiveness in speaking Japanese and acting as translator could be construed as equally freakish by an audience who might not expect a Black woman to communicate in this language.

A further cross-cultural and rather freakish alliance is established between Chris (a Caucasian) and Montana[16] (a Black woman), who couldn't be more different in a physical sense. Yet they are brought together in the film through their common desire for the same woman, Alex, and through an image of darkness. For example, Chris' last name is Black, and Montana's racial identity is Black. Montana also reinforces her alliance with Chris by telling Alex, "You must have me confused with Chris, a glutton for punishment." Here both characters are linked to self-abuse, which appears to be a consequence of establishing a relationship with Alex, who is very focused on her own aspirations. Both characters love Alex, but she appears to have difficulty fully integrating either character into her life. Like other aspects of multiculturalism, the idea of accepting a person who is constructed as a freak is often easier to do in theory than in practice. In Alex's case, directing a film about freaks is easy, but making freaks part of her personal life is not so simple, thus illustrating her tendency to express a desire which is not fulfilled in her real life. Similarly, the aesthetic appreciation for tattoos may prove easier than the real act of acquiring one. Alex's refusal to participate in the intimacy associated with getting a matching tattoo with Chris mimics her lack of commitment to nurturing her relationship with Montana.

Ironically, Alex, who is a member of various minority groups (Japanese-Canadian, lesbian, female filmmaker), actually takes on a rather centrist position and marginalizes others, thus challenging one of the assumptions of a multicultural ideal — that all minorities are somehow equal in their marginalized status. Her rejection of Chris reveals an underlying fear of various kinds of otherness, whether this otherness takes the form of Chris' tattoos, her own gender ambiguity, or even her otherness as a white individual from small-town Ontario.

An especially poignant scene in *Skin Deep* that highlights the film's concern with the concepts of the freak and the normal foregrounds the

Penny/Werner relationship. In the movie, a number of references are made to the absence of Werner, Penny's German lover who died of AIDS; he comes to represent yet another kind of cultural Other whose spirit enters into the film. Penny suggests that she led a life of deception; however, the film reinforces the idea that despite ambiguous physical appearances individuals can still experience a kind of truth. She is a woman "playing a man playing a woman" and illustrates the complexity of desire in the film as it is expressed by transgendered, lesbian and gay male individuals. She says that she did not find Abnormal" in her life, but that she found some kind of truth in her relationship with her German lover. Penny's former relationship with a German cultural Other who was a victim of AIDS, and her play with gender, indicate that she may be a part of freak culture. However, ultimately the concept of truth or desire should not be confused with a single, unambiguous and tidy form of representation. Truth and desire can be messy; they lie beyond essentialism and are often accessible through plurality rather than uniformity. In this sense the tattooed "freak," whose body resists images of the perfect, unmarked body, has parallels with other cultural outcasts such as drag queens, AIDS victims, and even ethnic minorities. At the same time, *Skin Deep* attempts to reclaim the term "freak" (whether applied to drag queens, lesbians, women filmmakers, transsexuals or tattooed individuals) by exploring the multifaceted aspect of relationships that transcend the classification of individuals into neat categories of ethnicity, race, sexual identity or aesthetic preference (e.g. tattoo art).[17]

Skin Deep depicts a vast array of groups that have been identified as freaks or which construct themselves in this manner. This film further questions the stability of categories such as normality and otherness, and it urges us to view the complex network of power relations and identity construction among marginalized groups, including tattooed individuals. The character of Eric in *That '70s Show* attempted to construct a tattoo as a dangerous image; however, his desire to live dangerously through a tattoo is deflated when his tattoo turns out to be an image of the funny little bird Woodstock. This image subverts his earlier desire and constructs him as a freak. Other tattooed individuals in fiction, film and television also subvert established images, albeit in a more serious fashion. These tattooed characters may be presented as transgressive freaks who destabilize established or hegemonic ways of viewing the body, whether they appear as sideshow oddities with unusual appetites, transgendered characters, or ethnically diverse women challenging traditional images of femininity. Fictional freaks like the tattooed Conundrum character in "Humbug" or Emma in *Tattoo Girl* or the character of Chris in *Skin Deep* demonstrate that the concept of a freak encompasses diverse people, but that the freak is still predominantly associated with a marker of difference. The tattooed character as perceived by non-tattooed individuals often fits this definition, but even individuals who may ordinarily be considered "normal," beautiful or handsome (like agent Fox Mulder in "Humbug") can be viewed as freaks of nature, thus reinforcing the shifting concept of freak identity.

Conclusion

Tattoos continue to be linked to a variety of narrative forms and tend to be presented in the context of alternative lifestyles. This even extends to contemporary baby books! *Baby's First Tattoo: A Memory Book for Modern Parents* (2002) uses the image of the tattoo to suggest alternatives for modern parents, or a path of resistance to established texts. A description of the book offers some insight into how it will provide an alternative to other "memory books" that encourage parents to document moments in their new baby's life. *Baby's First Tattoo* allows parents to inscribe all of "those 'alternative' precious moments that really should be written down, celebrated, and remembered — Baby's First Projectile Vomit, Baby's First Tantrum..." (Mullen, *Baby's First Tattoo.* "Product Description," http://www.amazon.com).

While this book does not deal with the actual tattooing of a baby, it does demonstrate how the tattoo still serves as a powerful metaphor for the desire to depict alternative and sometimes violent experiences.

Tattoos also continue to leave their mark on all kinds of fictional narrative forms from novels to films to television series like *The Simpsons,* which embeds the tattoo as an image of desire for an outlaw figure like Bart, who is always getting into trouble. Bart's desire for maternal acceptance of his outlaw self is fittingly portrayed when he imagines his mother saying, "Oh, Bart, that's so sweet. It's the best present a mother could get, and it makes you look so dangerous" (*The Simpsons:* 1.1). While the pervasiveness of tattoos in a popular television series like *The Simpsons* might suggest a certain mainstreaming of this visual art form, this is still not how tattoos are presented thematically in most fictional contexts and in many non-fictional contexts. Tattoos subvert social expectations even when they are linked to the recording of specific moments or memories. The tattoo is a key access point to memory, especially in autobiographical writing; yet, while it attempts to preserve certain moments (including those tied to desire), it remains elusive just like desire which can never be truly satisfied (Bart Simpson's mother does not condone his desire to acquire a tattoo!). Furthermore, for those who would view the tattoo as a mark of cultural authenticity or exclusivity (e.g., Trachtenberg's experience in *7 Tattoos*), tattoos also shatter expectations of restricted cultural categories. They can transcend cultural boundaries and allow the bearer to appropriate other identities and transform the self.

Since literature, film and television may be viewed as the expression of imaginative or creative desire, it is not surprising that when tattoos are presented in these narratives they are used as a device to reflect many kinds of desire (as in *The Simpsons*) even as they sustain an identification with resistance and the process of subversion. These desires include not only artistic desire or the desire to create, but also the desire to preserve a cultural memory, the desire to imitate a cultural Other, sexual desire, narcissistic desire, the desire to belong to a group or community, and the desire to reproduce suffering or pain. An important component of many tattoo narratives is that desire for a particular person or thing cannot be accessed directly, and so the tattoo simultaneously acts as a site of mediation and subversion. Tattoos may appear to facilitate the expression of desire and the act of communication, but even when they do so, they still have a subversive function since they often resist an individual's initial perception of the tattoo and create an interesting element of surprise. Tattoos may also show how desire is deferred or demonstrate how the achievement of an original desire is frustrated, as in the attempt of characters to reproduce the pain and suffering of a Holocaust survivor through the acquisition of a concentration camp tattoo.

As in "real" life, desires in tattoo narratives are not always linked to the expression of socially sanctioned practices. Cannibalism, sado-masochism, homoeroticism, domestic abuse, rape and various forms of violence in the form of criminal acts (e.g., murder) are presented in tattoo fictions and thematically linked to the pain and suffering that is implied in the image of a particular tattoo or through the tattoo experience itself. Tattoos often consist of images that embed an aesthetic of violence (such as the images of deadly beauty in yakuza tattoos or the tattoos on body of the "Illustrated Man" that depict the death of the person who views these tattoos). Violence is a key part of the tattoo's aesthetic image and sadomasochistic appeal for a number of people. One cannot overlook the fact that the very creation of the tattoo is a violation of the flesh as the ink is inserted into the skin. Narratives of violence also surround the creation of a tattoo, whether this tattoo takes the form of a prison tattoo (*Oz*), a concentration camp tattoo that honors a mother ("The Apostate's Tattoo"), a tattooed body that serves the aesthetic of bondage and masculine desire (*Tattoo*), or a mutilated, homoerotic textual body (Jerome in *The Pillow Book*). While many of the fictional characters survive their suffering and even find a way of recovering from the violent narrative of their past, all of them, like the Biblical figure of Cain, remain marked for life.

In all of the tattoo narratives presented in this book, gender identities and gender relations play significant roles. In fact, some of the most intriguing elements in the various tattoo narratives which merit even further exploration are the links between tattoos, desire, violence or violation, and gendered identity (including the concept of the freak) or gender relations. Masculinist perspectives have dominated tattoo culture and have been incorporated into tattoo narratives as well by privileging the male tattoo artist or his tattooing of women's bodies. Just as tattooed women have become more of a common sight in reality, tattoo narratives have incorporated tattooed women as images of an alternative story or aesthetic. However, in a novel and film such as *Foxfire,* women's experiences and desires are validated through the image of a common tattoo. This tattoo narrative and others like *Cover Me* or "Never Again" show women resisting patriarchal restrictions on women's bodies and minds through the liberating image of tattoos. The ability of a tattoo to highlight an alternative aesthetic also applies to sexual orientation in the form of lesbian desire or homosexual relations between men and to transgendered identity, the focus of the film *Skin Deep*. The tattoo's historical association with circus or freak culture and individuals who transgress what is perceived as "normal" can be related to the complexity of gender identity in contemporary narratives that depict individuals whose bodies resist easy categorization.

Tattooed bodies are clearly capable of crossing boundaries in terms of gender and cultural affiliation. But they also serve as markers and narratives of the self. They may symbolize past desires and may even convey an individual's current desires; they offer access to narratives of suffering and violence, and in this sense they resemble other scars on the body that also serve as a record of a person's pain. Yet, unlike most scars, tattoos can fulfill the double function of marking and subverting psychological scars. Whatever form tattoos may take (whether on real bodies or on the bodies of fictional characters), one thing is certain — they will continue to generate fascinating stories.

Notes

Introduction

1. Even though I tend to appreciate the diverse interpretations a single tattoo can generate, I have to admit that I was astonished and impressed when a young girl (probably around the age of 7), who was walking with her mother, pointed at my tattoo and said, "Dolphins!" Most people who have seen my tattoo without knowing what it is assume that it is simply a stylized pattern.

2. The study was completed in 2001, and the results are discussed in *Tattoo Study: The Cultural, Symbolic and Social Significance of Tattoos in a University Community* (Beeler and Wintemute).

Chapter One

1. The actress Angelina Jolie is just one example of someone who removed her tattoo of her former husband after their breakup: "No stranger to controversy, Academy Award–winning actress Angelina Jolie made headlines once again when, upon ending her marriage to actor Billy Bob Thornton, she had the tattoos of his name removed from her body" (Mann).

2. Neither Kisch's essay in the original German, nor Segel's translation, gives the name of the tattooist as it appears in the advertisement. However, in a German edition of this tattoo essay, there is an apparent reproduction of the poster which reads "Fred A. Lionsfield." The poster is full of exclamation marks and various typefaces. It includes statements such as "Whoever is untattooed, is naked"; "Whoever loves his wife, will get tattooed!"; or the phrase "!!Guaranteed painless!!" which even appears twice (Segel 87). Clearly the last phrase is a far cry from Kisch's own painful tattoo experience.

3. Kisch's racist comments are unusual, given the fact that he was dedicated to acts of left-wing resistance. In 1934 Kisch was "eager to promote the agenda of the antifascist movement" (Segel 7) after being imprisoned by the Nazis. He was released because of his Czechoslovak citizenship. Kisch's disturbing way of describing other races illustrates the selective nature of certain kinds of resistance groups or movements which do not always embrace the principles of racial and gender inclusivity.

4. Ekphrastic studies which focus on the "poetic" include Murray Krieger's *Ekphrasis: The Illusion of the Natural Sign* (Baltimore, MD: Johns Hopkins University Press, 1992) and James A. W. Heffernan's collection of essays *Museum of Words: The Poetics of Ekphrasis from Homer to Ashbery* (Chicago: University of Chicago Press, 1994).

5. According to Vincent Crapanzano, Lacan argues that desire cannot be satisfied directly. Desire must always be satisfied "by symbolic substitutes for that which it can never possess" (Crapanzano 89).

6. "All ekphrasis is notional, and seeks to create a specific image that is to be found only in the text as its 'resident alien'"; W.J.T. Mitchell as cited in Peter Wagner, ed., *Icons. Texts. Iconotexts: Essays on Ekphrasis and Intermediality.* (Berlin: Walter de Gruyter, 1996), 12.

7. The narrator's desire for cultural otherness is also experienced by the character Fletcher Christian in the 1984 film *The Bounty.* Fletcher Christian receives a Tahitian style tattoo according to the tradition of manual tapping while he rests his head in the lap of a beautiful woman.

8. In her article "Mimesis: The Dramatic Lineage of Auto/Biography," Evelyn J. Hinz indicates that auto/biography (her slashmark indicates a reference to both autobiography and biography) frequently uses pictorial metaphors and photographs: "'Portrait,' for example, repeatedly occurs in the titles of auto/biographies, and 'vivid' is the adjective used by reviewers to express commendation. Similarly, some of the earliest forms of biography is, the pictographs in Egyptian tombs are visual articulations; the autobiographical impulse of numerous modern artists such as Van Gogh takes the form of self-portraits, and photographs constitute a major component of many contemporary biographies" [Hinz 196].

9. This detour is another example of how the many stories the author tells are really about himself. This also signals the constructions and fictionality of memoir.

10. The author tells us that this term is used by Javanese émigrés to refer to the Dayak. It translates as "forest people" and is the origin of the word *orangutan* (Trachtenberg 102).

11. In the *Star Trek: Voyager* episode "Tattoo," Chakotay's facial tattoo serves as an alternate form of communication as well. While exploring a planet, he encounters another culture whose facial markings are similar to his own tattoo. They are unable to communicate until the alien individual sees Chakotay's tattoo and Chakotay remembers the word *chamozi* from his childhood. The word refers to circular lines of his tattoo that were also carved into the bark of a tree to indicate the potential for healing. Shortly thereafter, the alien individual uses some kind of translation device and is suddenly able to communicate in English. However, had it not been for the initial alternative visual marker of the tattoo, it is unlikely that Chakotay's life would have been spared. During his conversation with the alien, the Voyager character discovers that this alien race had visited the earth and disseminated their culture and language to the aboriginal inhabitants of Chakotay's culture. He then takes on the role of mediator as he speaks to these angry inhabitants, who had disabled Voyager with a cloaking device. The visual sign of his tattoo, his linguistic ability, and his awareness of cultural traditions shared with this alien race all contribute to the successful resolution of the conflict, but the visual sign permitted the further communication to take place.

12. Trachtenberg quotes from Joseph Conrad's *Lord Jim* in order to emphasize the futile search for the "full utterance": *"Are not our lives too short for that full utterance which through all of our stammerings is of course our only and abiding intention?"* (Trachtenberg 109).

13. "...I kept imagining the look on those bastards' faces when they saw the emblem of sabotage on my right arm, which might happen if someone photographed my ink for *Outlaw Biker Tattoo* and a copy of that magazine somehow found its way into a congressional mailbox or onto the coffee table of a corporate waiting room" (Trachtenberg 120). This statement may initially be read as the expression of the narrator's belief at the time that his tattoo would in fact make a political impact; however, when read from the perspective of the older, omniscient narrative voice, it can be read ironically, and we are asked to question the efficacy of the image as a symbol of resistance.

14. The 36-year-old ban against tattooing in New York City was repealed in 1997 by local law. The ban was introduced "when a hepatitis outbreak in New York heightened fears that practices such as tattooing could transmit infectious diseases" (Jason Gay, "The Stink over Ink: Two New Efforts

to Legalize Tattooing in Massachusetts," *Boston Phoenix*, October 14–21, 1999).

15. This sentiment is echoed by Mark Kingwell in *Dreams of Millenium* (213), who also questions the image of the tattoo in the 1990s as a sign of resistance. However, I would argue that the ability of the tattoo to serve as a symbol of resistance may vary depending on different cultural contexts or situations, since resistance is a complex idea that shifts depending on the political and cultural contexts.

16. Trachtenberg's images of pain with Leonard Cohen's linking of religious ecstasy in his poetry and songs to heroin addiction (e.g., see his song "Joan of Arc") are quite striking.

17. Roland Barthes' comments on the paradoxical nature of the photograph can be applied to this passage; the photograph is both a solid record of that which has occurred as well as a reminder of an absent object: "on the one hand 'it is not there,' on the other 'but it has indeed been'" (Barthes, *Camera Lucida* 115).

18. Henk Schiffmacher indicates how, among the Berbers and Samoans, tattoos have "achieved importance as a type of vaccination": for example, one can get "tattooed against rheumatism" (Schiffmacher and Riemschneider 11).

19. "Milton tells us that Lucifer was the first to fall and dragged us down behind him. But I can imagine a Gnostic gloss in which the Bright Son of Morning is ejected from heaven only later on, not because he tempted Adam and Eve, but because he questioned their fearful punishment. 'For God's sake, it was just a goddamn apple!' he yells up at the Throne. And the next thing the trapdoor has snapped open beneath his feet and he is falling" (Trachtenberg 262).

20. This statement is an adaptation of Trachtenberg's words: "All the time I'm watching those other people, I'm also watching myself" (31).

Chapter Two

1. According to Hilde Hein, the term masculinist "is gender-specific while leaving open the issue of power distribution," unlike other terms such as "phallocratic" or "phallogocratic" (note 1 to Hein's "The Role of Feminist Aesthetics in Feminist Theory"). Hein indicates that the term "masculinism" is defined by feminists as that "nameless 'default mode' of normal thought..." "It is so pervasive that we fail to recognize it and are oblivious to its influence upon all aspects of intellectual and social operation" (Hein 447).

2. An American tattoo artist, Tex, has made the following comment on the increase in the number of women tattooists: "In the near future, the imbalance between male and female tattoo artists will level off. In the last eight years, since I began tattooing, many women have taken up this occupation. They are slowly catching up. It just takes time before someone can make a name for themselves. If you start today, then maybe in five or ten years you would have earned a name. So pay attention, it is only a question of time until women have closed the gap." "Big, Bigger, Texas-Size" http://www.coldsteel.co.uk/articles/tex.html.

3. Japanese has various words for "tattoo," including *irezumi*, *horimono* and *shisei*.

4. Saralyn R. Daly mentions that Donald Keene discusses the presence of foot fetishism in a Kabuki play called *Love Suicides at Sonezaki* (1703) by Chikamatsu Monzaemon. However, while the image of a tattoo as fetish object may be part of Japanese tradition, contemporary Western style tattoos and their influence on Japanese culture may also contribute to the image of woman as fetish object. As Don Ed Hardy points out, during "the late 1980s and early '90s ... a new generation of Japanese youth extended its passionate embrace of 1950s American culture to include classic Western tattoos. These included pinup tattoos (Hardy, "Japanese Tattooing" 63).

5. This film is discussed in greater detail in chapter three in the context of crimes of passion.

6. Other tattoo narratives which depict the theme of imprisonment are discussed more fully in the chapter on prison tattoos.

7. The film version of *The Illustrated Man*, starring Rod Steiger as the marked man, is even more pervasive in its misogynist representation of woman as a femme fatale. It develops the seductive quality of the female tattoo artist more fully than

Bradbury's narrative and demonizes woman for her creative power.

8. Definitions of fantasy, fantastic literature and science fiction are varied; however, for the purposes of this study, Rabkin's concept of the fantastic seems the most inclusive. He defines the fantastic as a continuum which includes elements that are more or less realistic or fantastic. Science fiction is a subgenre on this continuum which may appear closer to the 1 range if it has more realistic elements or closer to the 10 range (defined by Rabkin as fantasy) if it has more fantastic elements. For Rabkin the key feature of the fantastic is the reversal of ground rules that are created within the text. According to Rabkin if there are a large number of reversals or many examples of subversion, the text has a higher degree of fantastic properties and approaches the genre of fantasy. Rabkin's definition of the fantastic therefore argues against the more polarized definitions of science fiction or fantasy that continue to inform popular culture or bookstore shelving practices!

9. "Riot Grrls" was a term used to describe "a loose network of young punk feminists in Washington, D.C., and Olympia, Washington" (Baumgardner and Richards 78). These women scrawled words such as "slut" and "fuck no fat chicks" on their bodies in order to challenge and reclaim phrases that had formerly restricted women (Ibid).

10. Chapter 6 provides further discussion of Tamaki's novel in the context of tattoos and freak culture.

Chapter Three

1. Brooke Stevens' novel *Tattoo Girl* (2001) replicates the captivity tattoo narrative presented in *Skin Art* and *Tattoo* by pairing a male tattoo artist with a woman as the object of his creative desire. However, it revises the convention by highlighting the narrative from the female characters' points of view and by showing the possibility of resistance on the part of the women who are held captive. This novel is examined further in chapter six in the context of freak culture.

2. In *The Tattoo Murder Case* Takagi establishes a parallel between the scarred bodies of Japanese victims of the bombing of Hiroshima and the tattoo.

3. Judith Berke's poem "The Tattoo" suggests images of female empowerment through the tattooing process by presenting a speaker who contributes to the process, unlike Maddy who does not choose to be tattooed. While the poem may be read as a way of subverting the image of a concentration camp tattoo, it also subverts the image of woman as a weak individual. The speaker's tattoo (based on a sketch that the speaker has made) depicts a woman looking up at a dragon, but the woman has claws and talons, thus investing her with the power to protect herself. The speaker of the poem wants everything to "be its opposite" (Berke 23) and likes the way the flames come out of the woman's mouth: "I *said* to the artist, more flames" (24). The ashes also evoke the transformative capacity of the tattoo in renewing identity and in rewriting a narrative of death. The reference to ashes suggests the mythical Phoenix, a bird which rises from the ashes, signifying rebirth. Clearly, the speaker wishes to create an alternative identity for herself by fusing the images of the woman and the dragon, thus creating an image that is more predatory than submissive. While woman as predator may have certain negative associations, in the context of her poem, Berke's hybrid woman/dragon is linked to agency and control. Since the speaker also gives instructions to the male tattoo artist to create more flames and ashes in the image, the poem demonstrates the liberating nature of the tattoo experience when the tattooed individual contributes to the process.

4. This separation of tattoo images into masculine and feminine types seems to be captured in the film version of *Tattoo*, where Karl bears an oriental lion pattern and Maddie, his victim, is tattooed with flowers. Florence Rome suggests that some tattoos may be more indicative of masculine imagery and that women within the yakuza tend to select flowers; however, tattoo patterns are not always divided according to masculine and feminine types. The designs may include images of the lion dog, which is associated with protection and fierceness or the yang concept and con-

trasted with the peony flower (symbolic of yin) for aesthetic balance (Fellman 26). In the case of Karl and Maddy, it is perhaps less important to differentiate between male and female tattoo types than to recognize that he still views Maddy as an extension of his artistic ability. In the film *Blue Tiger* (2000), red and blue tiger tattoos are associated with male and female bodies respectively, but instead of merely complementing one another, these images are part of a battle motif and reinforce a woman's appropriation of a man's tattoo image to serve her own ends. In a sense, the protagonist Gina subverts the sense of machismo that often pervades the yakuza world as well as the scenes in Japanese yakuza films where woman are presented as inferior.

5. Mascia-Lees and Sharpe inappropriately use the name of the actor instead of the name of the fictional character in this quotation.

6. If Maddy as a woman has merely represented an extension of Karl, then she cannot even be granted the agency of committing the act of murder; if we read the text/film as a narcissistic narrative of Karl's desire, then Maddy is only an extension of his aesthetic (appropriated Japanese aesthetic). It is therefore possible to view the final scene as Karl's re-enactment of yet another auto-erotic experience.

7. The lack of control that an individual experiences in relation to a tattoo is also represented in "The Background," a short story by the British writer Saki (H. H. Munro). In this text, a character by the name of Henri Deplis has the Fall of Icarus tattooed on his back by a famous Italian tattooist. However, Deplis loses control of his own work of art, as various institutions attempt to regulate the public display of his body. The story ends with Deplis experiencing an identity crisis: "He nurses the illusion that he is one of the lost arms of the Venus de Milo, and hopes that the French Government may be persuaded to buy him" (Saki 124). Saki's story is an intriguing exploration of how aesthetics can control an individual.

8. The idea of using a tattoo as a sign of ownership is not unique to a heterosexual relationship. In the prison drama *Oz*, the character Vern Schillinger marks his unwilling homosexual love-slave Beecher with a swastika tattoo to indicate that the latter is his property.

9. The parallel between tattoos and the scars of the Vietnam war is also presented in the American novel *Paco's Story* (1986) by Larry Heinemann. As Susan Jeffords indicates in her article "Tattoos, Scars, Diaries, and Writing Masculinity," Paco's body is "tattooed by the war" (Jeffords 208) since it is covered by 'dozens and dozens of swirled-up and curled-round, purple scars, looking like so many sleeping snakes and piles of ruined coins'" (quote from *Paco's Story* (174) as cited in Jeffords 208). His snake-like scars are also similar to the dragon tattoo of one of the members of his platoon, Gallagher. The latter's Bangkok R&R tattoo is a red and black dragon that covers his forearm from his wrist to his elbow.

10. In *Paco's Story* the scarring of American soldiers is equated with the soldiers' rape of a 14-year-old Vietnamese girl who had ambushed their night patrol; however, as in *Skin Art* (where the male artist's suffering is somehow equated with the difficult lives of prostitutes), this parallel is problematic (Jeffords).

11. *The Concubine's Tattoo*, by Laura Joh Rowland, depicts the relationship between Japanese culture, violence, eroticism and tattoos. This contemporary work of Asian-American detective fiction is set in the Japan of the 1690s during the Edo period. The plot involves the murder of Harume, a shogun's concubine, who was poisoned with the ink she used to create a tattoo of the Japanese character *ai*, or Love, in the "private place" of her body. A police investigator, Sano is charged with the mission of solving the murder, with the unsolicited assistance of his young bride, Reiko, who defies the model of the obedient Japanese wife (one of the details that betrays the contemporary bias of this novel, undoubtedly designed to appeal to feminist tendencies in a modern audience). Harume's body creates a current of instability in the novel, which is reinforced through the rocky relationship between Sano and his wife, Reiko, as well as through the power struggle at work within the court at Edo Castle.

12. In *Poetics*, Aristotle's theory of tragedy, he indicates that recognition and reversal are key components of the tragic action or plot. He identifies a variety of forms of recognition, one of which is a scar

or a mark of identification. However, the mark of recognition is also present in the narrative form of the epic, specifically in the *Odyssey*.

13. Kenzo not only kisses Kinue's skin, but he kisses the lips of the sorcerer (Takagi 44). This act has certain homoerotic overtones which add another subversive level to the tattoo.

14. Linda Hutcheon agrees with Susan Sontag, who indicated that a photograph is "both a record of 'reality'" and "a falsification of it" (Hutcheon 57).

15. The notion that a tattoo cannot be erased has been disproven by the development of laser surgery, which has allowed individuals to erase the "mistakes" of the past.

16. *The Concubine's Tattoo* presents a similar link between outlaw status and maternal biology and conditioning. In this novel, the character Harume, a tattooed concubine, unwisely consorted with Danzaemon, the chief of the *eta*, "a man whose outcast status had appealed to the low taste Harume had learned from her mother" (Rowland 274). The *eta*, as explained in the novel, were corpse handlers "who robbed body parts from the dead" to sell to brothel servants (272).

17. The magical "tattoo" in the Ranma anime video *Tattoo You* (based on the graphic novels of Rumiko Takahashi) establishes the parallel between the tattoo and calligraphy, thus blending the concepts of painting, writing and tattooing. In *Tattoo You* (based on the chapter "The Mark of the Gods" in Book 1/2 of the Ranma series) Ryoga finds himself lost in the forest and fights what initially appears to be a demon but ends up being an old hermit. After consuming all of Ranma's food, the old man examines Ryoga's abdomen and tells him that there is an energy center below the belly button in an individual. He claims that he can turn Ryoga into the world's strongest man with the assistance of martial arts calligraphy. The hermit then proceeds to dip a giant paintbrush in black ink and paint a design on Ryoga's abdomen. However, this act of painting is not exactly calligraphy, because Ryoga's painful reaction to the marking is presented more like a reaction to the burning or engraving of the flesh experienced during the process of tattooing.

18. Bridget Elliott and Anthony Purdy describe Greenaway as "a literary as well as a painterly director" ("Artificial Eye/Artificial You" 179).

19. Much of my analysis will concentrate on Greenaway's 1994 script rather than on the final film version, because the script contains translations of various texts that appear in the film in Japanese. Furthermore, as the director indicates, the 1994 script which was originally presented to the film's producer offers the reader/viewer "a fuller exposition of the intentions for the film rather than a script-description of the film itself" (Greenaway 11). Notwithstanding some of these differences, both the finished film and the script alone explore the intertwining of writing as a kind of painting (and tattooing) on the body in the context of Japanese and other cultures.

20. I am drawing on Marshall McLuhan's famous statement, "The Medium is the Message."

21. Hearn was influenced by many cultures: he was the son of an Anglo-Irish father and a Greek mother, was raised in Ireland, moved to Ohio at the age of nineteen, and lived in Japan. His book *Kwaidan* was published in 1904.

22. The image of Utamoro as a resistance figure illustrates how the concept of resistance shifts according to a historical moment. Today many of Utamoro's images of feminine beauty have become part of the Japanese mainstream and are evident in a multitude of visual art forms from prints to calendars to pottery. In the American film *Tattoo*, the tattoo artist who captures a woman and tattoos her body has an interest in Utamoro's art.

23. In *Tattoo*, Karl paints the bodies of fashion models before he abducts one of them and marks her with a permanent tattoo. He is also an admirer of the artist Utamoro.

24. This inability to remove a painted image is also presented in the *Ranma* anime film *Tattoo You*. A hermit dips a giant paintbrush in black ink and paints a design on a character's abdomen. However, Ryoga's painful reaction to the marking is presented more like a reaction to the burning or engraving of the flesh experienced during the process of tattooing. While the mark is never actually called a tattoo in the first part

of the *Tattoo You* episode, it has all the ear-marks of this art form. It is impossible to wipe off or remove with water or ordinary human methods.

25. As Angela Dalle Vacche has pointed out, and as discussed earlier in this chapter, *The Pillow Book* may also owe some of its imagery to the story of Hoichi the ear-less in the Japanese film *Kwaidan*, based on the stories of Lafcadio Hearn. In the story of Hoichi, a musician is bewitched by spirits to play to his music. In order to prevent this from continuing, one of the Buddhist priests writes a holy text on Hoichi's body to protect him. Unfortunately, he forgets to write on Hoichi's ears, which are taken away by the spirit. This scene of the painted and mutilated body has interesting parallels with the concept of mutilating a tattooed woman's body in Takagi's novel as well as with Greenaway's depiction of transform-ing a dead body into a book.

26. Despite the reluctance of tattoo artists to tattoo the name of a person's lover on their body, people still request this type of tattoo, only to have it removed or changed later. One high profile case was that of the actress Angelina Jolie, who had the name of her former lover, Billy Bob Thornton, removed.

Chapter Four

1. In addition to signifying gang mem-bership or inmate status in literature, film and television, the tattoo is also linked to membership in a political resistance group. The character of Chakotay in the *Star Trek Voyager* series, Commander Janeway's right-hand man, is a character of aboriginal de-scent who bears a facial tattoo. The show establishes Chakotay as a figure of resist-ance because of his membership in a resist-ance group called the Maqui who lived along the border of Federation space. When a race called the Kardassians started to ex-pand, the Federation gave the Kardassians some of the space in the borderlands, but the Maqui refused to give any of their land to the Kardassians. Chakotay's tattoo thus reminds the viewer of his past involvement in this resistance activity.

2. Florence Rome views the yakuza as nothing less than fascist (214).

3. An interesting development in an-other contemporary Japanese-made yakuza film is the complete absence of the Japanese tattoo. In *Tokyo Mafia: Yakuza Wars* (1995), for example, there is frequent use of the rit-ual of finger mutilation, a common practice among yakuza as a way of repaying a debt as well as a sign of sadistic punishment. However, tattoos are nowhere to be found. Could this be the result of making these films less "strange" to Western audiences and increasing the marketability of a film? Perhaps the filmmakers believed that the non-tattooed yakuza is a more generic kind of gangster character who might prove more appealing to an American or Euro-pean mainstream audience than a tattooed oddity? Whatever the reason, the absence of the tattoo suggests a departure from the previous image of the tattoo as a sign of Japanese difference or distinctiveness.

4. The American film *American Yakuza* (1994) also focuses on outsider figures and links them to the world of tattoos. In this yakuza film an American by the name of Nick ends up working for the yakuza after he saves one of their men from an attack. Nick is one quarter Native American and is described as "a bit of a loner"; perhaps be-cause of his time in prison and because of his American Indian heritage, he is an out-sider. Similarly, the Japanese yakuza are a "foreign" element in a world where the Mafia have established a presence in organ-ized crime. Tattoos do not occupy a signi-ficant place in this film, but they do link different members of outsider communi-ties. For example, the tattoo identifies the strangeness of one yakuza individual and his willingness to endure pain: "the guy's certainly not afraid of needles." Nick also acquires a tattoo as he becomes a member of the Tendo yakuza family, in order to join this group of outsiders. The tattoo thus serves as a symbol that suggests that he too will endure pain.

5. Florence Rome points out that some women who belong to yakuza circles also acquire tattoos, although she doubts that "there are 'his' and 'hers' patterns" (55). She states that the "lady yakuza patterns run more frequently to flowers and leaves and quiet figures of Buddha, with maybe a ser-

pent or so entwined throughout" (55). As Rome suggests, Japanese tattoo patterns are not always divided according to masculine and feminine types. The designs may include images of the lion dog, which is associated with protection and fierceness or the yang concept, and which is contrasted with the peony flower, symbolic of yin for aesthetic balance (Fellman, "The Japanese Tattoo" 26). An image of the dog and the flower may be placed on the male body.

6. This film was updated in the form of a later film, *Black Rain* (1989), starring Michael Douglas as a more "hip" Robert Mitchum character. However, while the film works hard at suggesting images of resistance through biker culture, the tattoo content is reduced even further to a few images of yakuza with body tattoos.

7. Despite the positive relationship between Harry and his Japanese friend, the film still seems to favor an American perspective. Mitchum's character returns to the U.S., and the film appears to uphold the message that Japanese culture is strange and foreign. In this sense *The Yakuza* reinforces the observations made by Harry's younger partner in the bathhouse: in Japan "everything's in reverse."

8. The tattoos of the yakuza signify a kind of deadly beauty, since those who bear these magnificent works of art on their bodies may also carry out heinous acts. In Chris McKinney's novel *The Tattoo*, a former gang member's tattoo signifies not only a memory of past violence, but also a desire to put a stop to the kind of violence that characterized his past. The tattoo that he acquires in prison, however, is not a traditional Japanese style tattoo like that of a yakuza, but a Japanese kanji symbol of *The Book of the Void*. In a sense this kanji tattoo serves as a way of subverting his past. While it still evokes a connection to his Japanese identity, it is not the conventional Japanese tattoo, and it symbolizes his desire to end the violence that has marked his family line. As Claudia, his former lover and mother of his son, realizes, the tattoo is not about the void in his life, but it represents "the fate of the son he would not raise" and a way of severing the ancestral threat "infected by a lineage of hate and pride" (McKinney 227). It is also interesting to note that some Japanese tattoo purists do not consider a kanji

tattoo to be a true Japanese tattoo. Michihiro Kono, a Raleigh, North Carolina, restauranteur from Japan, has said that "A true Japanese tattoo has meaning. Kanji is not a Japanese tattoo; it's just a tattoo" ("Kanji tattoos prickle traditionalists" E3). Perhaps the choice of the kanji tattoo reflects Ken's distancing himself from Japanese tradition. While Ken intends to sever contact with his family, he does so as a kind of sacrifice, and the tattoo is not so much a way of preserving cultural heritage as it is his way of protecting his son from experiencing a similar life of violence.

9. A film such as *Blue Tiger* (1994) redirects the focus away from the male yakuza to the image of a tattooed woman who becomes part of a yakuza network. In this film, the narrative of resistance is developed when a mother by the name of Gina Hayes witnesses the death of her son, who is shot by a Japanese yakuza. The latter bears a tattoo on his chest depicting a red tiger. Gina seeks revenge and decides to enter the world of the yakuza, eventually acquiring a tattoo of a blue tiger, the counterpart and rival of the red tiger according to Japanese legend. Her entry into the culture of the yakuza as a hostess in a club is reinforced through the acquisition of the tattoo according to the traditional, more painful technique of Japanese tattooing with multiple needles. Interestingly enough, the procedure is executed by an American tattoo artist, played by Harry Dean Stanton, perhaps as a way of highlighting the American perspective in the film. What this film does have in common with other yakuza narratives is that it depicts the world of chaos juxtaposed against tattoo imagery that highlights the aesthetic of balance and symmetry that are part of Japanese tattoos as well as the cultural aesthetic and ethos of the yakuza world.

10. The act of acquiring a tattoo may document the various experiences (birth, dreams, puberty, marriage) that are part of the narrative of life. There are countless examples of how the tattoo functions as a rite of passage; in his study *Tattooing and Face and Body Painting of the Thompson Indians, British Columbia*, James A. Teit writes that tattooing was carried out in connection with marriage and puberty and was also used as a sign of courage. In addition they

were used as a way of marking the significance of dreams (406).

11. Paradoxically, the increase in violence initiated by young women within and outside the school system over the last few decades seems to have coincided with one of the victories of feminism: more freedom of expression and independence for women.

12. In *Never Again*, agent Scully acquires a tattoo of an oroboros or a snake eating its own tail. However, she is accompanied by her new found love interest who watches her as she is tattooed. The scene is highly erotic. The act of the needle penetrating her skin and her reaction to the needle are intended to simulate or anticipate a sexual act between Scully and her lover.

13. Goldie also has a white "mother" in the film, so either she is adopted or one of her parents is a stepparent.

14. Oates' novel does suggest more creative reconstruction on the part of Maddy, perhaps because so much of the text is dominated by Maddy's first person perspective. The novel emphasizes Maddy's writing process through chapter titles such as "The Plot (I)" and "The Plot (II)" and the uncertainty surrounding the whereabouts of Legs, her friend and a car: "Maybe Legs and V.V. crossed the border into Canada?— hid LIGHTNING BOLT where it was never found, and fled on foot?" (321).

15. Angelina Jolie is the American actress who plays Legs Sadovsky, and she has a number of her own tattoos. Her tattoos include a dragon on her left arm, the letter "H" on her wrist, a Tennessee Williams quote on her forearm, a cross on her hip, a Latin motto on her abdomen, a blue rectangle on her black (Gerard 32). She used to have the words "Billy Bob" on her arm, which she had covered up after she broke up with her actor/director husband Billy Bob Thornton.

16. The relationship between membership in a gang and the prison experience is presented in Chris McKinney's novel *The Tattoo*. The frame story (excluding the epilogue) presents a prisoner by the name of Cal who tattoos a prisoner of Japanese descent called Ken. Most of the embedded narrative consists of Ken's story of his life of crime as told within the walls of Halwa Prison in Hawaii. One sign of Ken's rebellious life as a youth in Hawaii is evident in his tattoo, which bears the letters SYN, an abbreviation of the word syndicate (7). This cements his image as a member of a gang of youth who also harbors a hatred for *haoles* (or white people). His involvement in the gang may have been instigated by the beatings he received from his father. It is therefore doubly ironic that he has a tattoo of his family crest carved into his skin by a white tattoo artist.

17. In his study of the tattoo in Japan, Donald McCallum indicates that there is "very little information about tattooing during the historical periods from ca. 600–1600" (118). However, he mentions that W. R. van Gulik (*Irezumi: The Pattern of Dermatography in Japan*, 1982) refers to the Jōei Code of 1232, which has a reference to facial tattooing as a punishment (McCallum, Note 17).

18. In the DVD of *Oz: The Complete First Season* (2002), Fontana discusses how he offered up his own arm for the Oz tattoo that is shown during the opening titles. According to the Bar Association of Erie County *Bulletin*, Fontana's tattoo was created by a prison tattoo artist (BAEC *Bulletin*).

19. A community is usually defined according to the shared or common beliefs of the people within this social structure; however, it is also possible to view a community in terms of how its members define themselves as different from other groups or communities. This emphasis on difference seems to characterize the gangs or groups within *Oz*.

20. The official HBO site for *Oz* lists a bulletin board called *em city* and an Oz newsletter called "The Warden's Office Newsletter." http://www.hbo.com/oz/community.

21. One would expect many prison tattoos to be quite crude in their design because of the self-fashioning of tattoo materials and the amateur status of these tattooists. Yet this is not always the case. Photographs of some prison tattoos displayed in Madame Chinchilla's book *Stewed, Screwed and Tattooed* indicate some carefully crafted and complex designs as well as designs that are simpler with crude outlines. Many of the tattoos in *Oz* are aesthetically quite professional in appearance and are a far cry from the crude tattoos of some non-fictional

inmates, perhaps because some of these tattoos could have been acquired before these prisoners even entered *Oz*.

22. The character's act of cannibalism is a subversive replication of the communion scene when he accepts a wafer (the body of Christ) from the prison priest.

23. Hill's use of language is not precise here, because technically Emerald City is a section of the general prison called Oz

Chapter Five

1. For those not familiar with the history of hockey in Canada, Gordie Howe was one of the sport's greatest players.

2. A tattooed arm is also mentioned in Judith Berke's poem "The Tattoo" (1989); however, in this poem, the focus is on a new back tattoo. While this poem does not focus on a concentration camp experience in great detail, it does refer to a "camp" experience and to the fact that the speaker already has a tattoo on her arm, although it is not clear what kind of tattoo this might be: "The artist said we shouldn't detract / from the one on my arm" (1–2). The speaker of the poem, who is probably a woman, describes the process of acquiring a new tattoo on her back. This new tattoo depicts both a dragon and a woman and seems to subvert the memories of her camp experience when she had to move different parts of her body "to keep the muscle /from dying" (14–15). One reason to read Berke's poem in the context of a concentration camp is that the author has also written a poem and created a sculpture about Dachau.

3. Tatana Kellner's exhibition (*71125: Fifty Years of Silence* and *B-11226: Fifty Years of Silence*, Rosedale Women's Studio Workshop, 1992, 1994) consists of two books which include covers displaying images of fragmented arms that bear numerical tattoos. The books include words as well as "pictures on the alternating translucent and opaque pages of each book" (90). "In the middle of each book is the cast of an arm, whose making also required collaboration. The daughter had to ask her parents' permission to take casts and photograph the tattoos so as to be able to copy them ex-

actly onto the pink, handmade paper surface" (Hirsch and Suleiman 92).

4. Steinfeld also has another story about imprisonment that includes a brief reference to an arm tattoo. In "Anton Chekov Was Never in Charlottetown," he presents a former inmate who has a tattoo of a left arm on his right arm. "A tattoo of my deleted left arm. Not the greatest tattoo, but I wanted it badly at the time. About a year after the real one was deleted" (28). Here the tattoo also symbolizes an absent narrative just as Sam's tattoo is an attempt to record the narrative of his parent's concentration camp experience.

5. In acquiring a death-camp tattoo, Eve engages in a feminist act of challenging a masculine aesthetic that dominates tattoo culture (see chapter 2 on tattoos and a feminist aesthetic). Her tattoo is not typical of "feminine" floral designs that are still identified with women's tattoos. Because it is a number rather than an image, its aesthetic value is also questioned just as the tattoo artist questions Sam's choice of a blue numerical tattoo in "The Apostate's Tattoo." For example, her book editors think that the tattoo is ugly. In this sense, she is promoting an aesthetic of the ugly, which has been discussed as a feminist alternative to masculinist-inscribed notions of beauty (see Halprin's "*Look at My Ugly Face!*").

6. There seems to be one individual who does find Eve's tattoo desirable; he is a young musician who is "turned on" by Eve's story (Prager 102).

7. The tattoo narratives of breast cancer survivors are discussed in greater detail in chapter 2.

8. Tattooing has been practiced by numerous aboriginal cultures around the world for centuries. The Ainu, the indigenous inhabitants of Hokkaido in Japan, had a long history of tattooing (McCallum 118). Tribal tattoos have affirmed traditions, including the celebration of native spirituality, and may be viewed as a visual manner of communicating the beliefs and stories of aboriginal people. The Haida Indians of Canada of the nineteenth and early twentieth centuries had a range of animal symbols such as the wolf, the salmon, the thunderbird, and the bear that were commonly used as tattoo designs (Drew 73). According to Arnold Rubin, the Haida's tattoos

covered "the backs of the hands and upper surfaces of the feet, both arms from wrists to shoulders, chests, thighs and lower legs, and sometimes also cheeks and back" ("Introduction: Native America" 179).

9. Adrienne Kaeppler indicates that in Hawaiian culture, "Tattoo was also a genealogical commemorative device, especially of the death of important related persons of high rank" (169). Among the Haida Indians, various designs on their art and on their bodies "showed the owner's status and lineage affiliation was of prime importance" (Drew 72).

10. As Oettermann points out in his article on tattooed entertainers, Rutherford's narrative appeared as a biography in 1830 under the title *The Great White Chief John Rutherford* and "was the source of some confusion in the historiography of New Zealand" (198–99).

11. The Maori have been depicted in New Zealand film as early as 1913. *Loved by a Maori Chieftess* (1913), *Hinemoa* (1914), *How Chief Te Ponga Won His Bride* (1913), and *Maori Maid's Love* (1916) are some of the earliest films in this country's history, although — as is the case with many early films — no known footage of these films is available (Martin and Edwards). A photograph from the 1914 George Tarr film *Hinemoa* (Martin and Edwards 23) reveals an image of a Maori woman with a chin tattoo. However, other photographs depicting Maori characters from early films for which no known footage exists show faces that are unmarked. Perhaps the absence of facial tattoos on these actors reflected the Western aesthetic of the films' non-Maori creators. Even though Maori content has been a quite common feature of New Zealand films, it was not until 1987 that a Maori directed a film. Barry Barclay's *Ngati* (1987) was the first Maori-directed film, and *Mauri* (1988) is the first fiction feature to be directed by a Maori woman, Merata Mita (Martin and Edwards 14). The 1980s and '90s also witnessed an increase in the participation of Maori in the filmmaking process and the writing of fiction and, with this, films and fiction that resist earlier models dominated by non-Maori filmmakers. Some of the films in particular use representations of Maori tattoos as reflections of an aboriginal tradition and as a way of il-

lustrating narratives of resistance in a colonial or post-colonial context.

12. For Maoris, revenge was only one component of the word "utu." The word is also used in the context of a "reciprocal exchange" or return payment during the exchange of gifts (Salmond 176).

13. Peter Gathercole indicates that Maori moko or facial tattoos are also present on carved figures, especially the figures of Maori ancestors, which are ideal beings. He argues that the ancestor moko is a kind of ideal social personality and that, in acquiring a moko tattoo, the Maori are attempting to represent this ideal social personality in a symbolic manner (176).

14. H. G. Robley presents a variety of historical accounts of the process of moko tattooing but focuses on the nineteenth century improvements: "In the earliest days chisel work was the only method employed in tattooing; but later on the system of pricking was introduced and allowed the artist far more scope for his elaboration of detail. The general practice of operators in moko undoubtedly was however to dip the Uhi or chisel into the colouring matter before incising the skin, so that the process of cutting and colouring went on at the same time; the chisel was then withdrawn, wiped clean, and dipped again in the pigment for another insertion. Polack says: 'The process was one of intense pain, the recumbent figure of the victim wincing and writhing at every stroke of the operator and quivering under the torments inflicted'" (50).

15. Each of these lines has a corresponding name in the Maori language: TE KAWE: six lines on each side of chin. TE PUHAWAE: lines on the chin. NGA REREPI and NGA NGATAREWA: lines on bridge of nose. NGA KOKIRI: curved line on cheekbone. NGA TITI: lines on centre of forehead. (Robley 69–70). Tattoo artist Hanky Panky relates how the facial divisions of a Maori tattoo also signify different features: "your temples tell your rank or position in life. Cheekbones: the lines of your rank; where you came from, who your father was" (Vale and Juno 144).

16. The aunt of the girl who is murdered by Te Wheke also has a Maori tattoo, but, perhaps because of her affiliation with the non-Maori or perhaps because of her gender, she is spared the kind of demonization

that characterizes the depiction of Te Wheke.

17. In her summary of the film version of *Once Were Warriors*, Helen Martin indicates that "in adapting Alan Duff's controversial 1990 novel the producer, director and screenwriter felt that the story in which two of the Heke children die, Jake is implicated as his daughter's rapist and Beth is as negligent as her husband, was too bleak to form the basis for a successful feature film. Thus the focus was shifted from aggressive Jake, dispossessed of his culture and inarticulate in his rage, to his wife, Beth, who stays with Jake because, despite the violence and abuse, she still loves him. In changing her priorities Beth becomes the catalyst through whom change and hope for a better future can be effected when the cycle of violence is broken" (Martin and Edwards 175).

18. Henk Schiffmacher states that tattoos serve as a form of protection for various societies: "among the Berbers and Samoans, for example, you can get tattooed against rheumatism ... The Eskimos and North American Indians covered the skin with signs to protect against disease" (Schiffmacher and Riemschneider 11–12).

19. The partial moko style tattoo on the face of Chakotay in the television series *Star Trek: Voyager* has a positive function. In the episode called "Tattoo," Chakotay's mark functions as an alternative or alien form of language that paradoxically bridges gaps in communication with an alien race who had disabled *Voyager*, Chakotay's spaceship. The aliens' facial markings are similar to Chakotay's. They recognize his tattoo because they had visited Earth and disseminated their culture and language to the aboriginal inhabitants of Chakotay's culture. Chakotay thus becomes an empowered mediator figure whose cultural hybridity ties him to at least two groups. He has knowledge of the cultural traditions of the aliens as well as familiarity with the culture of *Voyager*. Thus his dual cultural status allows him to resolve a conflict between two worlds. His tattoo serves as a symbol of cultural memory and cultural difference from the rest of the *Voyager* crew while simultaneously connecting him to the many other different people and races that make up the *Voyager* crew.

20. In contemporary society, there are ongoing examples of how the tattoo is an extension of historical interaction with non-native colonizers and a sign of aboriginal empowerment. For example, the rise in popularity of tribal style tattoos reflects a new appreciation for aboriginal cultures among non-aboriginal people and has resulted in a new kind of cultural economy for indigenous tattoo artists. In Tahiti, the board of tourism invited tattoo artists and photographers from around the world to an International Tattoo Festival, April 28–30, 2000 (Zulueta 24–34). Many non–Tahitians acquired tribal tattoos. This is one example of how traditional tribal tattooing is turning into a commercial venture for indigenous cultures; however, at the same time, aboriginal people have expressed concerns about the commercialization and appropriation of traditional designs by non-aboriginals. The Haida (who live on the northwest coast of Canada) and other aboriginal groups have viewed the use of aboriginal designs by the mainstream fashion industry as an example of cultural appropriation.

21. This marginalization of women by aboriginal men living in post-colonial societies such as New Zealand and Canada may be due to the imposition of a Western patriarchal system onto native societies. This new system often changed the interaction between men and women. In traditional native societies, women were generally treated with greater respect.

22. In the film, a Maori lawyer introduces the art of Maori dance and spear fighting to Boogie but says that he carries his spear inside, thus suggesting a shift in the kind of strategy that the Maori must adopt in a post-colonial world.

Chapter Six

1. Portions of this chapter were previously published in Karin Beeler's "Visualizing Difference: Tattoos and Cultural Alternatives in Canadian Writing and Film." In *The Canadian Alternative*, edited by Klaus Martens. Würzburg: Königshausen & Neumann, 2003. Permission has been granted to reproduce sections of the article.

2. "Eric's Drunken Tattoo" first aired May 1, 2001. (http://www.tvtome.com/tvt ome/servlet/GuidePageServlet/showid-246/ epid-40452/

3. The subversion that takes place in "Eric's Drunken Tattoo" establishes the tattoo as an element of resistance. Eric's desire to acquire a tattoo was the result of his reading the diary of his girlfriend Donna. In this narrative, she had wished that Eric had a more dangerous side. He tries to realize this narrative but is ultimately left with a tattoo that falls short of this desire. In an earlier segment, the "stoned" character who creates the tattoo (played by Tommy Chong) also makes the mistake of tattooing "Debbie" rather than "Donna" on Eric's buttock and must re-write the tattoo.

4. The etiological tale provides a description of how a particular phenomenon occurred. For example, in many myths, there are narratives surrounding the coloration of an animal (e.g., how the robin acquired a red breast) or why a certain natural formation exists.

5. Fantastic narratives such as the *X-Files* episodes "Never Again" and "Humbug" offer images of the tattoo in conjunction with the supernatural. Other examples of fantastic narratives that include tattoo content are horror series such *The Hitchhiker Series* and *Night Visions*. "The Curse" (Episode 19 in The Hitchhiker Series) and "The Bokor" (a tale from the series *Night Visions*) highlight the magical properties of a tattoo as an element of otherness. In the Hitchhiker episode "The Curse," the owner of an apartment building discovers the mysterious appearance of a snake tattoo on his body and meets two different women who are actually the same person. In the *Night Visions* episode "The Bokor," a group of medical students work on a cadaver that has the tattoo of a voodoo priest. Apparently the tattoo prevents the cadaver from returning to life (Huddleston http://www. scifi.com/sfw/issue220/screen4.html).

6. The creation of the freak is not only a naturally occurring phenomenon (e.g., a freak of nature) but also a product of self-creation or choice. One has only to think of the seemingly extreme alleged cosmetic surgery of a performer such as Michael Jackson to realize that this is the case. An individual by the name of Erik Sprague has

also re-created his body to resemble that of a reptile. The "reptile man" has had "his teeth sharpened, bumps implanted into his forehead and green scales tattooed across his face and body in his quest to become a reptile" (*Prince George* (B.C.) *Citizen*, Friday, December 17, 1999: 39)

7. In a paper that he delivered at the Popular Culture Association conference in April 2000, Peter Goldstein focussed on the thematic use of the line "The Truth is out there" in the series. His paper "The Truth Is Out There, Sort Of: Darin Morgan's Scripts for *The X-Files*" included a discussion of the "Humbug" episode.

8. The fish became associated with Christ because, in Greek, a combination of the letters in the phrase Iesous CHristos Theou HUioS, or Jesus Christ, Son of God, Savior, spell the word for fish (ICHTHUS) (*Tattoo Girl* 103).

9. It is important to note that Gray discusses the concept of the tattoo's difference in the context of those who have "chosen to have an image indelibly stamped on his or her hide" (14). Emma's tattoo, on the other, hand is doubly different, because her tattoo was imposed upon her.

10. Pastor Joe/Grecco resembles the character of Harry Powell in *The Night of the Hunter* (1955). Powell is also a mad preacher figure. Like Pastor Joe/Grecco he is a freak, and he is linked to tattoos since he has the word love tattooed on his right hand and word hate on his left hand.

11. Embedded in Lucy's story is the mystery surrounding the baby that was taken from her at birth and put up for adoption (Stevens 70). The whereabouts of this lost child remain a mystery, but Emma becomes the symbolic replacement for it.

12. See note 19 in chapter 5.

13. Ross quotes Jennifer Terry, who refers to "xenophobic Cold War texts attacking homosexuality as a psychological condition that threatened the security of the family and the nation" (Ross 569).

14. In an article about Tamaki, Susan G. Cole says that "though she has a Japanese name, she hasn't got much of a stake in that identity. She adopted Mariko, her second name, when she was old enough to reject her first" name, which was Karen (Cole).

15. As a contributor to the multicultural work *Telling It: Women and Language across*

Cultures, lesbian writer Betsy Warland has argued that lesbianism is a culture.

16. Montana's name also suggests that Americans are part of Canada's multicultural context.

17. Even though *Skin Deep* appears to present a truly interactive world of cultural minorities, it still suggests that marginalization of specific individuals takes place (Alex's dismissal of Montana) and that ethnic minorities are somehow identified with freak culture. The longstanding history of viewing various races in the context of freak culture is too involved to discuss within the confines of this book; however, *Skin Deep* suggests this kind of identification while also attempting to dismantle the concept that freak culture and marginalized otherness are somehow stable or unchanging categories.

Bibliography and Filmography

Adams, Rachel. *Sideshow U.S.A.: Freaks and the American Cultural Imagination.* Chicago: University of Chicago Press, 2001.

American Yakuza. Dir. Frank Cappello. Overseas Filmgroup, 1993.

Anderson, Clare. "*Godna*: Inscribing Indian Convicts in the Nineteenth Century." In *Written on the Body,* edited by Jane Caplan, 102–117. Princeton: Princeton University Press, 2000.

Aristotle. *Poetics.* Trans. James Hutton. New York: Norton, 1982.

Bantock, Nick. *Griffin & Sabine: An Extraordinary Correspondence.* Vancouver, B.C.: Raincoast, 1991.

Bar Association of Erie County, (PA) Bulletin http://www.eriebar.org/bulletin/april_98/tomfontana.html, 22 July 2002.

Barnes, Linda. *The Snake Tattoo.* New York: Fawcett Crest, 1989.

Barthes, Roland. *Camera Lucida: Reflections on Photography.* Trans. Richard Howard. New York: Hill and Wang, 1981.

Baumgardner, Jennifer, and Amy Richards. *Manifesta: Young Women, Feminism, and the Future.* New York: Farrar, Straus and Giroux, 2000.

Beeler, Karin. "Visualizing Difference: Tattoos and Cultural Alternatives in Canadian Writing and Film." In *The Canadian Alternative,* edited by Klaus Martens, 133–42 Würzburg: Königshausen & Neumann, 2003.

_____, and Kelly Wintemute. *Tattoo Study: The Cultural, Symbolic and Social Significance of Tattoos in a University Community.* Prince George: English Department, University of Northern British Columbia, 2001.

Benson, Raymond. *The Man with the Red Tattoo.* London: Hodder and Stoughton, 2002.

Berke, Judith. "The Tattoo." *Massachusetts Review* (Winter 1989): 570.

"Big, Bigger, Texas-Size." http://www.coldsteel.co.uk/articles/tex.html.

Black Rain. Dir. Ridley Scott. Paramount, 1989.

Blue Tiger. Dir. Norberto Barba. Overseas Filmgroup, 1994; First Look Pictures, 2000.

Bradbury, Ray. *The Illustrated Man.* New York: Bantam, 1951.

Brady, Elizabeth. *Marian Engel and Her Works.* Toronto: ECW Press, 1987.

Brother. Dir. Takeshi Kitano. Cinema Club, 2000.

Buck, Sir Peter. *The Coming of the Maori.* 2d ed. Wellington, 1950. Cited in *Marks of Civilization,* edited by Arnold Rubin, 175. Los Angeles, Regents of the University of California, 1988.

Buss, Helen. *Mapping Ourselves: Canadian*

211

Women's Autobiogrphy. Montreal and Kingston: McGill-Queen's University Press, 1993.

Cape Fear. Dir. Martin Scorsese. Universal City Studios and Amblin Entertainment, 1991.

Caplan, Jane, ed. *Written on the Body: The Tattoo in European and American History.* Princeton: Princeton University Press, 2000.

Chevalier, Jean, and Alain Gheerbrant. *The Penguin Dictionary of Symbols.* Trans. John Buchanan-Brown. London: Penguin, 1996.

Chinchilla, Madame. *Stewed, Screwed and Tattooed.* Mendocino, CA: Isadore, 1997.

Chong, Denise. *The Concubine's Children.* Toronto: Penguin, 1994.

Clayton, Jay. "Narrative and Theories of Desire." *Critical Inquiry* 16.1 (Autumn 1989): 33–53.

Cole, Susan G. "Mariko Tamaki: Fearless Freak Gets Cheeky Tounges (*sic*) Wagging with High-Octane, Sexually Charged Performance." *Now* 20.19 (January 11–17, 2001). Http://www.nowtoronto.com/issues/2002–01011/cover.htm.

Crapanzano, Vincent. *Hermes' Dilemma and Hamlet's Desire: On the Epistemology of Interpretation.* London: Harvard University Press, 1992.

Dahl, Roald. "Skin." In *Someone Like You,* 108–26. London: Michael Joseph, 1961.

Dalle Vacche, Angela. *Cinema and Painting: How Art Is Used in Film.* Austin: University of Texas Press, 1996.

Daly, Saralyn R. "Tanizaki's West: A Fable of the Occident." In *Discovering the Other: Humanities East and West,* edited by Robert S. Ellwood, 103–21 Malibu: Undena, 1984.

DeMello, Margo. *Bodies of Inscription: A Cultural History of the Modern Tattoo Community.* Durham: Duke University Press, 2000.

"Les Derniers Géants." http://www.france-assoc.com/homeje/g8/num, 30 April 2001.

Drew, Leslie. *Haida: Their Art and Culture.* Surrey and Blaine: Hancock House, 1982.

Duff, Alan. *Once Were Warriors.* New York: Vintage Books, 1990.

"Easter Island tattoos." http://www.netaxs.com/~trance/tattoo.html.

Elliot, Bridget, and Anthony Purdy. "Artificial Eye/Artificial You: Getting Greenaway or Mything the Point?" In *Literature and the Body,* edited by Anthony Purdy, 179–211. Amsterdam: Rodopi, 1992.

_____. *Peter Greenaway: Architecture and Allegory.* Chichester: Academy Editions, 1997.

Emerson, Earl. *The Million-Dollar Tattoo.* New York: Ballantine Books, 1996.

Engel, Marian. "The Tattooed Woman." In *The Tattooed Woman,* Markham: 3–9. Penguin, 1985.

Epstein, Julia. "Remember to Forget: The Problem of Traumatic Cultural Memory." In Julia Epstein and Lori Hope Lefkovitz, *Shaping Losses,* 186–204. Urbana: University of Illinois Press, 2001.

_____, and Lori Hope Lefkovitz. *Shaping Losses: Cultural Memory and the Holocaust.* Urbana and Chicago: University of Illinois Press, 2001.

Fellman, Sandi. *The Japanese Tattoo.* New York: Cross River Press, 1986.

Fischer, Lucy. "*Irezumi*: Tattoo, Taboo, and the Female Body." *Post script* 18:1 (1998) 11–23.

Foxfire. Dir. Annette Haywood-Carter. Columbia Tristar Home Entertainment, 1996.

Gammel, Irene, ed. *Confessional Politics: Women's Sexual Self-Representations in Life Writing and Popular Media.* Carbondale: Southern Illinois University Press, 1999.

Gathercole, Peter. "Contexts of Maori Moko." in *Marks of Civilization,* edited by Arnold Rubin, 171–77. Los Angeles: University of California, 1988.

Gay, Jason. "The Stink Over Ink: Two New Efforts to Legalize Tattooing in Massachusetts." *Boston Phoenix*, October 14–21, 1999.

Gell, Alfred. *Wrapping in Images: Tattooing in Polynesia.* Oxford: Clarendon, 1993.

Gerard, Jim. *Celebrity Skin: Tattoos, Brands and Body Adornments of the Stars*. New York: Thunder's Mouth, 2001.

Goldie, Terry. *Fear and Temptation: The Image of the Indigene in Canadian, Australian, and New Zealand Literatures*. Montreal and Kingston: McGill-Queen's University Press, 1989.

Goodheart, Eugene. *Desire and Its Discontents*. New York: Columbia University Press, 1991.

Gray, John. *I Love Mom: An Irreverent History of the Tattoo*. Toronto: Key Porter Books, 1994.

Greenaway, Peter. *The Pillow Book*. Paris: Dis Voir, 1996.

Hall, James. *Illustrated Dictionary of Symbols in Eastern and Western Art*. N.P.: IconEditions, 1994.

Halprin, Sara. *"Look at My Ugly Face!": Myths and Musings on Beauty and Other Perilous Obsessions with Women's Appearance*. New York: Penguin, 1995.

Hardy, Don Ed. *Life and Death Tattoos. Tattoo time* 4. Honolulu: Hardy Marks Publications, 1993.

_____, and The Drawing Center. *Pierced Hearts and True Love: A Century of Drawings for Tattoos*. New York and Honolulu: The Drawing Center and Hardy Marks Publications, 1995.

_____. "Japanese Tattooing: Legacy and Essence." In Don Ed Hardy, *Pierced Hearts and True Love*, 58–71. New York and Honolulu: The Drawing Center and Hardy Marks Publications, 1995.

Härting, Heike. "'Chokecherry Tree(s): Operative Modes of Metaphor in Toni Morrison's 'Beloved.'" *Ariel* 29.4 (October 1998): 23–51.

Hays, Lee. *Tattoo*. New York: Pinnacle, 1981.

Hearn, Lafcadio. "The Story of Miminashi-hoichi." *Kwaidan: Stories and Studies of Strange Things*. Http://www.mtroyal.ab.ca/gaslight/kwaidanB.htm.

Heffernan, James A. W. *Museum of Words: The Poetics of Ekphrasis from Homer to Ashbery*. Chicago: University of Chicago Press, 1994.

Hein, Hilde. "The Role of Feminist Aesthetics in Feminist Theory." In *Feminism and Tradition in Aesthetics,* edited by Peggy Zeglin Brand and Carolyn Korsmeyer, 446–63 University Park: Pennsylvania State University Press, 1995.

Heinemann, Larry. *Paco's Story*. New York: Farrar, Straus, and Giroux, 1986.

Hinz, Evelyn J. "Mimesis: The Dramatic Lineage of Auto/Biography." In *Essays on Life Writing: From Genre to Critical Practice,* edited by Marlene Kadar, 195–212. Toronto: University of Toronto Press, 1992.

Hirsch, Marianne, and Susan Rubin Suleiman. "Material Memory: Holocaust Testimony in Post-Holocaust Art." In Julia Epstein and Lori Hope Lefkovitz, *Shaping Losses*, 87–104. Urbana and Chicago: University of Illinois Press, 2001.

The Hitchhiker Series. 19: "The Curse." Dir. Philip Noyce. 25 February 1986.

Hodgson, Barbara. *The Tattooed Map*. Vancouver: Raincoast Books, 1995.

Holman, C. Hugh, and William Harmon. *A Handbook to Literature*. 6th ed. New York: Macmillan, 1992.

Homer. *The Odyssey*. Trans. Robert Fagles. New York: Viking, 1996.

Honour, Hugh, and John Fleming. *The Visual Arts: A History*. 3rd ed. New York: Harry N. Abrams, Inc., 1991.

Huddleston, Kathie. "Night Visions." *On Screen,* http://www.scifi.com/sfw/issue 220/screen4.html, 4 May 2003.

Huntley, Pam. "In Celebration of a Scar: Women, Breast Cancer and Tattoos." http://www.triangletattoo.com/women.html, 1 Feb 2002.

Hutcheon, Linda. *The Canadian Postmodern: A Study of Contemporary English-Canadian Fiction*. Toronto: Oxford University Press, 1988.

The Illustrated Man. Dir. Jack Smight. Warner Bros., 1969.

Irezumi (Spirit of Tattoo). Dir. Yoichi Takabayashi. Pacific Arts Video Records, 1985.

Ito, Ken K. "*Seven Japanese Tales* by Tanizaki Jun'ichiro." In *Masterworks of*

Asian Literature in Comparative Perspective, edited by Barbara Stoler Miller. 428–438. Armonk, New York: M. E. Sharpe, 1994.

Jeffords, Susan. "Tattoos, Scars, Diaries, and Writing Masculinity." In *The Vietnam War and American Culture,* edited by John Carlos Rowe and Rick Berg, 208–25. New York: Columbia University Press, 1991.

Kaeppler, Adrienne. "Hawaiian Tattoo: A Conjunction of Genealogy and Aesthetics." In *Marks of Civilization,* edited by Arnold Rubin. 157–70. Los Angeles: Regents of the University of California, 1988.

Kafka, Franz. *In der Strafkolonie* (The penal colony). *Franz Kafka Erzählungen.* Frankfurt am Main: Fischer, 1983.

Kamboureli, Smaro, ed. Introduction to *Making a Difference: Canadian Multicultural Literature.* Toronto: Oxford University Press, 1996.

"Kanji tattoos prickle traditionalists." *Honolulu Advertiser,* Friday, December 1, 2000, E3.

King, Thomas. *All My Relations: An Anthology of Contemporary Canadian Native Fiction.* Toronto: McClelland & Stewart, 1990.

Kingwell, Mark. *Dreams of Millennium: Report from a Culture on the Brink.* Toronto and London: Penguin, 1996.

Kisch, Egon Erwin. "My Tattoos" ("Meine Tätowierungen") 1925. In *The Raging Reporter,* Edited by Harold B. Segel, 204–213. West Lafayette, IN: Purdue University Press, 1997.

Krich, Rochelle. *Blood Money.* New York: Avon Books, 1999.

Krieger, Murray. *Ekphrasis: The Illusion of the Natural Sign.* Baltimore: Johns Hopkins University Press, 1992.

Kwaidan. Dir. Masaki Kobayashi. Home Vision Entertainment, 1964.

Lawson, Kate, and Lynn Shakinovsky. *The Marked Body: Domestic Violence in Mid–Nineteenth-Century Literature.* Albany: SUNY Press, 2002.

Layton, Lynne, and Barbara Ann Shapiro, eds. *Narcissism and the Text. Studies in Literature and the Psychology of Self.* New York: New York University Press, 1986.

Lim, Shirley Geok-Lin. "Asians in Anglo-American Feminism: Reciprocity and Resistance." In *Changing Subjects: The Making of Feminist Literary Criticism,* edited by Gayle Greene and Coppelia Kahn, 240–52. London and New York: Routledge, 1993.

Long, William R. "Does 'Rapa Nui' Take Artistic License Too Far?" http://www.netaxs.com/~trance/costner.html

"Lydia the Tattooed Lady" (sung by Groucho Marx). Lyrics by E.Y. Harburg. http://www.geocities.com/~jbenz/lydia.html.

McCallum, Donald. "Historical and Cultural Dimensions of the Tattoo in Japan." In *Marks of Civilization,* edited by Arnold Rubin, 109–34. Los Angeles: Regents of the University of California, 1988.

McKinney, Chris. *The Tattoo.* Honolulu: Mutual Publishing, 1999.

McLuhan, Marshall. "Understanding Media." In *Essential McLuhan,* edited by Eric McLuhan and Frank Zingrone, 149–179, 151 Concord: Anansi, 1995.

Mäder, Markus. "Oh! No!" in Gregor von Glinski *Masters of Tattoo,* 7–15. Zurich and New York: Edition Stemmle, 1998.

Mann, Denise. "Tattoo Removal: Ta Ta Tattoos." *http://www.dermadoctor.com,* 3 Jan 2005.

Martin, Helen, and Sam Edwards. *New Zealand Film, 1912–1996.* Auckland and New York: Oxford, 1997.

Mascia-Lees, Frances E., and Patricia Sharpe. "The Marked and the Un(re) Marked: Tattoo and Gender in Theory and Narrative. "In *Tattoo, Torture, Mutilation, and Adornment: The Denaturalization of the Body in Culture and Text,* edited by Frances E. Mascia-Lees and Patricia Sharpe, 145–69. Albany: State University of New York Press, 1992.

Masciuch, John. *Haida Indian Tattoos.* n.p., Shorthorn Press, 1998.

Mifflin, Margot. *Bodies of Subversion: A Secret History of Women and Tattoo.* New York: Juno, 1997.

Morrison, Toni. *Beloved.* New York: Penguin, 1987.

Mullen, Jim. *Baby's First Tattoo: A Memory Book for Modern Parents.* New York: Simon and Shuster, 2002.

_____. *Baby's First Tattoo.* "Product Description." http://www.amazon.com.

"Native Images Tattoo." http://www3.sk.sympatico.ca/donham, 8 August 2002.

Night Visions. 2: "The Bokor." Dir. Keith Gordon, 12 July 2001.

Oates, Joyce Carol. *Foxfire: Confessions of a Girl Gang.* New York: Penguin, 1993.

Oettermann, Stephan. "On Display: Tattooed Entertainers in America and Germany." In *Written on the Body,* edited by Jane Caplan, 193–211. Princeton University Press, 2000.

Once Were Warriors. Dir. Lee Tamahori. New Line Studios, 1995.

Ovid. *Metamorphoses.* Trans. Allen Mandelbaum. New York: Harcourt Brace, 1993.

Oz. Dir. Tom Fontana. 1997.

Oz. 1.1: "The Routine." Dir. Darnell Martin. Writ. Tom Fontana. 12 July 1997.

Oz. 1.3: "God's Chillin.'" Dir. Jean de Segonzac. Writ. Tom Fontana. 21 July 1997.

Oz. 3.1: "The Truth and Nothing But ..." Dir. Nick Gomez. Writ. Tom Fontana. 14 July 1999.

Oz: The Complete First Season Dir. Tom Fontana. 2002.

"OZ website." http://www.hbo.com/oz/community.

Patterson, David. *Sun Turned to Darkness: Memory and Recovery in the Holocaust Memoir.* Syracuse: Syracuse University Press, 1998.

Persky, Stan. *Autobiography of a Tattoo.* Vancouver: New Star Books, 1997.

Pfouts, Chris. Book Review. *International Tattoo Art* (July 2000): 58.

The Pillow Book. Dir. Peter Greenaway. Kasander and Wigman Productions.

IBV/Alpha Films s.a.r.l. Woodline Films, 1996.

Place, François. *The Last Giants.* Trans. William Rodarmor. London: Pavilion Books, 1993. Orig. published 1992.

Plath, Sylvia. "The Fifteen-Dollar Eagle" (1959). In *Johnny Panic and the Bible of Dreams,* edited by Ted Hughes, 59–73 London: Faber and Faber, 1979.

Poirier, Michael. "*Tattoo Master.*" wysiwyg://51/http://www.ex.org/ex/5.124-anime_tattoonmaster.html.

"Polynesian lizard" or fish-man image. http://sorrel.humboldt.edu/~rwj1/POLY/poly047s.html.

Prager, Emily. *Eve's Tattoo.* New York: Random House, 1991.

Purdy, Anthony, ed. *Literature and the Body.* Amsterdam: Rodopi, 1992.

Rabkin, Eric S. *Fantastic Worlds: Myths, Tales, and Stories.* Oxford: Oxford University Press, 1979.

Ranma 1/2 Outta Control Vol 8: Tattoo You. Viz Video, 1999.

Rapa Nui. Dir. Kevin Reynolds. Easter Island Productions, Warner Bros. 1994.

"Reptile-man throws self into the role." *Prince George* (B.C.) *Citizen,* Friday, December 17, 1999, 39.

Robley, H. G. *Moko: The Art and History of Maori Tattooing.* Twickenham: Tiger Books, 1998. Orig. published 1896.

Rome, Florence. *Tattooed Men: An American Woman Reports on the Japanese Criminal Underworld.* New York: Delacorte Press, 1975.

Ross, Becki L. "Destaining the (Tattooed) Delinquent Body: The Practices of Moral Regulation at Toronto's Street Haven, 1965–69." *Journal of the History of Sexuality* 7.4 (1997): 561–95.

Rowe, Elizabeth. *Tattoos.* London: Haldane Mason, 2001.

Rowe, John Carlos, and Rick Berg, eds. *The Vietnam War and American Culture.* New York: Columbia University Press, 1991.

Rowland, Laura Joh. *The Concubine's Tattoo.* New York: St. Martin's Press, 1998.

Rubin, Arnold, ed. *Marks of Civilization: Artistic Transformations of the Human*

Body. Los Angeles: Regents of the University of California, 1988.

Saki. "The Background." In *The Complete Works of Saki,* edited by H. H. Munro, 121–24. Garden City: Doubleday, 1976.

Salmond, Anne. *Between Worlds: Early Exchanges between Maori and Europeans, 1773–1815.* Honolulu: University of Hawai'i Press, 1997.

Satin, Joseph, ed. *Reading Literature.* Boston: Houghton Mifflin, 1964.

Schiffmacher, Henk, and Burkhard Riemschneider. *1000 Tattoos.* Köln: Taschen, 1996.

Segel, Harold B., ed. *Egon Erwin Kisch. The Raging Reporter: A Bio-Anthology.* West Lafayette, IN: Purdue University Press, 1997.

Shakespeare, William. *Hamlet,* edited by Sydney Bolt. London and New York: Penguin Books, 1990.

The Simpsons. 1.1: "The Simpsons Christmas Special: Simpsons Roasting on an Open Fire." 17 Dec 1989.

Skin Art. Dir. W. Blake Herron,. 1993. Polygram Video, 1997.

Skin Deep. Dir. Midi Onodera. Water Bearer Films, 1997.

Sontag, Susan. *On Photography.* New York: Anchor Books, 1990.

Star Trek Voyager. 2.9: "Tattoo." Dir. Alexander Singer. Writ. Larry Brody. 6 November 1995.

Steinfeld, J. J. "Anton Chekhov Was Never in Charlottetown." In *Anton Chekhov Was Never in Charlottetown.* Wolfville, N. S. Gaspereau Press, 2000.

_____. "The Apostate's Tattoo." In *The Apostate's Tattoo,* 66–74 Charlottetown, Ragweed, 1983.

_____. "Weintraub's Education." In *Dancing at the Club Holocaust: Stories New and Selected,* 75–84 Charlottetown, P.E.I. Ragweed, 1993.

Stevens, Brooke. *Tattoo Girl.* New York: St. Martin's Griffin, 2001.

Swallow, Jerry. "Preserving Vintage Canadian Ink." *International Tattoo Art* (July 2000): 10–15.

Takagi, Akimitsu. *The Tattoo Murder Case.* Trans. Deborah Boehm. New York: Soho Press, 1998. Orig. published 1948.

Takahashi, Rumiko. *Ranma 1 / 2.* San Francisco: Viz Communications, 1999.

Tamaki, Mariko. *Cover Me.* Toronto: McGilligan Books, 2000.

Tanizaki, Junichiro. "Tattoo." Trans. Ivan Morris. In *Modern Japanese Stories: An Anthology,* edited by Ivan Morris, 90–100. Rutland and Tokyo: C. E. Tuttle, 1962.

Tattoo. Dir. Bob Brooks. Twentieth Century–Fox, 1981.

"Tattoo Museum Amsterdam." Information Guide. N.p., n.d.

"Tattoo Song for a Man," or "He Whakawai Taanga Moko." in Sir George Grey *Hakiraka O Nga Maori.* Cited in H. G. Robley, *Moko,* 117. Twickenham: Tiger Books, 1998.

Tattoon Master. A.D. Vision, 2000.

Taylor, Mark C. "Skinscapes." In Don Ed Hardy, *Pierced Hearts and True Love,* 28–47. New York and Honolulu: The Drawing Center and Hardy Marks Publications, 1995.

Teit, James A. *Tattooing and Face and Body Painting of the Thompson Indians British Columbia.* Extract from B.A.E. Annual Report #45, 1927–28. Edited by Franz Boas. Facsimile Reproduction. Seattle: Shorey Book Store, 1972.

Telling It Book Collective, ed. *Telling It: Women and Language across Cultures.* Vancouver: Press Gang Publishers, 1990.

That '70s Show. 3.22: "Eric's Drunken Tattoo." Dir. David Trainer. Writ. Joshua Sternin and Jeffrey Ventimilia. 1 May 2001.

_____. 4.1: "It's a Wonderful Life." Dir. David Trainer. Writ. Linda Wallem. 25 Sept 2001.

Thomas, D. M. Introduction to *The Japanese Tattoo* by Sandi Fellman. New York: Cross River Press, 1986.

Tokyo Mafia: Yakuza Wars. Dir. Seiichi Shirai. Central Park Media, 1995.

Trachtenberg, Peter. *7 Tattoos: A Memoir in the Flesh.* New York: Crown Publishers, 1997.

Utamoro and His Five Women. Kenji Mizoguchi. New Yorker Films, 1946.

Utu. Dir. Geoff Murphy. Utu Productions, 1988.

Vale, V., and Andrea Juno. "Hanky Panky." In *Research: Modern Primitives*, 137–149. San Francisco: V/Search Publications, 1989.

Verduyn, Christl. *Lifelines: Marian Engel's Writings*. Montreal and Kingston: McGill-Queen's University Press, 1995.

Von Glinski, Gregor. *Masters of Tattoo*. Zurich and New York: Edition Stemmle, 1998.

Wagner, Peter, ed. *Icons. Texts. Iconotexts: Essays on Ekphrasis and Intermediality*. Berlin: Walter de Gruyter, 1996.

The Wizard of Oz. Dir. Victor Fleming. Warner Studios, 1939.

The X-Files. 2.20. "Humbug." Dir. Kim Manners. Writ. Darin Morgan. 31 March 1995.

_____.4.13: "Never Again." Dir. Rob Bowman. Writ. Glen Morgan and James Wong. 2 Feb. 1997.

The Yakuza. Dir. Sydney Pollack, Warner Bros., 1975, 1990.

Zulueta, Leo."The 1st International Tattoo Festival, Raiatea-Tahiti." *Skin & Ink* (January 2001): 24–34.

Index

Index

Index

Index

Index

Index

Index

Index

Index

2476